THE DARKSIDE ZODIAC

WITHDRAWN

Stella Hyde

IVY PRESS

This edition published in the UK in 2016 by
Ivy Press
210 High Street, Lewes
East Sussex BN7 2NS, UK
www.ivypress.co.uk

British Library Cataloguing-in-Publication Data
A catalogue record for this book is available from the British Library

ISBN 978-1-78240-366-1

The dates for the zodiac signs in this book follow accepted standards, but people born at the beginning
or end of a sign should always check their birthchart; for technical, star-based reasons, the start and end
dates occasionally shift one day either way (and sometimes more), depending on the year.

This book was conceived, designed and produced by
Ivy Press
Creative Director **Peter Bridgewater**
Publisher **Sophie Collins**
Editorial Director **Steve Luck**
Design Manager **Tony Seddon**
Designer and illustrator **Tonwen Jones**
Zodiac icons **Tonwen Jones, Marina Murgioni**
Project Editor **Mandy Greenfield**

CONTENTS

INTRODUCTION

You know what you're really like ~ so do I

Before we go any further, look at the subtitle of this book. What does it say? Darkside. That means you are going to be reading some wince-making stuff about yourselves. There are no jolly Brightside platitudes, as there is quite enough of that kind of thing in the world, and every silver lining has to have a cloud. I don't want you writing in – you have been warned; anybody who is but a fragile blossom on life's maelstrom had better put the book down now; don't give it to anyone whose self-esteem is running at zero pressure.

DON'T BLAME ME, IT'S WRITTEN IN THE STARS

It's not just your sun sign; there are other dark forces out there to make things even worse:

• Your ruling planet: the Sun, Moon or any one of the solar system's nine aimlessly orbiting rocks (apart from Earth, of course), each of which looks after one or more signs and imposes its disgusting habits.

• The Moon, which is in charge of your dark, inner soul, frightful moods, and uncontrollable emotions; just how much of a prima donna you are depends on where the Moon was throwing a hissy fit when you were thrust into this vale of tears (see pages 392–395).

• Your rising sign: as the Earth creaks around on its axis, it appears to us that a new zodiac sign passes overhead every two hours or so. Your rising sign is the one that peeped balefully over the eastern horizon at the exact minute you fell to Earth.

• The psychotic duo, Venus (planet lust) and Mars (planet psychowarrior); you'll need a birthchart (see each sign) to find out what havoc they wreak.

• Your opposite sign – this is the fascinating badboy (six signs away from your own) your mum told you to keep away from.

Unredeeming features

Each sun sign hangs around street corners with one of four elements: Fire, Earth, Air, or Water – think of them as the style in which you express your cosmic sloth (*see box*). Plus, there are three sorts of qualities: cardinal, fixed and mutable. The qualities combine with the elements so that no single sign is exactly the same. This means we are all insufferable in our own special way. Each sign is also masculine or feminine. It's nothing personal; think of it as positive/negative.

Living with the Darkside

And how does all this affect you? Well, read on and weep. We look at your shameful personality; your pathetic work, relationship and sex lives; criminal tendencies; how appalling you are to live with and how you try to have fun in your own miserable way. And we end with a list of others who share your patch in the zodiac. So go on, suffer!

RIFFRAFF ELEMENTS

- Fire signs (Aries, Leo, Sagittarius): Brightsiders say impulsive! Darksiders say reckless sociopath.

- Earth signs (Taurus, Virgo, Capricorn): Brightsiders say solid! Darksiders say pig-headed fusspot.

- Air signs (Gemini, Libra, Aquarius): Brightsiders say intellectual! Darksiders say free-floating airhead.

- Water signs (Cancer, Scorpio, Pisces): Brightsiders say nurturing! Darksiders say moody whinger.

IT'S QUALITY TIME

Quality is just another word for attitude; on the Darkside, that's bad attitude.

- Cardinal signs (Aries, Cancer, Libra, Capricorn): bossy; this is the quality that initiates disasters.

- Fixed signs (Taurus, Leo, Scorpio, Aquarius): stubborn; this is the quality that never deviates.

- Mutable signs (Gemini, Virgo, Sagittarius, Pisces): fickle; this is the quality that ensures chaos and mess.

ARIES

21 March ~ 20 April

Aries is a masculine, cardinal Fire sign ruled by Mars. It is the first sign on the zodiac wheel, directly opposite Libra, and is named after the constellation Aries (the ram), which shouts and struts behind the Sun at this time of year.

On the Darkside, this makes you a loud, overconfident, aggressive thug with way too many Y chromosomes and a will of titanium-clad granite.

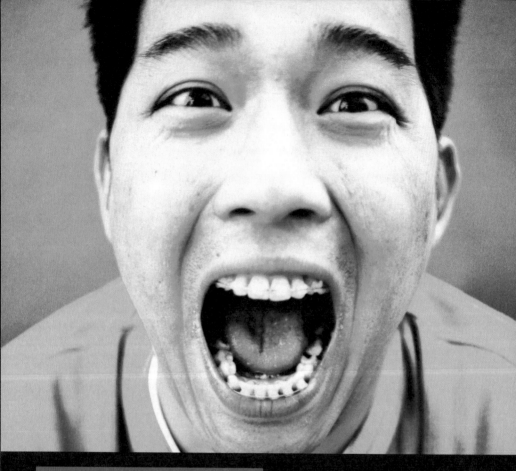

Punctuality

You are either 30 minutes early, raring to go and incandescent that everyone else is late, or you turn up four days later at a different venue and are outraged that the expedition went without you.

Toothpaste

After a five-minute rant in the bathroom when you throw everything out of the window looking for your tube of toothpaste, you finally find it in the laundry basket. You hammer it flat with your bare hands.

Temper gauge

$0°$ to boiling point is instantaneous, and occurs roughly every two minutes because people just won't do what you tell them, and you've lost the keys/hammer/remote control/plot.

PERSONALITY

Overwhelming, overbearing, overconfident

Brightside astrologers proclaim that you burst with creative energy and confidence, and that you prefer to express yourself through action. Well, they would, wouldn't they, especially with your knife to their collective throat? This is just salon talk for laying about you with a meat cleaver when you wish to make a point, isn't it, Aries? Your Instagram account is in permanent selfie overload, and your devices are all set to Me-Time – like there could be any other kind, RME, FOFL.

Greedy, aggressive, argumentative, restless, willful, confrontational, headstrong and self-obsessed, you are the zodiac's permanently enraged adolescent (and just look at the state of your room); you have what nice social workers call 'a problem with authority'.

Show you a no-entry sign and you are up the forbidden highway like a ferret up a drainpipe. No one has ever explained the phrase 'consequences-of-your-actions' to you (mostly because you won't stand still long enough, and even if you were nailed to the floor, you still wouldn't listen). Consequently the nation's A&Es are an Arien's second home.

Subtle you're not; no one will ever find you sitting quietly in a corner brooding on life's great mysteries, or sitting quietly anywhere. You blunder through the world like Tigger gone rogue, looking for new frontiers to smash. Fortunately you can be easily distracted by bright lights, loud noises, meat, blood, fire and knives. On good days, this means a neighbourhood barbecue; on bad days, World War III.

You generate a kind of low-frequency tetch field all around you, which unnerves the rest of us, and can be condensed into a stamping rage by practically anything. Lost your keys? House turned upside down, loved ones lambasted, doors slammed off hinges. And instructions for anything from a flat-pack to a cruise missile are torn up in a rage (nobody tells Aries what to do!) before you get past Step One.

Have you ever willingly finished anything in your life? You're just one big booster rocket, all fired up for blast off, and falling away as soon as your boredom threshold (usually around sea level) is reached. Some of you can't even get to the end of a sentence before moving on, which is probably why the military speak in speedily articulated acronyms.

Pathologically, addictively competitive, you have to come first in everything, even if it's only a spitting contest, and you will do anything to win, as your concept of fair play means that you triumph. This extends to your kids, whom you are likely to disown if they don't win a Nobel prize, the World Cup and an Oscar.

Your political opinions are strongly held: bigoted and extreme. The doctrine is irrelevant – it's the extreme part you like, along with the street fighting and mob violence. Many Ariens become politicians. How scary is that? Aberrant Ariens who show a mild interest in other life forms can clean up by running elite assertiveness-training courses – although the rest of you wonder why anyone would want to give ammo to the competition.

Bitch rating

C+. Think about it: bitching demands subtlety and finesse, neither of which your Bad Fairy Godmother left in your cradle. If you want to say something nasty about someone, you don't sneak around; you just open your mouth and blast away. Refreshing, in a strange way.

Collective noun

A safety tip for non-Ariens. You may find yourself, for some bizarre zodiacal reason, in a room full of Ariens (perhaps your local abbatoir is hosting an open evening in the spirit of community outreach). The air is thick with testosterone, and thrums with shouting and the sound of keen blade-whetting. You have rashly stumbled into a Headbutt of Aries. Run away.

FAVE DEADLY SIN

You simply do not have the time for anything intellectual or namby-pamby, so you go straight for Wrath, or Anger: a big, strong, all-terrain sin that's just as unhelpful halfway up K2 as it is in a motorway traffic jam. It's straightforward, uncomplicated and requires hardly any brain power (it's just a matter of coupling mouth and fists to your amazing irascibility drive). Plus you get to do the shouting. In your quieter moments, you might consider Greed; it makes a useful indoor sin for the older Arien whose form is slipping.

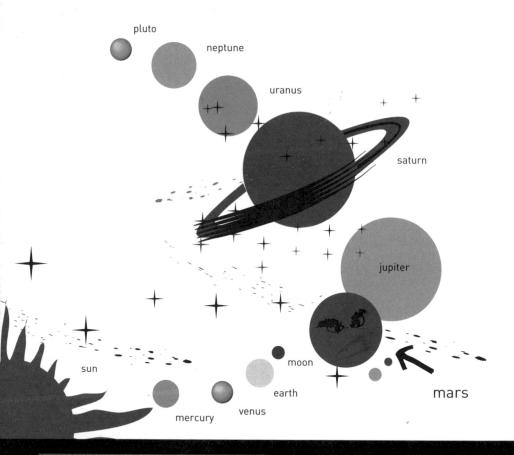

pluto

neptune

uranus

saturn

jupiter

sun

moon

earth

mars

mercury

venus

PLANET PLANET

Every sun sign has a planetary enforcer, whose job it is to strike the first blow, establish pole position and engage in a little pre-emptive defence to make it clear who is the leader around here. Before there were telescopes, astrologers could only see five planets in the sky, plus the Moon and Sun, so they counted these two as planetary rulers. It seemed a good idea at the time. Each planet babysat two zodiac signs – except for the Moon (Cancer's minder) and the Sun (which allows Leo to rule). Your planet is Mars. It's true that until 1930 you had to share it with Scorpio (*see page 238 for what happened*). Any other sun sign would have been toast, and Mars would have been all yours, but you respect Scorpio because, although you are headstrong and reckless, you like the idea of keeping all your organs on the inside.

BLAME YOUR PLANET

The red menace

If you are feeling even more hot-eyed and steam-driven than usual, your children are cowering behind a bunker of cereal boxes at the breakfast table, strong men are crossing the road to avoid you and the world is bathed in a red mist, is this your fault? Is it, punk? Not entirely. Blame your planet. In your case, it's Mars.

Mars knows where we live. In fact the red, glowering psychopath is our next-door neighbour, fourth rock from the Sun. Isn't that comforting? Somehow the fact that it's only half Earth's size doesn't really help. It stalks our orbit at half speed, so we can always see it just out of the corner of our eye. Worse, it has two hench-moons called – wait for it – Deimos and Phobos, or fear and loathing. They're tiny, but they do a menacing double act. Deimos, a midget made of black rock, is in synchronous rotation with the boss; this means it doesn't rise or set – it's a constant eyeball in the sky. Phobos, *au contraire*, the hyperactive one, pops up every five hours, just when you thought it was safe. The Martian atmosphere is almost entirely carbon dioxide; this is what happens when you are so angry with your mum and the cosmos that you hold your breath until you go red in the face.

Mars is named after the Roman god of war. Adored and worshipped by the Roman army, he was a remix of an ancient agricultural god and the Greek god of war, Ares, notorious on Mount Olympus as a violent but stupid, bloodlusty braggart. Ares/Aries – you see what's happening here?

BAD MOON RISING

The darkside of Aries' darkside

It's not all sunshine on the Darkside. You know just how power-crazed and monomaniac your innermost thoughts and secret fantasies are, but where do you think they come from? The Moon, that's where – or whichever area of your birthchart the Moon was moodily plodding when you were born. The Sun is our daytime self; the Moon represents our inner psycho. The nippy little blighter rushes around, plunging in and out of signs every few days, so throughout Aries' month in the Sun, the lunar nuisance dodges around like a *guerrillista* in a South American jungle. That helps to explain why two Ariens born only days apart stamp their feet in a different rhythm when thwarted, depending on which sign the Moon was bothering at the time.

CATCHING THE MOON

That's all very well, you say, but how do I know where the Moon was when I was born? There are long, complicated (and, frankly, dull) tables called ephemerides that tell you where every planet (and for tedious astrological reasons, the Moon is an honorary planet) stood in the heavens, atmosphere bated, as you made your sorry debut. However, we have provided a Moon itinerary at the back of this book to enable you to get a rough idea. If that sounds like too much hard work, and you have the techno technique, then try visiting the following website: www.alabe.com/freechart. If you know where you were born, and when, they will produce, for *free*, a rough-cut birthchart that will pin your Moon on the zodiac wheel.

Lunatic combinations

Here's what happens to Aries when the Moon marches off in a lust for glory.

Moon in Aries – twice as tetchy, twice as trigger-happy, twice as likely to start World War III.

Moon in Taurus – aggressively greedy for territory, but easily distracted by cakes and ale.

Moon in Gemini – soldier of fortune; a dirty fighter unencumbered by old-fashioned burdens such as loyalty.

Moon in Cancer – hard as nails mum; you like to bake a lovely apple pie for your enemies after you have knocked their teeth out.

Moon in Leo – will only lead the charge if you get to wear a big plumed hat and your troops all swear to adore you.

Moon in Virgo – Aries despises detail; Virgo lives for it; internecine strife and an obsession with uniforms.

Moon in Libra – you know that diplomacy is war continued by other means; your weapon of choice is the charm offensive.

Moon in Scorpio – scarily focused aggression, ideal for silent surgical strikes just before dawn.

Moon in Sagittarius – Captain Reckless: you can't see what was wrong with the Charge of the Light Brigade.

Moon in Capricorn – your preferred tactic is to bury the enemy in paperwork.

Moon in Aquarius – intellectual warrior; you avoid 'red mists' as you like to outbrain your opponents.

Moon in Pisces – aggressive but irresolute; unreliable under fire.

BORN UNDER A BAD SIGN

The scum also rises

And another thing. Your sun sign is modified by your rising sign. This is the zodiac sign that was skulking over the horizon at the very minute you were born. If your sun sign is your ego, then your rising sign gives you your public manners (such as they are), your Sunday worst. It's the painted smile behind which the real, disgusting you lurks. Some astrologers maintain that its malign influence affects what you look like. Be afraid.

You will probably be bitterly aggrieved to discover that, in the northern hemisphere, for tedious astronomical reasons, there are fewer people with Aries and Pisces rising, or ascending, than any other sign. (In other words, you have a short ascension span, ha-ha.) We say: good; there are only so many world dictators one little globe can take.

GOING UP

Now pay attention, because the following is quite brain-busting. There are 12 signs of the zodiac, and astrologers like to think of them as occupying a band of sky that spins around the Earth once every 24 hours. (This is a convention; it is not astronomically correct, and you will not see the signs if you look up, so don't write in.) So, every two hours or so another sign hauls itself blearily over the eastern horizon. This is going on whatever time of the day or night you were born, and whichever benighted spot you chose to appear in.

These astro-mechanics help to explain why rams born at either end of the same day take a different route as they charge through life. There are long, nerdy ways to discover your rising sign, but the easiest way is to get hold of a birthchart (*see page 16*).

Upwardly mobile

If your rising sign is Aries, your public persona is a fierce, pushy extrovert on a short fuse, obsessed with coming first. This is to distract the rest of us from discovering your plan for a Thousand-Year Reich. Here's what happens when other zodiacal upstarts rise above their station.

Taurus rising

It's all calm, bovine tranquillity until you catch sight of a red rag.

Gemini rising

Cheat, lie and con your way to the front; if that fails, bring on the heavy artillery.

Cancer rising

Mother knows best; after all, you know that the hand that rocks the cradle rules the world.

Leo rising

Swagger all you like in that dress uniform, but we all know it's a gun you've got in your pocket and that you're not particularly pleased to see us.

Virgo rising

Don't you find, Lady Macbeth, that however hard you scrub at ingrained bloodstains, they just won't shift?

Libra rising

Handsome, dashing freedom-fighter, armed with Weapons of Mass Seduction.

Scorpio rising

You appear darkly, hypnotically menacing; actually, you are just menacing.

Sagittarius rising

Our knight in unpolished armour.

Capricorn rising

Your papers are always in order and your jackboots gleam like a raven's wings.

Aquarius rising

Aren't you far too cool for all this petty squabbling over world domination?

Pisces rising

When you are World Dictator, they will all be sorry they didn't appreciate you.

DON'T YOU LOVE ME, BABY?

Venus and Aries

Just how much of a high-maintenance tease or bunny-boiler you are may depend on where the solar system's heartless tart (Venus) was blushingly dropping her handkerchief when you were born (*see below*). Oh, and Venus also has a say in how harmoniously you blend in with the rest of the world, but what do words like harmony have to do with the Darkside? Now, for astrological reasons that will fry your brain if I explain them here (basically, Venus is far too luxury-loving to move too far away from the Sun, and her orbital rate is in bed with Earth's), Venus only ever appears in your sun sign, or two signs on either side of it. In your case, rams, that means Venus will be in Aries, Aquarius, Pisces, Taurus or Gemini. And this is what it does to your love and lust life.

MAKE LOVE AND WAR

Venus is the girlie planet of lurve, right? And Mars is planet lad, the warlord. You may also have a sneaking feeling that men are from Mars and women are from Venus. Don't be upset if I tell you this is not true. All of us, of all genders, have a stake in both planets. Where they are in your birthchart has what I shall call consequences. You may think your sun sign makes you a born babe-magnet, but Venus in a chilly sign will cut you off at the knees; you may think that your sun sign means you are the twin soul of the dove of peace, but you may go red-eyed with bloodlust when beaten to a parking space. Mars will be somewhere irascible. You'll need a birthchart (*see page 16*) to find out what Venus and Mars were getting up to when you were born. It is far too complicated – and, frankly, dull – to work out here.

Venus in Aries

You always get your man (or woman), often at gunpoint, and you are a tough love fanatic: whips, pain, domination – and that's just when you're on your own. You always hurt the one you love, on principle.

Venus in Aquarius

You may be gung-ho to storm love's citadel, but you know better than to charge at it with all flags waving. You have cunning plans involving decoys, disinformation and playing dead.

Venus in Pisces

You are not above faking a war wound, or a duelling scar (so romantic!) or three, to incite pity and admiration in the heart of your love object. You know there's

nothing more alluring than a wounded hero, even though you aren't one.

Venus in Taurus

Once the love target is in the crosshairs, you lock on and don't let go until you've brought him or her down; but you do provide a very cozy prisoner-of-love nest.

Venus in Gemini

Heavy-duty extreme flirting, usually while bear hunting, base jumping, gunrunning or liberating small countries, and usually with the whole platoon. You know you're irresistible in distressed combats.

ARE YOU LOOKING AT ME?

Mars and Aries

Ariens and Mars have a special relationship (*see page 15*). But just how confrontational, paranoid and gagging for a fight you are depends on which area of your birthchart the bruiser planet Mars is being held back in by his mates (leave it, Mars, he's not worth it). Mars is the next planet out from Earth, but paces its orbit more slowly (presumably to get some effective eyeballing in). It takes 2½ years for Mars to get around, and on the way it spends about two months of quality menacing time in each sign. As an Arien, you don't tolerate opposition (or even a mild difference of opinion); anybody who says otherwise is just asking for a good kicking. However, if you find your aggression comes out in an uncharacteristic peacenik mode, check out Mars' alibi at the time of your birth.

Mars in Aries
Wherever you go, people smile brightly as they put knives and sharp objects on the top shelf and send their children for extended stays in neutral countries.

Mars in Taurus
It may take a while for your war machine to rumble into action, but when it does — boy, are your enemies confounded.

Mars in Gemini
Your favourite wargame is 'let's you and him fight', while you clean up as an international arms dealer. Taureans and Capricorns fall for it every time.

Mars in Cancer
You only go to war over prehistorical grudges and your battle plans are drawn up according to the phases of the Moon.

Mars in Leo
A warrior king who loves to give the troops a pre-battle man-to-man pep talk in blank verse; they can call you Hal.

Mars in Virgo
The trouble with war, as you constantly remind everyone, is that everything ends up so filthy, and nobody but you ever tidies up properly afterwards.

Mars in Libra
You rattle a mean sabre, but when it comes down to it, you find that covert ops and treachery do the job so much better than carpet-bombing.

Mars in Scorpio
You have very few declared enemies (apart from foolhardy Sagittarians), because you can focus all that ambient aggression into one laserlike beam that cuts through armour plating.

Mars in Sagittarius
Life and soul of the barracks, you live for the adrenaline rush of the charge. Collateral damage? It happens.

Mars in Capricorn
Call you old-fashioned, but you just can't bear launching an all-out war unless you have made a plan for every eventuality; by which time it will all be over.

Mars in Aquarius
You're never swept away by patriotic fervour, but you might be found developing a ghastly new secret weapon, just for the intellectual challenge.

Mars in Pisces
Your lightning mood swings mean you are never entirely certain whose side you are on, and neither is anyone else; you are in danger of being executed out of sheer exasperation by your own troops.

Aries

Libra

POLAR BEARS

Your polar sign sits on the opposite side of the zodiac wheel, six signs away, giving you knowing looks. You have a dark umbilical link with it. If Darkside you is your evil twin, then your polar sign is your evil twin's evil twin. It's got your number – but then you've got its, so that's alright, isn't it? Brightside astrologers maintain that there is a strong complementary relationship between you and your polar sign, and that this relationship is positive and fruitful, especially at work, because you share the same energy quality (cardinal). Well, excuse me; on the Darkside it's more like a Mexican standoff between rival street fighters, both trying to get the drop on each other without moving, blinking or dropping their weapons; it's a matter of willpower, you see? Neither can bear to be second best.

WHO'S GOT YOUR NUMBER?

check out the opposition

Your polar opposite sign is Libra: duplicitous, insincere, detached and terminally indecisive. (For more about your darkly fascinating opposite number, *see pages 200–231*.) What would an adrenaline-fuelled action junkie like you want with an indolent, vacillating, self-indulgent sofa hogger like your average Libran? How did you come to this – shall we say – understanding? Well, like good cop and bad cop, or arch villain and superhero, you need each other to make the Darkside work for you. It's all about elements (undesirable ones, of course). You are Fire; Libra is Air. So it's only right that Libra should stand around admiring your big red fire engine as you rush to put out fires you probably started in the first place. Fire cannot burn without oxygen…

As you thrust and strut about the world, issuing orders and going purple in the face if everyone does not leap to attention at once, don't you sense deep down the enigmatic smile and raised eyebrow of the zodiac's lounge lizard, mocking the way you waste so much energy on pointless shouting and tantrums? Ever wonder how a reckless, headstrong, inconsiderate bigot like you has managed to stay alive for so long?

Respect your inner Libran; it's the one thing that makes you look *before* you leap (sometimes); it surrounds you with a low but adequate mental guardrail of self-preservation that counteracts your death wish. Of course, if it gets too harmonious in there, you are stripped of your rank and made to get a real job.

DARKSIDE DATE

Not getting a date is not an option. You are a stranger to low self-esteem. You are so insensitive and persistent that people usually give in and accept, just for a quiet life. Mind you, then the game is half over for you; what you like best about dating is the chase.

You are oppressively ardent and romantic, forever sending vulgar bouquets or organizing platoons of troubadours to warble all night long under your love object's window, even after the noise police have been summoned. Your ideal date, achieved after much enjoyable

hunting, is with a gorgeous socialite who is way out of your league, so that you can show off in front of your rivals. This glittering prize must not criticize anything you do, or look at another person in your presence, but when you are bored, they can leave.

SEX

Hard, fast, competitive

Sex is just another extreme sport as far as you are concerned, and you don't like to waste time; foreplay is for wimps. You are strictly a notches-on-the-bedpost kinda guy (or girl), so you like to multitask sometimes. Your Little Black Book is almost ready to be catalogued by the British Library. You always need to be told that you are the first (and, naturally, best) lover that your partner's had, ever; you don't bother to do the social maths that proves this is impossible without virginity becoming a renewable resource. Your affairs burn with a gemlike flame for, oh, several days, during which time you are extravagantly possessive and jealous every time your prey steps out for a comfort break. Lust does not, however, quench your competitive spirit. Of course,

you have to do it harder, faster, longer and quicker than anybody else, and naturally you always have to come first. (You silently count your partner's orgasms – just to make sure you are not being outclassed.)

What kind of love rat are you?

The worst. It's the winning, you see; the fighting off of all rivals, or defeating overwhelming odds (you are in Sydney, they are in Alaska; they are a Druid, you are a lumberjack, etc.) Once you've got the prize, it's no longer what you want. You wander off to find a new challenge, abandoning the poor sap who believed you when you said you'd slash your wrists with a rusty blade if they did not come with you to be your love.

Aries – this is how two tribes end up going to war.

Taurus – you want to command the world; they want to own it.

Gemini – they swear loyalty, but are on a mission from the enemy.

Cancer – you want to find the final frontier; they insist that you take a packed lunch.

Leo – you'll let them be king, if you can drive the tanks.

Virgo – secretly love clearing up all your mess and rubble.

Libra – will sap your strength with luxury, then betray you.

Scorpio – effective double act: noisy, violent bad cop and menacingly silent bad cop.

Sagittarius – they outclass you in the reckless daredevil stakes.

Capricorn – they control your war chest and ration the bullets.

Aquarius – always have a superior chess strategy.

Pisces – slavishly ready to play soldiers to get your approval, but only pack a water pistol.

RELATIONSHIPS

Leader of the pack

It's not that you don't want to relate, it's just that you can't do one-to-one, because you are the only one in the world. Do you see the difficulty? If only your friends and lovers would think of themselves as your flock, everything would fall into place. All they have to do is follow the flock rules you have kindly drawn up, which are: 1) do everything you say; 2) admire your every action; 3) never, ever criticize anything you do.

For all your leadership skills, you are a very poor judge of character, mainly because all sheep look the same to you, and you think empathy is a mild skin disease. You have no idea how a network functions, since you only know about linear chains of command that extend from you to everyone else. You have to be in control at any social event, even when you're a guest. Secretly you'd love there to be an emergency, so that you could show off. You insist on running your friends' and family's lives for them: they call you the drill sergeant behind your back; you're flattered. Plus, you get ragingly jealous if any of your friends demonstrates the slightest ability to do anything a nanometre better than you (and that includes breathing), or wins a prize in a competition you didn't enter. Then you are forced to cut them loose from your circle and get in new stock.

When it comes to romance, you have to make the running, otherwise the game is declared null and void. You fall in love hard and often, but out of love just as frequently, often just hours later.

It's strange how everyone in your office keeps finding ads for jobs in faraway places and leaving them on your desk, or desktop. Perhaps they sympathize with your restless spirit; perhaps they just want some peace and quiet. Here are a couple of useful suggestions:

Explorer

Fantastic! Be the first to hack your way through virgin rainforest, scale an unclimbed alp or cross an uncharted desert. Spit in the face of caution and local advice. Win a posthumous knighthood.

Firefighter

Now you're really in your element! Fire, danger, big sharp axes, shiny red appliances to ride on and the chance to be a real hero every day. Avoid starting the odd conflagration just because the day's a bit slow.

WORK

My way or nothing

Some of the workforce simply will not follow your orders without question. Alright, so you are 'only' the caretaker, but is that the point? You resign or, more likely, smash your broom over your knees, toss the pieces at the boss and march off, leaving others to clear up the mess.

You see, you have to run the show (although you don't need to be seen to, like Leo). Obviously you know better than anyone else how to do any job, even though you have no experience. You work on the principle that shouting with confidence and acting aggressive are the answer to everything, and the sad thing is you are almost right. Myopic employers hire you for your energy, direction and drive (why, if you're that good, are you so available?). So you crash around, alienating the workforce and tearing down all the old systems, but not putting in anything to replace them, because you don't do detail; then they pay you off before the writs are served. Astute employers hire you to run down perfectly viable companies for barely legal tax reasons.

Brash, crass and insensitive, you are a nightmare to work with because you never listen, you are morbidly competitive, you are always throwing hissy fits and you can't stand being told what to do. The most you can deal with is one boss above you, usually a Scorpio with a big stick.

And if it all goes wrong, and you're fired, you don't go for the boring option of the tribunal and reconciliation services; you sneak around on a dark night with a Molotov cocktail and torch the place.

WHEN RAMS GO WRONG

Aries crimes nearly always get spectacular media coverage, mostly because you almost always get caught (unless you're working with Scorpio). What did I tell you about attention to detail and keeping schtum? And do you listen? However, there are a couple of little jobs...

Enforcer

Many a Mr Big relies on your notorious Irritable Thug Syndrome when clients get out of order; but you can get overenthusiastic and end up, quite unintentionally, on a manslaughter charge. Doh!

Arsonist

Burn, baby, burn! Herostratus is your role model: he was the tenth-rate architect who burned down the Temple of Artemis squillions of years ago, just so that people would remember his name. That's not crime; that's art.

CRIMES AND MISDEMEANOURS

How bad could it get?

So what sort of crim would you be, if sociopathy became the new world order? How would you spend your days (or maybe your nights) if you really lived on the Darkside? Well, you are the zodiac's bit of rough, and you're not telling me that in your younger days you weren't pretty damn lucky not to be caught red-handed at the scene of various juvenile crimes. Ramraiding, for instance. Threatening behaviour. Grievous Bodily Harm.

And after you had paid society's price for your infant crime spree, you would be well connected enough to set up a gang of your own. Mind you, this might be a bit of a disaster, as you lack the cool brain and meticulous planning gene that typifies a criminal mastermind; your big heist would go wrong because you lost the getaway vehicle keys, or even the vehicle itself. Your short fuse and physical strength make you a useful bit of muscle, which is fine by you, but you report only to Mr Big. You are far too impatient for cerebral stuff like fraud, but safe-blowing might be alluring.

It's not that you disrespect the law, not as such. It's just that you just can't stand being told what to do. So you do as you like. Then you end up before the judge, where you can't stand being told what to do, again, and get extra time for contempt of court. And when you can no longer get bail and are banged up, you may find it's not so bad. You love a challenge, and pretty soon you will be the leading light of the escape committee, going over the wall at regular intervals.

AT HOME

The mess hall

A few millennia from now, archaeologists will think grateful thoughts about those ancient Ariens (tentatively classified as the Gadget People) who never even considered tidying up and so left a rich seam of artefacts to illustrate life in the 21st century. The purpose of all those lockless keys, mobile phone carcasses, nostril hair cutters, Swiss army knives and unidentified bits of plastic will tax the greatest brains. They will deduce that you used to worship the god Honda, symbolically represented by a stripped-down motorbike kept on a table-like altar, and so sacred that the whole household used to eat their meals around it.

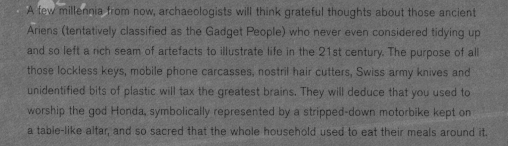

DOMESTIC DISHARMONY

Aries – you will be blacklisted by the cleaning agency.

Taurus – they may be good for a new kitchen, but they won't let you share it.

Gemini – they will find and pawn your granny's silver teaspoons that you thought you'd lost.

Cancer – will tidy up, but gripe about it; as you never listen, that won't bother you.

Leo – only desperate, exiled, rogue lions need apply.

Virgo – constantly tut-tutting under their breath about something they call bleach.

Libra – will leave when they find out about the bathroom, and that all the mirrors are cracked.

Scorpio – they step over your muck into the pristine minimalist cube of their own room.

Sagittarius – true mess mates; won't notice anything.

Capricorn – will put things away in a logical place so that you can never find them.

Aquarius – it's OK, because they're from planet Zog, so believe all Earthlings live like this.

Pisces – tetchy about mess, but happy to add more to it, especially empties.

Decor

How best to describe the Aries home style? Junkyard Transitional perhaps? A DIY repeat offender, you have never knowingly finished a renovation job. So wallpaper is half stripped, there are 49 shades of paint on the woodwork and you unplumbed the entire bathroom last year and now use a system of buckets. Your more zeitgeisty friends suspect you may be in the vanguard of a hot new trend.

Sharing the Aries slum

You find it difficult to retain partners, staff or housemates, but can't think why. Alright, the spare room is full of back copies of *What Car?* and the fridge only works when you kick it, but it's great for parties, and your sound system is bangin'.

Aries paint chart

Red alert

Red hot

Blood red

Code red

Red Adair

Fire engine red

Crimson tide

Red beret

Seeing red

Black

PLAYTIME

The darkside of fun

Like all Fire signs, you are unbearable anywhere the Sun don't shine. No Arctic breaks with extreme lemming racing for you, then. Avoid holidays that involve just you, a quiet tropical beach and your partner – especially on your honeymoon – because it will end in divorce: you don't do repose, and there is no fun bossing just one disciple around. Foreign city breaks find you braying at bar staff, hoteliers, taxi drivers and anyone else whose language you don't speak, just to assert yourself. And don't even think about hiring a villa with a bunch of mates, unless you have established that you will be running the temporary household (make sure the group contains a Cancerian to mop up after you).

What you'd really like is an action adventure holiday with the lads (even if you're a girl). And what would make it even better would be the outbreak of a smallish local war, so that you could do a little leisurely freedom fighting.

ZODIAC CULL

Suppose you were marooned on a desert island/up an alp/in a rainforest/ at sea with 11 others, each one a different sun sign. Who would you eliminate in order to survive? Well, you would need to leave a respectable-sized pack, otherwise there would be nothing to be leader of, but you would have to get rid of Gemini (argues too fluently and sways the others), Leo (might claim the leadership), Libra (too girlie for adventures) and Capricorn (picks you up on every last detail).

Holidays from hell

★ A luxury world cruise with Taurus, Leo and Libra; you have to throw yourself over the side or die of cabin fever.

★ A guided tour of anywhere; although you've never been there before, you know far more about the place than the guide who's lived there all his life, and you will not hesitate to say so. Loudly.

★ Anywhere on your own; you'd be lost without a docile pack to boss around and lead into dangerous new pastures.

Road rage

Although you single-handedly invented this social phenomenon, you think road rage is a base slur; it's just legitimate issue-raising with the visually challenged incompetents who throng your roads, idling along in your lane at the tired old national speed limit rather than at the Arien version. You don't need a map, because you always know where you're going; anyway you tore it up in a fit of rage and threw it out of the window 50 miles back. You always drive, even if it's not your car.

Gamesmanship

The universe will cease to be if you don't win every game you play, and every race and competition you enter. A founder member of Competitors Anonymous, you could turn a pensioners' bingo night into *Fight Club*. If the laws of physics are repealed and you lose, you must kill the winner and all other competitors, to blot out the shame; and take your ball home.

BAD COMPANY

Your hall of infamy

You may be feeling a bit emotionally fragile after a session on the Darkside, so to cheer the soul, let's look at a few of the famous, infamous, notorious and just plain bad Ariens who might feel the same if they read this book. You will be impressed (but not surprised) by the number of monomaniacs, superegos, politicians, warlords and self-centred artists there are: you're in very good bad company. And, despite your formidable (and frankly overwhelming) Darkside, there are a number of people who appear to want to be you, but who have missed the target. Think of any swaggering know-it-alls with an unshakable belief in their own fabulousness and the sensitivity of a house brick. All wannabe Ariens. If they're not, someone's lying. Look at the panel below if you don't believe me.

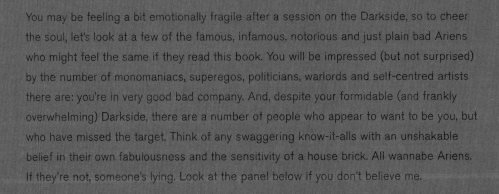

WANNABES

All soldiers, corporate raiders and fitness trainers are honorary Ariens, regardless of their actual sun sign. They should really have an official birthday – 1 April, perhaps – like Her Majesty the Queen. But what about Red Adair, the daredevil oil-fire supremo, whose life is one long thrilling round of infernos and adrenaline? Aries incarnate, wouldn't you say? Gemini. How about Mao Zedong, China's Red Emperor, who forged a nation (killing several million of them on the way, but so what!) with his bare willpower? Capricorn. Margaret Thatcher, the Iron Lady, who imposed her own agenda and took no prisoners? Libra (but that is Aries' opposite sign, so you can see a link). And you'd think John Wayne, the Dook, doer of what a man's gotta do, would be leading the Aries patrol, wouldn't you? Nope: Gemini.

Charlemagne *2 April, 742*

Charles the Great, King of the Franks, the first Holy Roman Emperor and the man who put Europe together in the Middle Ages. Top empire builder, military campaigner and scholar, but never a fan of delegation.

Leonardo da Vinci *15 April, 1452*

Renaissance man, and all that: a fount of new ideas, futuristic inventions and revolutionary techniques, but never actually quite finished anything, unless threatened at Pope-point.

Giovanni Giacomo Casanova *2 April, 1725*

Top-class serial lover, combining energy, stamina, lust and a dedication to the chase that puts tomcats everywhere to shame; he claims a hit rate of 122. A career fidget, he was a soldier, spy, diplomat, writer and adventurer, but ended his days as a librarian.

Vincent Van Gogh *30 March, 1853*

Flame-haired Dutch rebel artist, who hated his teachers, exploited his family, loathed fellow artists who sold more than he did, annoyed the pants off absolutely everyone and got so cross with everything that he chopped off his own ear. He just knew he was right! As it turned out, he was.

François 'Papa Doc' Duvalier *14 April, 1907*

One-time doctor turned Haitian dictator and self-proclaimed voodoo adept, who ruled by fear, military might, mass execution and curfew; created a personal police force, the Tontons Macoute, to enforce his will.

TAURUS

21 April ~ 21 May

Taurus is a feminine, fixed Earth sign ruled by Venus. It is the second sign on the zodiac wheel, directly opposite Scorpio, and is named after the constellation Taurus (the bull), which plods and bellows behind the Sun at this time of year.

On the Darkside, this makes you a stubborn, sybaritic, rut-bound bully, fuelled by dull resentment and an insatiable love of money.

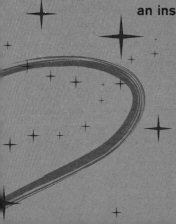

ANNOYING HABITS

Punctuality

You are never late; you have never been late; you will never be late. People in Switzerland set their clocks by you, train companies call you for advice. Strangely, everyone else is always late meeting with you

Toothpaste

The Taurus toothpaste tube always lives in a toothpaste-tube cozy on the third shelf down and is always rolled up from the bottom. If anyone moves it – let alone squeezes it in the middle – you kill them

Temper gauge

0° to boiling point in about six months, but on a regular five-year cycle. Much earth-shaking; small buildings fall down; you gore everyone within reach. Ten days later people armed with chocolate can approach you

PERSONALITY

obdurate, opinionated, overpowering

Brightsiders have enough trouble trying to gloss over your Darkside, so I don't know what you expect me to do. They call you things like slow but sure, steady and reliable, when we know they mean that you are stupendously dull and will move only when poked with a stick; they refer coyly to your love of beautiful things and traditional values, when we know they mean that you are a hidebound, reactionary Übermaterialist, superglued into a rut several metres deep; but even the most loopily starry-eyed of them fail to dress up the fact that you are a stubborn, obstinate, opinionated authoritarian, and all of them throw in the towel in the face of your overpowering urge for money.

Alright, being soul-sappingly boring isn't the most Stygian you can get on the Darkside (although tell that to your desperate family, mouthing 'Kill me now' through the windowpane at passersby as you get out the Monopoly board for your biweekly game). But being a dull boy is the least of it.

What you really like is stuff: in your mouth, on your plate, in your bank, in your bed, in the bag. You stubbornly refuse to accept the folk wisdom that tells us we can't always get what we want. You can! And when you've got stuff, you hold on to it with a grip that it would be laughable to describe as vicelike. Possessive seems too weak a word. It's a brave astrologer who tries to take anything away from you (even if only to clean it). And the evil spawn of paranoid possessiveness is murderous jealousy and resentment.

However much you've got, you resent the fact that: 1) you haven't got any more; 2) other people may have stuff; and 3) other people may have more stuff than you.

You are not a people person (of course you'd sell your grandmother – she's depreciating quickly and will soon be worthless, but if you shift her now, you could pick up a nice little investment Hockney print or two), but while you have them under your hoof you are possessive, jealous and resentful of them too. You timetable their every hour, always want to know where they are and stamp your feet if they are not back on the dot specified by you. Your children try to leave home the minute they can crawl. They won't get far. You fitted GPS tracking devices into their comfort blankets.

Your pig-headed obstinacy, obdurate opinions and refusal even to say the word 'adapt', let alone 'change', are all a result – Freud may possibly have said – of a lack of imagination. (He was a Taurean; it takes one to know one.) Your little bully brain can't compute more than two variables at once, so when faced with something complex or unusual, you go rigid and do what you have always done. Often that is nothing, so you tend to get buried alive by avalanches you refuse to notice, or dispatched by clever matadors.

What softens your tough hide (and makes it easier for the rest of us to lead you by the nose) is your self-indulgent hedonism. A case or two of Margaux, a 10-course banquet, a team of sunkissed masseurs – and you're anybody's.

Bitch rating

C+. Others think this is because you are naturally kind and charitable, but they are wrong; it's not that you don't want to bitch, you're just too slow-witted to really make an impact. When you do try, you make dull, painful remarks about other people's lack of fashion sense or money.

Collective noun

A field tip for non-Taureans. You may find yourself, for some bizarre zodiacal reason, in a meadow full of Taureans. No one is talking, but the rhythmic sound of regular grass-chomping syncopates smoothly with the soft rustle of bank statements being filed. You are corralled in a Stodge of Taureans. Stay awake, or get trampled to death in the rush for the buffet.

FAVE DEADLY SIN

'I'll have all them, now' is naturally your first thought as a rush of desire for some new stuff fogs your brain. When you finally understand you've got to choose, you go away to ruminate, and come back some days later with the obvious answer: Greed, with a substantial side dish of Gluttony (maybe served in a *jus* of Lust). You think having and holding until death do you part is sensible behaviour, and nothing is ever going to change your mind. As for Gluttony, what's wrong with liking your fodder, especially if it comes at a *prix fixe*?

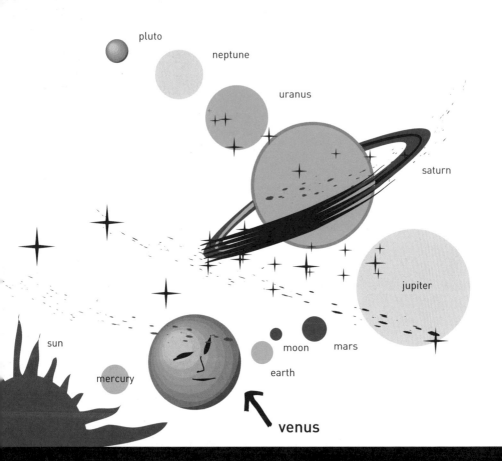

pluto

neptune

uranus

saturn

jupiter

sun

mercury

moon   mars

earth

venus

PLANET PLANET

Every sun sign has a property and portfolio manager, whose job it is to ensure that funds and assets are positioned to maximize growth and attract minimum tax. Before there were telescopes, astrologers could see only five planets in the sky, plus the Moon and Sun, so they counted these two as planetary rulers. It seemed a good idea at the time. Each planet babysat two zodiac signs – except for the Moon (Cancer's minder) and the Sun (which allows Leo to rule). Your ruler is Venus, planet of love (*see page 52*); maddeningly, this inconstant baggage also sees to Libra. Since you strongly resent sharing anything, you strongly resent sharing your beautiful planet. You have tried to argue about it, but Libra just laughs indulgently at you, tickles you under your chins and tweaks your nose ring.

BLAME YOUR PLANET

Mighty aphrodite

You have just thrown the widows and orphans out of the 19th-century workhouse you bought for a snip and plan to develop into loft-style apartments; you have shifted all your funds from ethical stocks to the industrial-military sector; you've just eaten all the pies. Even you think you are acting like a City Boy tool. So shift the blame onto your planet. In your case, it's Venus.

Surprised? Expecting something a little more – how shall I put it – substantial? Don't be. Venus is named after the Roman goddess of love and harmony, which is a politically correct disguise for Aphrodite, the Greek goddess of love and just plain having it. She is renowned for going after the many objects of her desire with a singularity of passion and purpose that is admired and emulated by land-grabbing evil emperors, asset strippers and eight-year-old girls everywhere. Trust me, you couldn't have a more effective mentor.

Venus is the second rock from the Sun, and our nearest neighbour (which is nice for you, because you don't like straying far from your paddock). It likes to be chased, so it orbits the Sun just that little bit faster than we do, but not so fast that we don't get the chance to admire its beautiful, creamy, luminous complexion.

It has the kind of atmosphere you are at home with: solid, reassuring, you could cut it with a knife and, stubbornly, it refuses to spin anticlockwise on its axis like the rest of us. It's your kind of place. If it wasn't so hot on the surface, you might put in an offer.

BAD MOON RISING

The darkside of Taurus's darkside

It's not all sunshine on the Darkside. You know just how power-crazed and monomaniac your innermost thoughts and secret fantasies are, but where do you think they come from? The Moon, that's where – or whichever area of your birthchart the Moon was moodily plodding when you were born. The Sun is our daytime self; the Moon represents our inner psycho. The nippy little blighter rushes around, plunging in and out of signs every few days, so throughout Taurus's month in the Sun, the lunar nuisance charges around like two tons of potential roast beef breaking angrily out of the abattoir. That helps to explain why two Taureans born only days apart store their money in entirely different offshore accounts, depending on which sign the Moon was bothering at the time.

CATCHING THE MOON

That's all very well, you say, but how do I know where the Moon was when I was born? There are long, complicated (and, frankly, dull) tables called ephemerides that tell you where every planet (and for tedious astrological reasons, the Moon is an honorary planet) stood in the heavens, atmosphere bated, as you made your sorry debut. However, we have provided a Moon itinerary at the back of this book to enable you to get a rough idea. If that sounds like too much hard work, and you have the techno technique, then try visiting the following website: www.alabe.com/freechart. If you know where you were born, and when, they will produce, for *free*, a rough-cut birthchart that will pin your Moon on the zodiac wheel.

Lunatic combinations

Here's what happens to Taurus when the Moon sets off to plod around the paddock.

Moon in Aries – on hot nights you dream of blood, sand, bright lights, stamping and death in the afternoon.

Moon in Taurus – you shall not be moved.

Moon in Gemini – you occasionally suspect it might be possible to charge in more than one direction.

Moon in Cancer – you prefer to be alone in a gloomy barn, where you moan about how none of your herd ever calls.

Moon in Leo – royal bull, glued to the throne; they will have to tear the sceptre and orb from your cold, dead hand.

Moon in Virgo – why does it always have to be you who remembers to take the ball of string into the labyrinth?

Moon in Libra – you feel sure there must be more elegant ways to open a gate than just charging at it.

Moon in Scorpio – other people never know when you're going to charge; you like it that way.

Moon in Sagittarius – easily excited by red rags, or rags of any colour; and strangely attracted to ceramic shops.

Moon in Capricorn – you find it hard to really indulge yourself: bleak experiments with sugar-free chocolate and no-fat cake.

Moon in Aquarius – cud-chewing is interrupted by occasional puzzling thoughts; surely it couldn't be right to give away all your money to the poor?

Moon in Pisces – always wandering off the beaten track and having to be brought home by the farmer's boy.

BORN UNDER A BAD SIGN

The scum also rises

And another thing. Your sun sign is modified by your rising sign. This is the zodiac sign that was skulking over the horizon at the very minute you were born. If your sun sign is your ego, then your rising sign gives you your public manners (such as they are), your Sunday worst. It's the painted smile behind which the real, disgusting you lurks. Some astrologers maintain that its malign influence affects what you look like. Be afraid.

If you were born around dawn (unlikely, I know, given your slowness on the uptake; midwives would have to lure you out with chocolate creams and a lucrative contract), your rising sign will almost certainly be the same as your sun sign. This means that your image is only a slight spin away from the grim actuality beneath the mask. Yuck!

GOING UP

Now pay attention, because the following is quite brain-busting. There are 12 signs of the zodiac, and astrologers like to think of them as occupying a band of sky that spins around the Earth once every 24 hours. (This is a convention; it is not astronomically correct and you will not see the signs if you look up, so don't write in.) So, every two hours or so another sign hauls itself blearily over the eastern horizon. This is going on whatever time of the day or night you were born, and whichever benighted spot on the globe you chose to appear in. These astro-mechanics help to explain why bulls born at either end of the same day dig in their hooves at a slightly different angle. There are long, nerdy ways to discover your rising sign, but the easiest way is to get hold of a birthchart (see page 48).

Upwardly mobile

If your rising sign is Taurus, then your public persona is a slow-moving, low-wattage gâteau-blaster. This is to distract the rest of us from your plans to rob the world bank. Here's what happens when other zodiacal upstarts rise above their station.

Aries rising

Raging bull.

Gemini rising

Who would've thought that so much prime rib could turn so niftily?

Cancer rising

You look rather worried; is it free-floating anxiety, or have you just found out exactly what *boeuf wellington* means?

Leo rising

Zeus, king of the gods, once manifested himself as a handsome white bull to seduce an unwary maiden; and you believe that, in certain favourable lights, you have rather a look of Zeus about you.

Virgo rising

No bovine excrement here, thank you.

Libra rising

Oiled hooves, polished horns, gleaming nose ring; who's the lucky heifer, big boy?

Scorpio rising

You appear darkly, hypnotically resolute; actually, you're just stubborn.

Sagittarius rising

Maverick bull; always up for a good stampede, especially if it's near a precipice.

Capricorn rising

You'd lead the herd into an abattoir if you thought there was a fat deal in it for you.

Aquarius rising

Looks like a bull; bellows like a bull; charges like a bull; is actually a Tauroid alien from the Aldebaran star region.

Pisces rising

Sacrificial bull; so set on martyrdom you try to light the sacred flames yourself.

DON'T YOU LOVE ME, BABY?

Venus and Taurus

Taurus and Venus have a thing going on anyway (*see page 47*), but just how much of a high-maintenance tease or bunny-boiler you are may depend on where the solar system's heartless tart was blushingly dropping her handkerchief when you were born (*see below*). Oh, and Venus also has a say in how harmoniously you blend in with the rest of the world, but what do words like harmony have to do with the Darkside? Now, for astrological reasons that will fry your brain (basically, Venus is far too luxury-loving to move too far away from the Sun, and her orbital rate is in bed with Earth's), Venus only ever appears in your sun sign, or two signs on either side of it. In your case, bulls, that means Taurus, Pisces, Aries, Gemini or Cancer. This is what it does to your love and lust life.

MAKE LOVE AND WAR

Venus is the girlie planet of lurve, right? And Mars is planet lad, the warlord. You may also have a sneaking feeling that men are from Mars and women are from Venus. Don't be upset if I tell you this is not true. All of us, of all genders, have a stake in both planets. Where they are in your birthchart has what I shall call consequences. You may think your sun sign makes you a born babe-magnet, but Venus in a chilly sign will cut you off at the knees; you may think that your sun sign means you are the twin soul of the dove of peace, but you may go red-eyed with bloodlust when beaten to a parking space. Mars will be somewhere irascible. You'll need a birthchart (*see page 48*) to find out what Venus and Mars were playing at when you were born. It is far too complicated – and, frankly, dull – to work out here.

Venus in Taurus

You always get what you want, even if what you want doesn't want you. You cut your prey off from the herd, corner them in a remote field, then shower them with kisses, chocolate and inappropriately expensive presents. This is to distract them while you tether them to the spot.

Venus in Pisces

You nuzzle your beloved needily, lowing plangently for declarations of love; when they respond, you show your joy by running off with their best friend.

Venus in Aries

You come back victorious from the fight, with El Cordobés' ears in a silk bag slung around your throat. Your muscles ripple powerfully as you choose one of the adoring herd to celebrate your triumph. Two seconds later, you choose another.

Venus in Gemini

You're too insensitive to notice when your embarrassingly terrible, clunky chat-up lines (you've been using the same ones since you first trotted into the sexual arena) are ridiculed; someone (it doesn't matter who) will fall for you.

Venus in Cancer

Homemade cakes are your aphrodisiac of choice. You take them on every date. If they don't work, you can always bring them home and eat them yourself.

ARE YOU LOOKING AT ME?

Mars and Taurus

Taureans don't get much hassle; standing still, looking solid, usually does it for you. But just how confrontational, threatening, paranoid and gagging for a fight you are depends on which area of your birthchart the bruiser planet Mars is being held back in by his mates (leave it, Mars, he's not worth it). Mars is the next planet out from Earth, but paces its orbit rather more slowly (presumably to get some effective eyeballing in). It takes 2½ years for Mars to get around, and on the way it spends about two months of quality menacing time in each sign. As a Taurean, you can be prodded into action only if your food or money supply is threatened. If your brute force expresses itself in a style that doesn't reach *corrida* standards, check out Mars' alibi at the time of your birth.

Mars in Aries

The farmer has put a big warning notice in red writing on your gate; luckily for him, you can't read it.

Mars in Taurus

Not easy to get this war machine into action; requires an enormous run-up time, and plenty of ground-pawing space. Devastating, but often too late.

Mars in Gemini

A bullring favourite, you dive and swerve amid the pikes on twinkling hooves, then lightly gore your opponents while they're looking for you under their cloaks.

Mars in Cancer

You charge down your enemies on their blindside, out of the blue, usually about 10 years after they have upset you.

Mars in Leo

A slight to your royal house? You order your guards to hunt down the villains in question, then challenge the leader to a one-to-one tournament with your champion (Aries).

Mars in Virgo

There had better be a really good reason for the mud and blood spattered all over your pristine paddock.

Mars in Libra

Smile diplomatically at your enemies. Invite them round for tea and cake. Poison the cake.

Mars in Scorpio

Everybody's worst nightmare: an unchallengeable combination of physical force and psychic menace. No one is going to risk making you angry, which is a bit disappointing, really.

Mars in Sagittarius

Easily baited, and quicker on your hooves than most, you love a good ruck, with plenty of barging and horn action.

Mars in Capricorn

Impressively implacable, even by Taurean standards; you not only fight all enemies to the death – however long it takes to achieve this – but also bankrupt their friends and families and sell their children into slavery.

Mars in Aquarius

You don't like to get your horns bloody, so when you get mad, you buy the land from under your enemies, evict them and make them watch while you burn their houses down.

Mars in Pisces

Lots of ineffectual tilting, mostly at windmills who don't appreciate you.

Scorpio

Taurus →

POLAR BEARS

Your polar sign sits on the opposite side of the zodiac wheel, six signs away, giving you knowing looks. You have a dark umbilical link with it. If Darkside you is your evil twin, then your polar sign is your evil twin's evil twin. It's got your number – but then

you've got its, so that's alright, isn't it? Brightside astrologers maintain that there is a strong complementary relationship between you and your polar sign, and that this relationship is positive and fruitful, especially at work, because you share the same energy quality

(fixed). Well, excuse me; on the Darkside it's more like the ancient, mutually understood confrontation between man (OK, human) and beast in the Plaza de Toros – brute force against mind power amidst the blood and dust. Both of them want the same trophy: the ears

WHO'S GOT YOUR NUMBER?

check out the opposition

Your polar opposite sign is Scorpio: the scary, cool, brooding control freak. (For more about your darkly fascinating opposite number, *see pages 232–263*.) What would a bloody-minded, bovine breadhead like you want with a moody, manipulative mind gamer like your average Scorpio? How do you have this – shall we say – understanding? Well, like good cop and bad cop, or arch villain and superhero, you need each other to make the Darkside work for you. It's all about elements (undesirable ones, of course). You are Earth; Scorpio is Water; put them together and you get mud, ideal for slinging, or for making voodoo dolls of people who look at you in a funny way.

Chomping your way stolidly through your usual catering-size wheel of strawberry cheesecake while you check your bank statements – as you do every second Thursday – don't you sense, deep down, the shadowy inner presence of a fierce-eyed, black-clad guru, urging you to use the force? Ever wonder why it is that the rest of us do not instantly dismiss you as an obstinate, ineffectual stick-in-the-mud who doesn't realize it's the Age of Aquarius? It's because we, too, can feel a flicker of the force.

Respect your inner Scorpion; it slips you that little bit of true menace that gives you cred, makes you a serious person and forces people to admit you are a contender. Too much, and your eyes turn red, you paw the ground, become a dangerous chunk of psycho muscle and have to be put down.

DARKSIDE DATE

You will always get a date because most of you are quite handsome, in a solid, thick-necked sort of way, and you just keep charging at the gate until it gives way. Once you have decided on a datée, they don't really stand a chance or get much say in the arrangements.

You have always given your dates flowers and chocs, and no power on Earth will stop you now, even if your current beloved is diabetic and has hay fever. (You can always eat the chocs yourself.) You are the sign that thinks oversized cuddly toys are sweet, romantic

gestures. Your ideal date sees you supine on a velvet couch in a private five-star restaurant with a pretty, fluffy airhead who is willing to do all the work, won't demand too much in the way of conversation and will love peeling post-prandial grapes for you as you sleep.

SEX

Slow, sensuous, suffocating

Brightside astros are always blathering about how sensuous, languorous and lollingly delicious a night between the sheets with you is, and how they all appreciate a lover with a slow hoof. Well, yes, it may be an improvement on the wham-bam-thank-you-Aries approach, but you can have too much of a good thing.

The trouble is, once you've learnt how to make the earth move, you just keep on singing the same old song. It gives a whole new meaning to the word 'rutting'. Good men and women have suffocated from boredom in your bed, their hopeless sobs mistaken for whimpers of desire. And you resent any attempt to bring a little novelty or spontaneity into the routine. Show you a *Kama Sutra* and you'd try to eat it. But you do rather like

the one where you smear each other with chocolate body paint and spend all night licking it off (although you can't help thinking you'd get more of the actual chocolate if you ate it straight from the jar with a spoon while watching a nice film, like *The Sound of Music*).

What kind of love rat are you?

Love ratting is not your sport. When you've got something, you hang on to it. To you the code words 'I just need some space' mean let's buy a bigger field. So even if your lover tries all 50 ways to leave, including servicing the entire Manchester United team simultaneously, you still follow them around the meadow bellowing piteously. This is called stalking.

INCOMPATIBILITY RATING

Aries – is that a suit of lights in their wardrobe, or are they just pleased to see you?

Taurus – irresistible meets immovable: cliché of the titans.

Gemini – they dance round you flapping red rags until you finally snap.

Cancer – they scuttle sideways when you charge at them.

Leo – impoverished royalty trying to ally themselves with bourgeois money.

Virgo – OK they're neat, but they don't do neat in the way you have always done neat.

Libra – all style; you can deal only with substance.

Scorpio – they can outstare you; you can outsit them.

Sagittarius – sudden action and loud noises always spoil your digestion.

Capricorn – they have more bank accounts than you.

Aquarius – think it's an insult to call you a materialist.

Pisces – they sink their fishy little hooks into your wallet.

RELATIONSHIPS

In a field of your own

There is a reason why bulls stand on their own in a field, you know. Partly it is because, although your murderous temper shows itself only once in a blue moon, the more pusillanimous members of the zodiac would rather be safe than sorry, and prefer to conduct social affairs with a big strong gate between you and them. Mostly it is because, after a few days in your field staring at your collection of numbered buttercups, discussing your varied pension plans and tax-exempt offshore investments, people begin to lose the will to live.

Of course you have friends; they are those whom you meet in the same bar, at the same time, on the same day of every month. If for some trivial reason they don't turn up (their house has burned down,

their only child has been kidnapped) or, even worse, suggest you meet half an hour earlier or even in a different place, you begin to snort and bellow and have to be placated with soothing words, food and gifts.

In any herd activities, everybody always does what you want to do; you think this is because they agree with your choice. In fact, they are being pragmatic; they just know that life's too short to go up against your Olympic obduracy (unless they are another Taurean).

When you get married (of course you will), after the initial flowers and babytalk business, you make it very clear that it's going to be your way or nothing. If your partner goes for the 'or nothing' option, you just won't let them out of the field.

DREAM JOBS

You don't really have the imaginative powers to dream of a job you're not actually in. And if somebody offered you the plummiest, most chocolate-covered job in the land, you wouldn't take it, because you don't do change. But even you might consider these two:

Property magnate

We see industrial wasteland; you see executive urban homes. We see designated historical sites; you see executive apartments. We see unspoilt fishing villages; you see executive holiday homes.

Asset stripper

Round peg, round hole: your ability to spot a wounded beast, a bargain and a money-making opportunity, and your genuine insensitivity to job losses, starving families and pensioner suicides, make this a bull's-eye.

WORK

Jobsworth

You would not miss the nobility of work if the Bad Fairy swung it so that you could have all of the money and none of the effort. Some bulls achieve this state by being born rich (you know who I am talking about Queen Elizabeth II of England). The rest of you have to work, just like the rest of us, but steer clear of anything marked vocation or social conscience, because the only thing you care about is the paycheque. This means you will do more or less anything, as long as you don't have to respond to emergencies or get too sweaty, and there's a canteen. Maybe you once dreamed of a more active job in Pamplona, or a china shop, but that was just youthful high spirits.

Colleagues soon learn not to walk on your patch of carpet, never to rearrange the ornaments on your desk and never, ever to use your special mug. They also learn not to ask you for a decision unless they have a month hidden in the schedule, or to ask you to do anything not specified in your job description.

Of course you join your trade union, because 'restrictive practices' sounds so you. Employers are impressed with you at first because you positively embrace mind-numbing routines and follow orders. They promote you; you demand a pay rise. They laugh; you point out clause 287b (ii) in your contract. They prevaricate; you take them to cumulative industrial tribunals and eventually the High Court, wiping out company profits at a stroke. You win. You cannot be fired. Result! Meal ticket for life.

Audacious and imaginative they're not, but Taurus crimes put food on the table; they are money in the bank (or, rather, out of it). If a plan works, stick to it: that's your motto. You aim to make every job as routine as possible; the nine-to-five ethic is just as valid on the Darkside.

Bank robber

Assume balaclava (or stocking). Enter bank. Point gun. Give me the money. Collect specified amount of cash in unmarked notes. Stuff in holdall. Exit bank. Take off balaclava. Home to view self on evening news.

Art thief

Shoplift art encyclopedia and Swiss army knife. Identify target painting and location. Attend gallery. Bribe security. Slice canvas from frame. Roll up and stuff down trouser leg. Limp home. Invoice punter.

CRIMES AND MISDEMEANOURS

How bad could it get?

So what sort of crim would you be, if sociopathy became the new world order? How would you spend your days (or maybe your nights) if you really lived on the Darkside? Well, show me the money. You're suspicious of invisible, complicated stuff like fraud or electronic crime because you suspect you will be done out of your cut by nimbler-brained Geminis (you're right). You like a simple plan and a payoff you can roll around in. Traditional bank robbery; antiques stolen to order; stripping the town houses of the obscenely rich when they are in Mustique, and vice versa.

Violence is not an issue. You make a very focused bounty hunter. And you are Mr Big's hitman of choice, since you don't get distracted, are insensitive to victims' pleas and will sit for days on a stakeout,

as long as there are enough doughnuts. You respect the law. Anything that gives property and money such protection is a good thing; but that doesn't stop you breaking it, if the law comes between you and what you want. Trouble is, you never change your MO, so the police always get you in the end.

You blow it in court. Lawyers (even your own) goad you into murderous rages and, before you know it, you have kicked in your stall, gored the judge and copped extra time for contempt of court. When you are sent down, it's not so bad. You could buy your way out, but you may find that prison life suits you: established routine, regular meals, exercise yard with a pleasantly beaten track, people who like to talk about money – what's not to like?

AT HOME

The comfort trap

You invite someone around to see your home movies. They fight their way past a security system that makes Fort Knox look like a corner-shop pushover. The house is warm, full of herds of huge furniture. They feel comfortably dozy. You pour them a vase of sherry and force-feed them a paving slab of madeira cake. They are getting drowsy. There are doilies everywhere, even under the doilies. Their eyelids droop. It's getting warmer. The furniture seems to be getting bigger. Light classical tunes tinkle. They are falling asleep. Then, with quiet determination, knowing they have no way out, you start selling them a pension.

DOMESTIC DISHARMONY

Aries – constant barbecues make you obscurely uneasy.

Taurus – you sit silently in opposite armchairs waiting for each other to see reason.

Gemini – they move the furniture around when you're not looking.

Cancer – they spend far too much time in the kitchen, worryingly near your food hoard.

Leo – their retinue and baggage take up too much territory.

Virgo – constantly trying to find something to tut-tut under their breath about.

Libra – they will win any fights over sofa space and the TV remote.

Scorpio – you suspect they are secretly eating all your cakes, but don't care to mention it.

Sagittarius – they use your special mug for swilling mouthwash, then accidentally drop it.

Capricorn – they get up early in the morning to open your bank statements before you can.

Aquarius – they have reset all your security codes, just for fun.

Pisces – every day your wine cellar gets a little roomier.

Decor

You have an exclusive network of interior designers able to take all your money and spend it on schemes that are guaranteed free from any imagination or creativity. Your home is every speculative contractor's dream show-house. Any inadvertent interest or individuality comes from an art collection that you were advised to buy for its investment value.

Sharing the Taurus home

You don't want to share with anybody, although you do accept – grudgingly – that you probably have to let your family in. Others who move in with you had better be ready to relinquish all their idiosyncratic little ways in favour of your one intractable little way.

Taurus paint chart

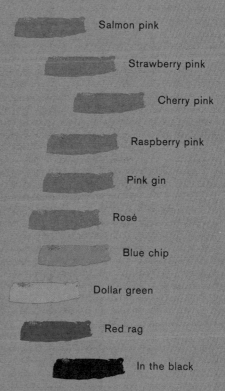

Salmon pink

Strawberry pink

Cherry pink

Raspberry pink

Pink gin

Rosé

Blue chip

Dollar green

Red rag

In the black

PLAYTIME

The darkside of fun

Every year you plod off to the little place you went to last year (and the year before that, and the year before that; you probably discovered it in your reckless, madcap days as a young bullock when you thought

ZODIAC CULL

Suppose you were marooned on a desert island/up an alp/in a rainforest/at sea with 11 others, each one a different star sign. Who would you eliminate in order to survive? Hmm, difficult; all of them, you think at first, to make sure there will be enough food for you until rescue comes. But suppose the food runs out? Maybe better keep the meatier ones in reserve; so a *coup de grâce* to the skinnies – Gemini, Virgo and Capricorn – and maybe Sagittarius, who eats a lot.

nothing of just upping and going into the next field – wild times!). It's not too hot, not too cold, with a guaranteed food supply, comfortable armchairs, no loud noises or sudden movements and nothing you haven't done before. Your family always seems strangely glum on these holidays, but you don't really know why. You are addicted to guided tours, which you like because you are used to being led around by the nose.

Your ideal would be an inaction-packed fortnight in Switzerland, where you can visit your money and eat chocolate in a heady atmosphere of affluence. Or in Liechtenstein (to visit your other money), because on a clear day you can see all the country's borders, and you do like to feel fenced in.

Holidays from hell

★ Snowboarding with Gemini and Sagittarius: cold, wet, dangerous, unpredictable and no regular meals.

★ Anywhere you have not been to before, unless it has been recommended by your Capricorn bank manager, who understands.

★ Anywhere with Virgo tightwads and Pisces incompetents; you will end up paying for everything because you are the only one with a functioning credit card.

Road rage

Traffic jams always seems to happen when you are at the wheel, but then you didn't get where you are today by giving way, and that applies to junctions and roundabouts. There always seems

to be a lot of beeping and shouting going on as you proceed along at a steady rate just two miles below the posted speed limit in the middle of the road, but you think that is normal. If anyone scrapes your beautiful car, you turn on a penny and go for them at ramming speed. You don't need a map because you are never going anywhere that you don't already know how to get to.

Gamesmanship

You are capable of holding up any game for days while you go head-to-head with the umpire/ref/line judge. If crossed, you will take home your ball, everybody's equipment and the goalposts, then set up a development company to buy the ground and turn it into a retail park.

BAD COMPANY

Your hall of infamy

You may be feeling a bit emotionally fragile after a session on the Darkside, so to cheer the soul, let's look at a few of the famous, infamous, notorious and just plain bad Taureans who might feel the same if they read this book. You will be truly impressed by the sheer number of long-lived, world-class dictators who share your field; you're in very good bad company. And, despite your formidable (though somehow tedious) Darkside, there are a number of people who appear to want to be you, but on whom the zodiac's bankers have foreclosed. Think of any pigheaded career materialists who move slow and think slower and are obsessed with making money long after they need it. All wannabe Taureans. If they're not, someone's lying. Look at the panel below if you don't believe me.

WANNABES

Well, how about Bill Gates, dull hero of the revenge-of-the-nerds movement? Enough money to buy two planets, but doesn't seem able to think of anything radical to spend it on; insists on keeping Joe Public waiting for the next operating system until he's good 'n' ready? A shoo-in for Taurus, wouldn't you say? No, Scorpio — but then you now know about the Scorpio-Taurus connection, so maybe you can see what's happening here. Consider Earl Tupper, inventor of those plastic boxes to keep food safe in, and father of a whole new way to alienate your friends by inviting them round and selling things to them? Leo. Martha Stewart, the doyenne of unnecessary detail and décor, who has made a fortune out of cake? Leo again. All bankers, property developers and supermarket squillionaires are honorary Taureans.

Genghis Khan *5 May, c.1162*

The world dictators' world dictator – *Khan* means universal ruler. Took over the Mongol horde at the age of 13, and slowly but surely built up an empire that stretched from the Black Sea to the Pacific. Died aged 70 (-ish) in his bed, with a nubile young friend.

Karl Marx *5 May, 1818*

Opinionated German philosopher who constructed an entire political theory around the idea of materialism. His greatest work, *Das Kapital* (all about money and the free-enterprise system), took him 30 years to produce and was never finished.

Adolf Hitler *20 April, 1889*

Wins the Darkside Superstar prize: everyone's choice for top world-class villain! The most hated and evil man in modern history – a coup for Bullkind! Although born on 20 April (usually Aries), zodiacal differences led him to annex a neighbouring sign; start as you mean to go on.

Tito *7 May, 1892*

Leader of the feuding, factionalist states formerly known as Yugoslavia. Tito ran the country his way, tolerating no opposition. He must have done well: it all fell to pieces less than 10 years after his death in 1980.

Saddam Hussein *28 April, 1937*

Successfully imposed his notions of how things should be done as president of Iraq's one-party state from 1979 to 2003, mainly by staffing the regime with family members. Famous for his innumerable palaces and the solid-gold taps in their innumerable bathrooms.

GEMINI

22 May ~ 21 June

Gemini is a masculine mutable Air
sign, ruled by the planet Mercury.
It is the third sign on the zodiac
wheel, directly opposite Sagittarius,
and is named after the constellation
Gemini (the twins), which constantly
ducks and dives behind the Sun at
this time of year.

On the Darkside, this makes you
an unreliable, roguish sociopath
with a light finger and the attention
span of a hyperactive mayfly.

Punctuality

You're rarely late (you'd hate to miss any good pickings), but never stay long since you are usually on your way to somewhere else that you think might be more interesting, or

Toothpaste

You have a shiny new electric toothbrush 'borrowed' from somewhere, and toothpaste picked up from unguarded retail displays – you didn't pay for it, so why should you give a damn

Temper gauge

0° to boiling point in five seconds, inventive invective, blistering bitchery, then back down again in two, mostly because your attention has wandered off. You prefer to

PERSONALITY

Feckless, reckless, two-faced

Brightside you is famous for your irresistible charm and sprightly wit. But you (and I) know that it's all a façade, isn't it? It's all sparkly patter to shift the eyes of the gullible away from what you're really up to. Underneath that layer of stage-school sincerity lurks a cold-eyed, cold-hearted, bad-mouthing rumour-monger, scavenging information so that you can shaft someone later or maybe even initiate a satisfactory little feud.

There is no cunning so low you can't limbo under it; no scam so complex that you can't get your devious, slippery mind around it. You are the con artist with the cheeky grin who detaches widows from their mites and babies from their candy, and yet leaves them laughing. What's the problem? It's all a game, isn't it?

Yet in spite of all your conning and conniving, you are never satisfied with what you get, are you? You carry colour swatches around so that you can check the greenness of the grass on the other side of whoever's garden you're drinking daiquiris in at the time. You always suspect that somewhere, just over the next rainbow, there's a more exciting party going on and you're not on the guest list. To block out such gloomy notions you have to be entertained at all times, otherwise you might get bored – and then the dark thoughts will come again. You charge about in a restless miasma of noise, change, bells and whistles, and the manufacturers of Ritalin rub their hands in glee as they airfreight yet another shipment out to you.

Brightside astrologers (just as easily bamboozled as anyone else) twitter on about your eternally youthful exuberance; this is code for saying that you are in a permanent midlife crisis of your own making: a discontented, self-obsessed commitment-phobe who refuses to grow up and is still wearing a baseball cap backwards at the age of 45.

Call you irresponsible? Yes, and unreliable, inconsistent, impractical, immature, incorrigible and a whole lot of other words with a negative prefix. If it came to a choice between feeding your children and the last pair of Blahniks in the sale, or an invitation to join an exclusive, high-stake poker game at the classy end of town – no contest. You might even sell the kids.

Of course, to live by your wits (i.e., lying, cheating and swindling) you need to have some wits to start with. You don't have any more than the rest of us, but you cunningly spread them very thinly over a large area, so that from a distance – and as long as you keep moving – you appear brighter than you are.

And it must have been you who invented ligging: basking in the limelight of the rich and famous; you're far too much of a feckless shapeshifter (plus there are your previous convictions to take into account) to build your own glittering career. Besides, being best friends with a rockstar gives you all the kudos without any of the hard work and tedium. And you'll never be called upon to deliver that difficult third album.

Bitch rating

A++. We bow to the zodiac's Bitch Queen. Your lightning rapier zigzags with such sparkling wit and style that many bitchees don't notice they've been slashed for at least three weeks; and your apologies are always so transparently heartfelt and sincere.

Collective noun

A confidential tip for non-Geminis. You may find yourself in a room full of Geminis (probably lured there by an impossibly cheap timeshare deal: watch your wallet, your reputation and your partner). The air buzzes with the sound of plausible grifters getting top dollar on their grandmothers. This is an Attention Deficit of Geminis. Sign nothing.

FAVE DEADLY SIN

Oh, come on! Only one deadly sin? For you, the dilettante of depravity? I don't think so. You need at least four: two for each twin. Choose from the following: Pride, for sure, although you prefer to use its other name, Vanity (you know you look good, so why not say so?); Lust, because it's fun; Envy (why should the rich have all the nice, shiny things? Indeed, why should anybody have anything you want? And how can you prize it from them without them noticing?). And Greed. Greed is good. What's wrong with wanting it all?

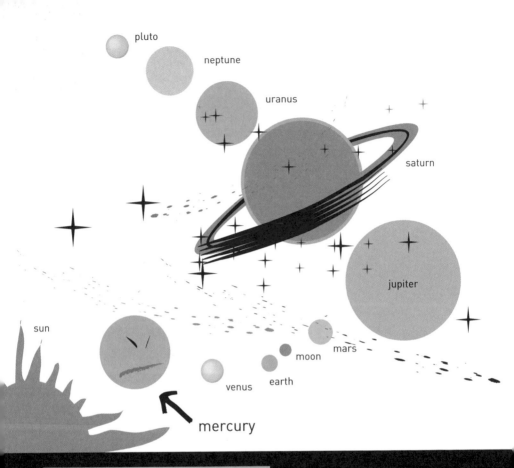

pluto

neptune

uranus

saturn

jupiter

sun

moon

mars

venus

earth

mercury

Every sun sign has a planetary lookout man, whose job it is to sweet-talk the authorities and keep the engine running in case a speedy getaway is called for. Before there were telescopes, astrologers could only see five planets in the sky, plus the Moon and Sun, so they counted

these two as planetary rulers. It seemed a good idea at the time. Each planet babysat two zodiac signs – except for the Moon (Cancer's minder) and the Sun (which allows Leo to rule). Your planetary ruler is Mercury. The great celestial irony for you, as a sign for whom the concept of

undivided attention simply does not compute, is that Mercury has a day job, metaphorically speaking, looking after Virgo (*see pages 174–175*). So it is a two-faced flirt, sneakily running a whole other household in another part of zodiac town. Does this sound at all familiar?

BLAME YOUR PLANET

Bright, fast and deadly

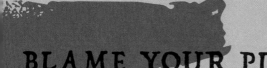

If you have been more devious than usual, have found yourself engaged to three separate admirers, have triple-crossed the local drug baron – if even you can't come up with a good excuse to explain why you are behaving so badly, then celestial help is at hand. Blame your planet. In your case, this is Mercury.

Mercury is a small, dense busybody that scurries sycophantically around the Sun in just 88 days, practically joined at the hip with our local star. It doesn't mind the heat as long as it can be self-important in the kitchen. It's got no moon (Mercury subjects like to travel light and, anyway, it wouldn't want to share the glory). Its showbiz twinkle is outclassed by the Sun, so it's mostly seen low in the east at dawn (like a party animal reeling back from a celeb-infested all-nighter) or low in the west at sunset (like a skulking burglar casing the joint).

It's called Mercury (like the shiny, silvery, shapeshifting, deadly metal) after the Roman god, but he is just a later version of Hermes, the Greek god of practically everything, but especially merchant bankers, mobile phones, gypsies, tramps and thieves.

And Mercury is a tricksy planet. It follows a charmingly eccentric orbit, speeding up and slowing down as the mood takes it, but rotating only on its axis three times every two years. This means that, if you stood on Mercury, you'd see the sun rise twice in the morning and set twice at the end of the day. Now you see it, now you don't.

BAD MOON RISING

The darkside of Gemini's darkside

It's not all sunshine on the Darkside. You know just how power-crazed and monomaniac your innermost thoughts and secret fantasies are, but where do you think they come from? The Moon, that's where – or whichever area of your birthchart the Moon was moodily plodding when you were born. The Sun is our daytime self; the Moon represents our inner psycho. The nippy little blighter rushes around, plunging in and out of signs every few days, so throughout Gemini's month in the Sun, the lunar nuisance slipslides around like a double agent looking for a safe house. That helps to explain why two Geminis born only days apart come up with such radically different con-artist schemes, depending on which sign the Moon was bothering at the time.

CATCHING THE MOON

That's all very well, you say, but how do I know where the Moon was when I was born? There are long, complicated (and, frankly, dull) tables called ephemerides that tell you where every planet (and for tedious astrological reasons, the Moon is an honorary planet) stood in the heavens, atmosphere bated, as you made your sorry debut. However, we have provided a Moon itinerary at the back of this book to enable you to get a rough idea. If that sounds like too much hard work, and you have the techno technique, then try the following website: www.alabe.com/freechart. If you know where you were born, and when, they will produce, for *free*, a rough-cut birthchart that will pin your Moon on the zodiac wheel.

Lunatic combinations

Here's what happens to Gemini when the Moon sets out to fool all of the people some of the time.

Moon in Aries – a lack of finesse and forethought scuppers your scams and ruins your punchlines.

Moon in Taurus – not so much a rapier wit, more like being clubbed with a double-edged broadsword.

Moon in Gemini – so sharp you'll cut your own throat: could end up conning yourself under a different name.

Moon in Cancer – too grumpy to dazzle; you rely on your grandmother's tried and tested box of con tricks.

Moon in Leo – you are the rightful heir to the throne, in exile; so you're not thieving, just taking what is legally yours.

Moon in Virgo – too anal to be charming, and your little schemes to separate fools and their money are so well organized they're almost no fun anymore.

Moon in Libra – professional charm merchant, more gigolo than gangster.

Moon in Scorpio – it's power games with gullible little minds that you really enjoy.

Moon in Sagittarius – a dead cert to blow any subtle, sophisticated stings.

Moon in Capricorn – your practical schemes appear so sensible that they invariably pay off; how dull is that?

Moon in Aquarius – a master of complex, brain-blowing schemes, but too cool to actually carry them out.

Moon in Pisces – emote with sincerity and quiver with pity as you rattle your bogus charity tin.

BORN UNDER A BAD SIGN

The scum also rises

And another thing. Your sun sign is modified by your rising sign. This is the zodiac sign that was skulking over the horizon at the very minute you were born. If your sun sign is your ego, then your rising sign gives you your public manners (such as they are), your Sunday worst. It's the painted smile behind which the real, disgusting you lurks. Some astrologers maintain that its malign influence affects what you look like. Be afraid.

If you were born around dawn (no doubt trying to sneak out before anyone noticed the spoons were missing), your rising sign will almost certainly be the same as your sun sign. This means that your image is only a slight spin away from the grim reality beneath the mask, and the rest of us get a double shot of your unedifying personality.

GOING UP

Now pay attention, because the following is quite brain-busting. There are 12 signs of the zodiac, and astrologers like to think of them as occupying a band of sky that spins around the Earth once every 24 hours. (This is a convention; it is not astronomically correct and you will not see the signs if you look up, so don't write in.) So, every two hours or so another sign hauls itself blearily over the eastern horizon. This is going on whatever time of the day or night you were born, and whichever benighted spot on the globe you chose to appear in. These astro-mechanics help to explain why twins born at either end of the same day flutter their eyelashes in a different way. There are long, nerdy ways to discover your rising sign, but the easiest way is to get hold of a birthchart (see page 80).

Upwardly mobile

If your rising sign is Gemini, your public persona is a shallow dilettante with a micro attention span and gorgeous shoes. This is to distract the rest of us from your plans to steal the planet. Here's what happens when other zodiacal upstarts rise above their station.

Aries rising

You may be wearing the gamekeeper's uniform, but that doesn't mean you've given up poaching.

Taurus rising

Who'd have thought it, say your neighbours as you are taken away in a plain van. You looked so respectable.

Cancer rising

A mother's work is never done, but shoplifting is so much easier with a double baby-buggy.

Leo rising

Like all royals, you never carry your own cash, but you will spend someone else's.

Virgo rising

Neat and tidy with a clipboard means that you will always get away with anything.

Libra rising

Handsome is as handsome does.

Scorpio rising

You appear darkly, hypnotically plausible; actually, you're just plausible.

Sagittarius rising

Life and soul of the party, but you leave with the spoons and the host's partner.

Capricorn rising

Dullness is a great disguise.

Aquarius rising

Your victims believe they were abducted by aliens who took all their earthly possessions for research purposes.

Pisces rising

Poor little you, all wet and cold with no home to go to. Surely some kind sap will take you in, so that you can do likewise?

DON'T YOU LOVE ME, BABY?

Venus and Gemini

Just how much of a high-maintenance tease or bunny-boiler you are may depend on where the solar system's heartless tart (Venus) was blushingly dropping her handkerchief when you were born (*see below*). Oh, and Venus also has a say in how harmoniously you blend in with the rest of the world, but what do words like harmony have to do with the Darkside? Now, for astrological reasons that will fry your brain if I explain them here (basically, Venus is far too luxury-loving to move too far away from the Sun, and her orbital rate is in bed with Earth's), Venus only ever appears in your sun sign, or two signs on either side of it. In your case, twins, that means Venus will be in Gemini, Aries, Taurus, Cancer or Leo. And this is what it does to your love and lust life.

MAKE LOVE AND WAR

Venus is the girlie planet of lurve, right? And Mars is planet lad, the warlord. You may also have a sneaking feeling that men are from Mars and women are from Venus. Don't be upset if I tell you this is not true. All of us, of all genders, have a stake in both planets. Where they are in your birthchart has what I shall call consequences. You may think your sun sign makes you a born babe-magnet, but Venus in a chilly sign will cut you off at the knees; you may think that your sun sign means you are the twin soul of the dove of peace, but you may go red-eyed with bloodlust when beaten to a parking space. Mars will be somewhere irascible. You'll need a birthchart (*see page 80*) to find out what Venus and Mars were playing at when you were born. It is far too complicated – and, frankly, dull – to work out here.

Venus in Gemini

Despite your smoothly spun sweet-talk and bulk purchasing of love tokens, your four fiancé(e)s, five spouses and 39 live-in lovers suspect they are not alone in the kingdom of your heart.

Venus in Aries

You're the best thing that happened to your band of lovers, whom you command with a whim of iron. Sex games tend to involve a lot of collateral damage and friendly-fire incidents.

Venus in Taurus

You own a whole treeful of love nests, which you won in a dodgy poker game. You like to line them with almost undetectably forged banknotes to attract the unwary.

Venus in Cancer

You bind your lovers to the bed with apron strings and do everything for them, then you get tetchy when they don't eat the cake you baked (it's their favourite), they don't call, they don't write …

Venus in Leo

You are already married (for dynastic reasons), but you feel you are free to lead your own love life and like to have new lovers sent in batches as tributes from smaller kingdoms. If you like any of them, you might even marry them as well.

ARE YOU LOOKING AT ME?

Mars and Gemini

Geminis tend to prefer the long knife slid between the ribs to noisy confrontation in which they might get hurt. But just how confrontational, threatening, paranoid and gagging for a fight you are depends on which area of your birthchart the bruiser planet Mars is being held back in by his mates (leave it, Mars, he's not worth it). Mars is the next planet out from Earth, but paces its orbit rather more slowly (presumably to get some effective eyeballing in). It takes 2½ years for Mars to get around, and on the way it spends about two months of quality menacing time in each sign. As a Gemini, you move so fast that you leave enemies lashing out at your shadow. If you find your light but deadly touch is losing some of its subtlety, check out Mars' alibi at the time of your birth.

Mars in Aries

Incidents that you should shrug off fog your brain with red mist. You lose your detachment and make silly mistakes.

Mars in Taurus

Turf warrior: slow to anger, but you will not tolerate unauthorized trespass on your 'hood (usually Leo and Sagittarius). Frequently guilty of overkill.

Mars in Gemini

You challenge enemies to a one-to-one fight, then cheat, buy off the ref, hide a stiletto up your sleeve, tamper with your opponent's weapon and win.

Mars in Cancer

You spend far too much time coming up with killer ripostes to perceived injuries and affronts received 10 years ago.

Mars in Leo

Although you have your own rapier, you don't fight, because that would take up valuable planning time. There is a court champion for that kind of thing.

Mars in Virgo

Messy fighting disturbs the grazing of the punters you have lined up for fleecing. So you always carry a gun with a silencer.

Mars in Libra

Too lazy to actually fight, you shop any enemies to their enemies (who instantly and temporarily become your friends). That way, they get knee-capped; you get to stay on the sofa with your alibi.

Mars in Scorpio

Only new guns in town don't know that you are surrounded by spies, cunning snares, traps for the unwary and a forcefield generated by sheer willpower.

Mars in Sagittarius

You really like it when scams go wrong and you can get down to some exhilarating straightforward scrapping without blowing your cover.

Mars in Capricorn

You don't like conspicuous warfare, so you hack into enemy bank accounts and siphon them dry; then you place a couple of anonymous calls to the Inland Revenue.

Mars in Aquarius

Fighting is so hot-making; you prefer a war of words, whispers, propaganda, lies, rumour, disinformation and more lies. You're the only one with the brain to remember who's on whose side.

Mars in Pisces

You beg those you have deceived for mercy, swear it will never happen again, then stab them when you get the chance.

Sagittarius

Gemini

POLAR BEARS

Your polar sign sits on the opposite side of the zodiac wheel, six signs away, giving you knowing looks. You have a dark umbilical link with it. If Darkside you is your evil twin, then your polar sign is your evil twin's evil twin. It's got your number — but then

you've got its, so that's alright, isn't it? Brightside astrologers maintain that there is a strong complementary relationship between you and your polar sign, and that this relationship is positive and fruitful, especially at work, because you share the same energy quality

(mutable). Well, excuse me; on the Darkside the relationship is more like the impressive impasse displayed by the colourful gangsters in *Reservoir Dogs*: each one is held at gunpoint by the other, and no one gives an inch because they are all after the same thing

WHO'S GOT YOUR NUMBER?

check out the opposition

Your polar opposite sign is Sagittarius, the thoughtless, reckless, obsessional extrovert, who likes to live now and default later. (For more about your darkly fascinating opposite number, *see pages 264–295*.) What would a fast-moving, fast-talking, nimble-witted artful dodger like you want with a clumsy, blundering, foot-in-mouth liability like Sagittarius? How come you have this – shall we say – understanding? Well, like good cop and bad cop, or arch villain and superhero, you need each other to make the Darkside work for you. It's all about elements (undesirable ones, of course). You are Air; Sagittarius is Fire. Fire cannot burn without oxygen, and don't you two just love breaking into the fireworks factory and throwing lighted matches around.

Unlike any other polar pairings, you two have a relationship that shows up above the subatomic particle level. You know the pattern: the little weaselly motormouth who fights dirty and initiates trouble, and the big, dumb oaf of little brain who is dragged along in the slipstream. Think of Laurel and Hardy, Pooh and Piglet and, for the intellectuals among you, Vladimir and Estragon.

Respect your inner Sagittarian; it provides a tiny inner flame of humanity (even Darkside Sagittarians love their mums), which thaws that cold, hard little heart of yours, secretly sneering at how easily the rest of us can be taken in. Of course, if it melts in there, you might begin to consider giving the suckers an even break. And you couldn't have that.

DARKSIDE DATE

Your trick is to cast a wide net, then you get to pick and choose the catch. You are such a broad-spectrum flirt that there is no chance you won't get a date – and probably two or three for the same evening. This is the kind of romantic challenge you relish, and you thank your lucky

planet for the invention of the mobile phone. Your date(s) must bring a well-stuffed wallet with them, as one of your favourite gambits is 'Let's you and me go and have a wonderful time spending your money'. One of your career goals is to become arm-candy to the filthy rich.

Your ideal date would be with identical-twin, world-famous Brazilian supermodels with their own Swiss bank accounts, playing strip poker and drinking Cristal champagne in their Lear jet. You'd bring your own sex toys and parachute – in case anyone mentioned commitment.

SEX

Fun and games

As your gonads are wired up firmly to your head, not your heart, you love sex because it's a game you're really good at. Singles, mixed doubles, five-a-side: you excel at all of them, at amateur and professional level.

Not for you the long, languorous nights in satin sheets with just the one lover. You must never be bored in bed. Lots of your sex takes place in unusual places (you are a founder member of the Mile High Club, the K2 It's Great on Top Collective and the Mariana Trench Going Down Slow Society). Or it has the frisson that comes from possible discovery: in the next room to your mother-in-law, on the boardroom table, in church.

You always like a nice old-fashioned orgy because, the minute dullness rears

its head, you just shift your leg slightly and move on. While not in the Scorpio class, you do appreciate a bit of designer deviance of the cross-dressing, velvet handcuffs, role-playing kind. Top sex for you is pleasuring one lover while flirting with the next two over their shoulder.

What kind of love rat are you?

You blarney your way into the hearts of the vulnerable, your friends' partners or useful work colleagues and keep them all sweet despite behaving atrociously. You move on (almost immediately), but you don't dump; you prefer to keep your options open to ensure a warm welcome in every port. And let's stop with the love-rat abuse – your rat is a smart, resourceful player who never goes hungry.

INCOMPATIBILITY RATING

Aries – this may be character forming: a megadose of your own love potion.

Taurus – they will try to tie you down with food and flattery.

Gemini – exhausting; how will the four of you keep it up?

Cancer – inevitably ends in tears (not yours, of course).

Leo – come on like royalty, but they're just another frog to you.

Virgo – will smother your every betrayal with understanding and forgiveness. Aargh!

Libra – see what happens when con artists collide.

Scorpio – social butterfly meets professional insectivore.

Sagittarius – *folie à deux;* bungee jumping without strings.

Capricorn – you leap at the chance of leading astray the zodiac's Mr Repression.

Aquarius – no good at all – way too cool to rise to your bait.

Pisces – perfect: the zodiac's amphibian, your natural prey.

RELATIONSHIPS

Round, round, get around

For Princess Gemini, it's all in the game: you love the pursuit of poor besotted frogs and will even kiss them, but when they turn into dull handsome princes, the thrill is gone and the spell wears off. You go to the next ball and they get thrown back into the pond.

Born to network, you cannot live without great swathes of lovers, but for you the words 'relationship' and 'permanent' go together like peaches and plutonium. In your case, it's never mind the depth, feel the quantity. At parties you constantly look over the shoulder of whoever you are currently bewitching with your coruscating badinage, your radar on high alert for anyone prettier, more famous or more likely to get you that job.

For you, flirting is an extreme sport, and one that you play at professional level. Even when not going for the burn, you lightly trash other people's marriages and flit onto your next victim, leaving the broken shards behind with never a backwards glance.

Your idea of commitment is restricting yourself to three (or four) concurrent partners, to whom you are faithful in your fashion. To be fair, you know this about yourself – although, of course, you see nothing wrong with it – and Brightside twins warn prospective lovers. But do they listen? Of course not. They immediately want to be the one who nails down your particularly bright, elusive butterfly of love. Which of course just makes you even more fascinating.

DREAM JOBS

You may spend your days idly fiddling the petty cash, trawling the Internet on company time and dropping your colleagues in it with a casual smile and a shrug, but you are only human after all, and you dream of much higher things. Gemini superjobs include:

Triple agent

It doesn't matter whose side you start out on (you have no moral perceptions), it's the game you love: inventing bogus info and outwitting the slow. You might get shot, but that just adds a frisson of danger to the fun.

Tabloid journalist

Digging dirt, spreading ugly rumours, doorstepping the unfortunate, hacking phones and email accounts, all-night papping, ruining marriages – getting paid to do what you do for free anyway.

WORK

Trust me, I'm a doctor

Your native instinct to deceive and dissemble means that you survive well in the workplace. You can blag your way into almost any position – what do a few boring qualifications matter? It's only brain surgery. And once there, you naturally gravitate to the influential people, where you ingratiate yourself with shameless fawning and flattery.

You clamber up the work ladder like a monkey up a coconut palm, using wit, charm, blackmail and a long, sharp blade for backstabbing; you are the original smiler with the knife. Astute MDs often hire you for this very reason. Eventually, you will nail the boss. Iago is, after all, your role model.

In the field of office politics, your weapon of choice is gossip. It's an easy option for an Olympic-class, two-faced dirt-disher like you. You are, naturally, smart enough to pinpoint key personnel lower down the food chain (receptionist, accounts clerk, office cleaner) whom you can bedazzle into submission without even breaking sweat, and who can give you all the information you need to apply a little leverage in the right places, if the promotions and perks aren't coming your way as quickly as you deserve.

You expend a lot of energy arranging things so that you get maximum reward for minimum effort. (You would never just do the work instead – where's the fun in that?) And you are a natural for all those jobs requiring a sociopathic ability to lie without blush or stumble: politics, the law, advertising, PR, customer relations.

WHEN TWINS GO WRONG

Gemini crimes are among the most entertaining because they all come across as working scripts for a Hollywood caper movie. You avoid pointless violence (*so* last season) and never really got over your Robin Hood obsession, did you? What about these little numbers...?

Getaway driver

A great combination of speed, thrill, skill, quick-wittedness and instant payoff, without having to do much – and at once removed from the bit that might get sticky. If the heist goes wrong, just drive off and act innocent.

International jewel thief

Irresistible! Unites shiny things, sophistication, high society and shopping (for free) in one package: glamour, thrills, a frisson of danger and the excitement of a heart-in-mouth, laser-dodging masterplan.

CRIMES AND MISDEMEANOURS

How bad could it get?

So what sort of crim would you be, if sociopathy became the new world order? How would you spend your days (or maybe your nights) if you really lived on the Darkside? Well, it has to be said that Brightside Gemini is not averse to a little light fingerwork and recreational scamming, and on the Darkside you'd like more of the same, but with some class. What you really love about the gangster life are the sharp suits, fast cars, laconic one-liners and the Rolexes. The weaker twins among you (of either sex) are quite happy to be a gangster's moll if you can't hack it as a hard man.

You like your crime risky, adventurous and fast-paced, so gunrunning, dope smuggling, insider trading and smash-and-grab raids all have their appeal. Your quick, shiny little mind and persuasive,

shiny little tongue make confidence trickery, blackmail and selling chunks of the Moon to the gullible easy options.

Of course you don't give a fig for the law – everyone knows it's an ass, and snook-cocking at authority is just one of your many specialities. If you do get pinched and it ends up in court, you hire a bent lawyer (who will be a sign-mate) or conduct your own defence, because you are sure no judge or jury could resist your cheeky grin or baby-blue eyes.

But if all your plutonium-grade charm does not penetrate the hide of the judiciary, and you do go down, it doesn't take you long to pickpocket the keys, sweet-talk the screws, disguise yourself as a simple washerwoman and make a break for freedom.

AT HOME

... or maybe not

The trouble is, Geminis are rarely at home. When not on the run, you are found on a futon in a friend's garage (maxing out their phone credit and blasting through their gigabytes), in the penthouse suite of a trillion-star hotel at somebody else's expense or on holiday. Those of you who have hit pay dirt, who launder money for the mob or live off immoral earnings like to rent look-at-me residences in tax havens, with a helipad or private airstrip for quick getaways. Those who have let the sign down may be found trashed in a trailer park, illegally parked in an untaxed camper van or in a cardboard box.

DOMESTIC DISHARMONY

Aries – they set fire to the place; you collect the insurance.

Taurus – easily flattered into cooking the dinner.

Gemini – neither of you will pay the rent or clean up, but since both of you will be out all the time, you won't notice.

Cancer – easily flattered into domestic drudgery; you don't listen to the nagging.

Leo – easily flattered into paying all the rent.

Virgo – constantly tut-tut under their breath about something they call the phone bill.

Libra – will seduce all your lovers – and even you – if there's nothing on the television.

Scorpio – even you wouldn't dare to 'borrow' anything from their scarily tidy room.

Sagittarius – bring all their dogs with them and throw wild parties; fun, then eviction.

Capricorn – it's their house and, boy, are they boring about getting the rent on time, or at all.

Aquarius – too smart to be conned into extra chores.

Pisces – they will guzzle all the freebie champagne you score at celeb bashes.

Decor

If Geminis do have to hole up in a normal house for a bit, you can be sure it will be decorated with small, shiny, portable gadgets, as befits a magpie's nest. Don't ask why the various antiques, Georgian teaspoons, Old Masters and so on don't reflect a coherent personal taste, but appear to come and go mysteriously – usually at night. In fact, just don't ask. At all.

Sharing the Gemini space

Neat! You get to scan their credit cards in the night and take their money, but forget to pay the landlord or the mortgage company; so they'll soon be back out on the street, but at least they won't have any possessions to worry about.

Gemini paint chart

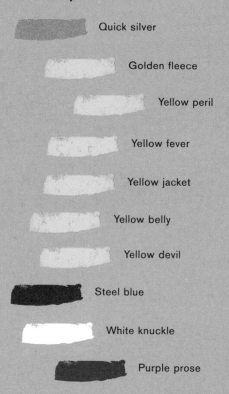

Quick silver

Golden fleece

Yellow peril

Yellow fever

Yellow jacket

Yellow belly

Yellow devil

Steel blue

White knuckle

Purple prose

PLAYTIME

The darkside of fun

Just as the Masai people believe that all the cattle in the world belong to them, so you (that's all four of you: Brightside and Darkside twins) believe that all holidays are yours by Divine Right; otherwise you'd have to go to work, or, worse, you might get bored. Don't, however, go on holidays with small groups – at least, not for longer than a weekend, which is the time it will take for everyone to realize that you have been bitching about them behind their back and that it was you who borrowed their best Louboutins and danced until dawn on the beach in them; then they will gang up on you, and for once there will be nowhere to run.

You want an about-to-be fashionable venue, full of A-list celebs, where you can do white-water rafting by day (you seduce the raftmaster and go for free) and clean up at poker in the evening. Although you like flirting with the croupier, Plan A is to seduce a filthy-rich admirer or several, to finance your fun.

ZODIAC CULL

Suppose you were marooned on a desert island/up an alp/in a rainforest/at sea with 11 others, each one a different star sign. Who would you eliminate in order to survive? You would be the most lenient of cullers in the zodiac, mainly because you need to have lots of suckers about you for entertainment and fleecing purposes, but even you would have to get rid of Virgo (nit-pickery saps your will to live), Capricorn (probably a Police Chief back home) and Taurus (bores you to death).

Holidays from hell

★ A cultural coach tour of ancient ruins with Cancer. You will seize the steering wheel out of sheer boredom and drive over the nearest cliff.

★ Anywhere with Taurus (absolutely no sense of adventure) or Pisces (you didn't sign up to babysit).

★ An out-of-season budget fortnight with Capricorn and Virgo in an unfashionable resort where the sun don't shine.

Road rage

You don't get mad, you get ahead. You are the one in the small but turbo-driven sportscar, with the wind in your hair and someone else paying for the gas. Or you are the one on this year's fashionable motorbike ('borrowed'). Either way, you burn rubber. You cut corners, jump lights, don't even register the speed limit and laugh as you give the finger to apoplectic Ariens whom you leave standing. You don't need a map: where's the adventure in that? You flirt with attractive natives if you get lost. Likelihood of you being at the wheel of the stolen car with the gigawatt sound system? About 90 per cent.

Gamesmanship

You have a Master's in undetectable cheating and hacking when the ref isn't looking and where the bruises don't show. Your witty wind-ups and under-the-breath taunts make your opponents mad and careless. You always play to win, but know better than to show naked greed; your smiling poker face is a work of art.

BAD COMPANY

Your hall of infamy

You may be feeling a bit emotionally fragile after a session on the Darkside, so to cheer the soul, let's look at a few of the famous, infamous, notorious and just plain bad Geminis who might feel the same if they read this book. You will be impressed by the number of revolutionaries, irresistible cads, plausible charlatans, career flirts and main chancers who share your sign; you're in very good bad company. And, despite your formidable (and, regrettably, seductive) Darkside, there are a number of people who appear to want to be you, but who are just a sliver too slow off the mark. Think of any silver-tongued charmers with the sincerity of an unfrocked televangelist. All wannabe Geminis. If they're not, someone's lying. Look at the panel below if you don't believe me.

WANNABES

How about Al 'Scarface' Capone, the gangster's gangster, instigator of the St Valentine's Day Massacre, but only ever nailed for tax fraud? A class-A Gemini, wouldn't you say? Wrong – Capricorn. David Blaine, street wizard, friend of the stars and fast-talking cool dude? Aries. Irresistible smooth-talking charmer and one-time, now reformed, self-styled commitment-phobe, George Clooney? Taurus. Frank Abagnale Jr., America's most gifted conman, now immortalized on film by Leonardo DiCaprio? Aries. All twins, magicians, gigolos, wandering minstrels and chatshow hosts are honorary Geminis; and they may very well be actual Geminis, but of course you should not believe a word they say, because they are probably trying to blag extra birthday presents.

Marquis de Sade *2 June, 1740*

Olympic-class sexual athlete with an 'ism' all his own. Invented an exquisitely painful self-pleasuring device, and favoured whips, beatings and torture for foreplay. When imprisoned for sexual vices, he wrote down his every fantasy, which is how we know all about him.

Paul Gauguin *7 June, 1848*

Impressionist painter who dumped a sensible day job as a Parisian stockbroker, abandoned his family and ran away to the South Seas to paint gorgeous Tahitian lovelies. Died romantically amid poverty and disease.

Jean-Paul Sartre *21 June, 1905*

French philosopher who built a whole doctrine (existentialism) on the idea that you could choose who, what and how you wanted to be, and thus change roles every day. Constantly searching for new ways to be free. A formidable womanizer despite looking like a squashed toad.

Errol Flynn *20 June, 1909*

Handsome, hard-drinking, hard-living Hollywood hellraiser, adored by women, envied by men; a notorious sex machine and career swashbuckler, he died young(ish) at 50, but didn't stay pretty.

Che Guevara *14 June, 1928*

Revolutionary poster boy and thorn in the side of US imperialism, Che was born wealthy in Argentina, but got restless and travelled all over South America on a Norton 500 motorbike. After helping Castro establish Cuba, he moved on to help liberate Bolivia, but was shot dead in 1967. Still cool.

CANCER

22 June ~ 22 July

Cancer is a feminine, cardinal Water sign ruled by the Moon. It is the fourth sign on the zodiac wheel, directly opposite Capricorn, and is named after the constellation Cancer (the crab), which frets and snaps behind the Sun at this time of year.

On the Darkside, this makes you a grumpy, secretive, passive-aggressive grudge-hoarder, with bipolar mood swings and a positive genius for pointless worrying.

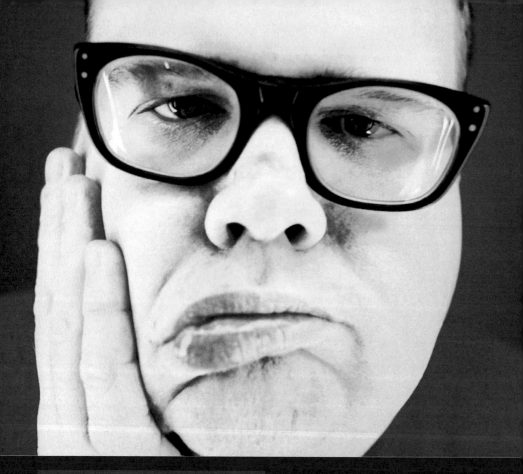

Punctuality

You are never on time for anything; who'd want to see you? Who'd even notice you weren't there? Plus, it's a classic way to control the event without appearing to – passive-aggressive or what?

Toothpaste

New moon: new toothpaste, cap firmly screwed on, tube squeezed from end; half moon: cap quite near tube, squeezed anywhere; full moon: cap lost, tube cut open; moonless night: no toothpaste at all.

Temper gauge

0° to snapping point in one second or several decades, depending on the Moon. Either short outbursts of unfocused tetch and filthy temper or centuries of insoluble sectarian intransigence and filthy temper.

PERSONALITY

Graceless, gloomy, grudge-encrusted

Grumpy, moody, wingy, snappy, tetchy, devious and fretful; not the cast list for a Darkside production of *Snow White* (with Crabby, Demanding and Spiteful as understudies), but a summary of your defining gracelessness. Depressing, isn't it? Notice that they are all diminutive Disneyfied versions of big, bad feelings. You yearn to be Wagnerian, but are too negative – and who ever heard of Valkyries riding down to snatch squashed crabs off the battlefield to glory in some crustacean Valhalla? You'll never be more than just another pebble on the beach, negligible in the scheme of things and you are perversely proud of your strong grip on the essential futility of existence.

Let's cheer ourselves up some more, why don't we? You distrust life and have no faith in the future – not surprising really, considering the behaviour of the tides. One minute there you are on a nice, wide moonlit strand, with executive rockpool, plenty of lugworms; then whoosh – everything's covered in saltwater, and your whole life is sucked away; you regroup, restart, then six hours later it happens all over again. What's the point?

To build immunity against fate's random cruelty, you look for homeopathic doses of gloom wherever you scuttle; to you, everything is a potential Bambi's-mum moment, and you can well up over anything lonely, plangent and hopeless that can't fight back: pieces of string too short for use, individual fruit pies, the last Christmas turkey in the shop (a pointless sacrifice left unsold in the deep freeze). And let's not get you started on the potency of cheap music. At the same time (I did mention mood swings, didn't I?) you love to whine about everyone and everything and are shamelessly addicted to Schadenfreude – that delicious trickle in the heart that you get when a dear friend falls off life's carousel.

You remember everything nasty anybody ever said about you (you dismiss the good stuff) and all your friends' transgressions (people tell you the oddest things), but you never, ever give away your own emotional secrets. The undiscerning think this is because you are shy and diffident, and you work hard to promote that illusion; actually, it's because you are afraid people might use them against you, just as you would against them.

You are always looking through the blue glass (which is of course half empty), scanning for anything that could, at a certain angle, be defined as an insult or a slight, to add to your impressive grudge-mountain. You may forgive, but you never forget (actually, delete forgive – you don't do that, either). Bygones? Ha! Closure? Never; you may remember some other slight, and have to reopen the whole feud. Move on? You?

If you ever feel in danger of enjoying yourself, you activate your powerful fret drive, so that you can worry ceaselessly about stuff you can do nothing about. This stops you having to take action about stuff you *can* do something about; you are constantly crossing bridges that have not even got planning permission.

Bitch rating

B+. For someone who likes to appear as the caring queen, you are a mistress of the snappy put-down (you sit at home in your shell, practising). You usually spoil the effect by muttering your pearls of acid wit under your breath as the bitchee departs, and then grovelling immediately.

Collective noun

A self-protective tip for non-Cancerians. You may find yourself, for some bizarre zodiacal reason, on a nighttime beach crammed with Cancerians. Tidal pools of angst lap about your ankles, and in the silence (no Cancerian ever initiates a conversation), you can hear the soft swish of umbrage being taken. This is a Grudge of Cancerians. Try not to despair.

FAVE DEADLY SIN

How you wish you could work up to a full-grown deadly sin, but all you can manage is watery own-brand versions; you don't do Anger, you do Irritability. However, there is a low-profile deadly sin that you could claim; it's the quiet one that usually lurks at the back in group photos, hiding behind Gluttony. Modern sinners call it Sloth (bone idleness), but its historical name is Accidie, a medieval attempt to define the paralyzing immobility that comes about when you let despair get you in its grip. You're really good at that.

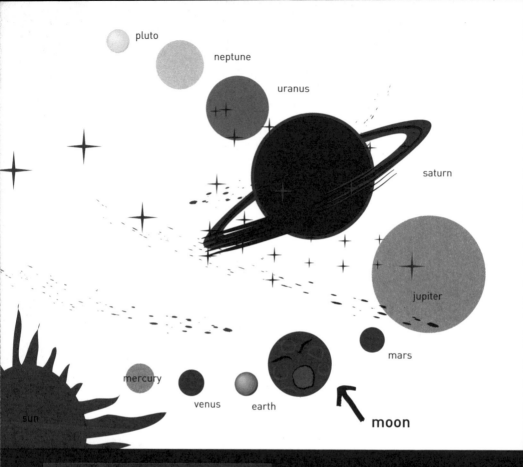

pluto

neptune

uranus

saturn

jupiter

mars

mercury

venus

earth

moon

sun

PLANET PLANET

Every sun sign has a planetary mum to make sure that ears are washed behind, homework is done, street corners are not hung around, meals are regular (if unwanted) and that a potent maternal mix of guilt, gratitude and exasperation is ground indelibly into the soul.

Before there were telescopes, astrologers could see only five planets in the sky, plus the Moon and Sun, so they counted these two as planetary rulers. It seemed a good idea at the time. Each planet babysat two zodiac signs – except for the Sun (which allows Leo to rule)

and the Moon, which is forever popping into Cancer's room, pretending to change the sheets, but actually reading your secret diaries. Yes, your planetary ruler is the Moon, our nearest and dearest celestial object (only 238,857 miles away, but do you ever visit, do you ever call?).

BLAME YOUR PLANET

Nearest and dearest

When you're not snapping at friends who have upset you in ways that you are not prepared to specify (if they don't know, you're sure as hell not going to tell them), you are baking cakes for them; and when you are not baking cakes, you are remembering how they didn't send you a birthday card four years ago, and cutting them dead in the street. You are a moody git; is this your fault? Not entirely; blame your planet. In your case, it's the Moon.

The Moon may loom large in our small sky, but cosmically speaking, it is just a little rock fussing fretfully around the Earth, just as your mother looms large in your life (part love object, part Kali the Destroyer), but has zero effect on the larger universe. It doesn't generate any light of its own – most of that silvery glitter comes from the Sun, and some of it is Earthshine, stray sunbeams bouncing off us. So the Moon lives in a state of constant reflected glory, experiencing life at one remove: the stage mum of the solar system (sound familiar?).

It compensates by constantly changing. One night it's a big silver disc in the sky, poets barking at it, lovers going at it like knives beneath it, werewolves morphing in its eerie argent glow; the next it's grumpy as sin with its back turned to us; then it disappears completely, gradually sidling back into view as if nothing's happened. It wouldn't be so bad, except that it does this once a month; you'd think the Moon could see some sort of pattern here, and get help, or at least acknowledge the problem.

BAD MOON RISING

The darkside of Cancer's darkside

It's not all sunshine on the Darkside. You know just how power-crazed and monomaniac your innermost thoughts and secret fantasies are, but where do you think they come from? The Moon, that's where – or whichever area of your birthchart the Moon was moodily plodding when you were born. The Sun is our daytime self; the Moon represents our inner psycho (and in your case, Cancer, the inner psycho has powerful outside help, because the Moon is your planetary ruler and can kick down the asylum doors whenever it likes). Throughout Cancer's month in the Sun, the lunar nuisance scuttles about like a mother woodlouse on a burning log, which helps to explain why two Cancerians born only days apart moon all over the place looking for completely different reasons to be cheerless.

CATCHING THE MOON

That's all very well, you say, but how do I know where the Moon was when I was born? There are long, complicated (and, frankly, dull) tables called ephemerides that tell you where every planet (and for tedious astrological reasons, the Moon is an honorary planet) stood in the heavens, atmosphere bated, as you made your sorry debut. However, we have provided a Moon itinerary at the back of this book to enable you to get a rough idea. If that sounds like too much hard work, and you have the techno technique, then try visiting the following website: www.alabe.com/freechart. If you know where you were born, and when, they will produce, for *free*, a rough-cut birthchart that will pin your Moon on the zodiac wheel.

Lunatic combinations

Here's what happens to Cancer when the Moon stomps off in another black mood.

Moon in Aries – übertetchy; you leap out of your shell and kebab anyone fool enough to believe what it says on Cancer's Brightside astrology label.

Moon in Taurus – are you sure you weren't swapped at birth with the baby from that limpet family next door?

Moon in Gemini – fiddler crab at heart, dancing the night away on pale moonlit beaches with all your friends.

Moon in Cancer – be one with the hermit crab; barricade yourself into an extra shell for double protection.

Moon in Leo – imperial-strength mood changes mean that none of your favourites should ever feel smug and secure.

Moon in Virgo – in your waterproof information-retrieval system you keep all your grudges, filed by date and cross-referenced by name and category.

Moon in Libra – the sadness of the world defeats you, so you withdraw; this is so that you can idle your days away on the sofa.

Moon in Scorpio – one glare from your rockpool and crab catchers run screaming.

Moon in Sagittarius – you're not homesick, just sick of home, so you run away to sea as soon as you can.

Moon in Capricorn – you may be tough and hard on the outside, but inside beats a heart of solid stone.

Moon in Aquarius – two removes from life's blood, sweat and tears.

Moon in Pisces – mood swings like windshield wipers on maximum.

BORN UNDER A BAD SIGN

The scum also rises

And another thing. Your sun sign is modified by your rising sign. This is the zodiac sign that was skulking over the horizon at the very minute you were born. If your sun sign is your ego, then your rising sign gives you your public manners (such as they are), your Sunday worst. It's the painted smile behind which the real, disgusting you lurks. Some astrologers maintain that its malign influence affects what you look like. Be afraid.

Here's something else to worry about. In the northern hemisphere, for tedious astronomical reasons, there are more people with Cancer (and Leo) rising than any other sign. Oh dear! This can only end in tears; so many people with such a strong grip on despair must unbalance the cosmic karma and plunge the world into eternal night.

GOING UP

Now pay attention, because the following is quite brain-busting. There are 12 signs of the zodiac, and astrologers like to think of them as occupying a band of sky that spins around the Earth once every 24 hours. (This is a convention; it is not astronomically correct and you will not see the signs if you look up, so don't write in.) So, every two hours or so another sign hauls itself blearily over the eastern horizon. This is going on whatever time of the day or night you were born, and whichever benighted spot on the globe you chose to appear in. These astro-mechanics help to explain why crabs born at either end of the same day hide under different pebbles in different rockpools. There are long, nerdy ways to discover your rising sign, but the easiest way is to get hold of a birthchart (see page 112).

Upwardly mobile

If your rising sign is Cancer, your public persona is a frowning, irritable recluse capable of raining on any parade. This is to distract the rest of us from your plans to sacrifice yourself until the world is properly grateful. Here's what happens when other zodiacal upstarts rise above their station.

Aries rising

Hermit with attitude.

Taurus rising

What a lovely big shell! Plenty of crab meat here; did anyone remember to bring the mayonnaise?

Gemini rising

Amazing how you are so nimble and light-hearted – you must have left all that emotional baggage in storage.

Leo rising

Gilded claws, royal monogram on your shell, but you'd rather stay in and trace royal bastards than greet your subjects.

Virgo rising

Hyperneat insult-hoarder; you've crocheted dust covers for every grudge.

Libra rising

Always lolling about in the warmer, shallower pools, dazzling naïve bivalves.

Scorpio rising

You appear darkly, hypnotically moody; actually, you're just moody.

Sagittarius rising

You leap before you look – and invariably end up in the *fritto misto*.

Capricorn rising

Cash hoarder; spending it only makes your collection look incomplete.

Aquarius rising

You stare up at the Crab nebula on moonless nights and wish you were home.

Pisces rising

Always forgetting the tide times and getting stranded on strange beaches.

DON'T YOU LOVE ME, BABY?

Venus and Cancer

Just how much of a high-maintenance tease or bunny-boiler you are may depend on where the solar system's heartless tart (Venus) was blushingly dropping her handkerchief when you were born (*see below*). Oh, and Venus also has a say in how harmoniously you blend in with the rest of the world, but what do words like harmony have to do with the Darkside? Now, for astrological reasons that will fry your brain if I explain them here (basically, Venus is far too luxury-loving to move too far away from the Sun, and her orbital rate is in bed with Earth's), Venus only ever appears in your sun sign, or two signs on either side of it. In your case, crabs, that means Venus will be in Cancer, Taurus, Gemini, Leo or Virgo. And this is what it does to your love and lust life.

MAKE LOVE AND WAR

Venus is the girlie planet of lurve, right? And Mars is planet lad, the warlord. You may also have a sneaking feeling that men are from Mars and women are from Venus. Don't be upset if I tell you this is not true. All of us, of all genders, have a stake in both planets. Where they are in your birthchart has what I shall call consequences. You may think your sun sign makes you a born babe-magnet, but Venus in a chilly sign will cut you off at the knees; you may think that your sun sign means you are the twin soul of the dove of peace, but you may go red-eyed with bloodlust when beaten to a parking spot. Mars will be somewhere irascible. You'll need a birthchart (*see page 112*) to find out what Venus and Mars were getting up to when you were born. It is far too complicated – and, frankly, dull – to work out here.

Venus in Cancer

Everybody's impressed by your unswerving loyalty and heart-warming devotion, except for your desperate partner, who has tried every known love-rat manoeuvre and still cannot shake you off: the prison warder of love.

Venus in Taurus

Love bully; most likely to appear in the tabloids under headlines like 'Spurned Lover Slays Partner and Self in Remote Love Nest'; if you can't have them, you'll make sure that no one else can.

Venus in Gemini

Clamber out of your shell and go for a little flirting in the dark; you are such a speedy scuttler than you can be safely back inside at the first sign of love danger, ready to snipe and snap.

Venus in Leo

King crab. Lurk behind the rocks, spring on your unsuspecting prey, knock them senseless with your great big masterful claw, then take them home to your palace by the sea.

Venus in Virgo

You cruise the beach looking for the inadequate, whom you lure in with tea and sympathy; this is to get yourself a live-in punchbag, always available to be criticized, nagged and picked to pieces, and psychologically unable to depart.

ARE YOU LOOKING AT ME?

Mars and Cancer

Cancerians don't do confrontation; sniping and pre-emptive defence are your preferred attack modes. But just how confrontational, threatening, paranoid and gagging for a fight you are depends on which area of your birthchart the bruiser planet Mars is being held back in by his mates (leave it, Mars, he's not worth it). Mars is the next planet out from Earth, but paces its orbit rather more slowly (presumably to get some effective eyeballing in). It takes 2½ years for Mars to get around, and on the way it spends about two months of quality menacing time in each sign. Only a very lost cause, or a slight to your great-grandmother's honour, will winkle a Cancerian out to fight. If you do feel an urge to lead the charge over the top, check out Mars' alibi at the time of your birth.

Mars in Aries
According to Greek myth, a bold crab once undertook a suicide mission to harass the hero Heracles; as it held grimly on to his big toe, he smashed it with his club. That's your kind of crab.

Mars in Taurus
At your best in a long-term siege; you always have huge stockpiles of food.

Mars in Gemini
Superlative sniper, popping up from behind the sea walls with your deadly assault wit locked and loaded.

Mars in Cancer
Defence is the best defence; you always wear your armour, even if you're alone, and repel all boarders before enemy warships are off the slipway.

Mars in Leo

You strategically bind your enemies with regal apron strings by contracting marriages between your cousins and theirs, with small print that points out that you will have their firstborn killed if they even think about criticizing your cooking.

Mars in Virgo

You bleach your shell to blinding whiteness and dazzle your enemies to death.

Mars in Libra

You seduce potential foes (that's everybody then) into your honeytrap, so you will always have something handy to blackmail them with if they ever cross you.

Mars in Scorpio

You build an impenetrable defensive forcefield all around yourself and your family, generated entirely by the glare-power of your beady little eyes.

Mars in Sagittarius

You yomp up the beach in your marine commando outfit, firing indiscriminately – you're bound to hit someone you love.

Mars in Capricorn

You sit in your shell and plan dreadful, cruel tortures for your enemies, with detailed diagrams. If they only knew …

Mars in Aquarius

Safe in your hazard suit, you deploy deadly slow-acting viruses, using your great pincer as tongs. Then you make notes on the results for the research paper that will get you that prestigious professorship and government pension.

Mars in Pisces

You eject from your shell on full whinge-power and fall at your enemies' feet; few can resist the temptation to stamp on you, and you just love that.

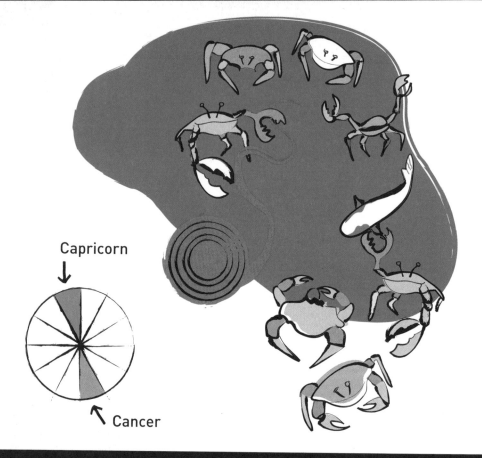

Capricorn

Cancer

Your polar sign sits on the opposite side of the zodiac wheel, six signs away, giving you knowing looks. You have a dark umbilical link with it. If Darkside you is your evil twin, then your polar sign is your evil twin's evil twin. It's got your number – but then you've got its, so

that's alright, isn't it? Brightside astrologers maintain that there is a strong complementary relationship between you and your polar sign, and that this relationship is positive and fruitful, especially at work, because you share the same energy quality (cardinal). Well,

excuse me; on the Darkside it's more like the tension between two ancient clans who have been feuding since 1349, after clan A did not return clan B's garden hose, and clan B stole clan A's ornamental carp; both want the same thing, but can't remember what that is.

WHO'S GOT YOUR NUMBER?

check out the opposition

Your polar opposite sign is Capricorn: the cruel, cold-eyed, calculating pragmatist. (For more about your darkly fascinating opposite number, *see pages 296–327.*) What would a hypersensitive, sentimental, pincer-wringing worryguts like you want with your average Capricorn: a hard-nosed, greasy-pole climber who thinks Weltschmerz and Schadenfreude are society accountants? How do you have this – shall we say – understanding? Well, like good cop and bad cop, or arch villain and superhero, you need each other to make the Darkside work for you. It's all about elements (undesirable ones, of course). You are Water; Capricorn is Earth. And together they make mud, just the stuff for building huge defensive ramparts, or walling up your enemies alive.

As you skitter diffidently through the world in your self-generated fog of unworthiness and inferiority, can't you hear the tiny clicking of the Capricornian abacus as the zodiac's bookkeeper carefully audits your vast hoard of grudges? And who do you think planted the seed of your shameful secret conviction that, underneath it all, everything you think, say and do is actually perfect and beyond criticism?

Respect your inner Capricorn; it's that bit of toughness that gives you enough nous to come in out of the monsoon, and stops you short of boiling yourself alive to provide a supper for your family. Of course, if it gets too reinforced in there, you will become a hard-boiled, soulless entity and have to work for the Inland Revenue.

DARKSIDE DATE

You will never get a date; who would want to go out with a worthless loser like you? (Go on, rub salt into those self-inflicted wounds until you bleed.) You certainly wouldn't, because – like Groucho – you wouldn't want to join a club that had people like you as members. If you see someone you fancy, your strategy is to go into another room (or country) and ignore them in a pointed fashion. Struck by your moody mystery (who is that fascinating enigma?), they do the chasing; that way, when it all goes wrong, no one can jeer at you. Your ideal date is with a dysfunctional therapee who needs to talk. That way, you don't have to speak, but you are in control; what's great is when you put them back on their feet, they gallop away with a feckless Arien, and you lie back and enjoy some serious suffering.

SEX

Hard to get

If they weren't blinded by lust, a little bit of forethought would have told your lovers that sex with an armoured personnel carrier is not much of a turn-on (unless one of them was Aries, who always packs anti-tank grenades and gets wet over anything military). You won't come out; they can't get in. It's partly your briar-rose complex (anyone who really loves me would jolly well hack through this almost impenetrable barrier to reach my inner secret loveliness); and partly because you have noticed in your shrewd, beady little way that deferred gratification is the key to keeping people hanging on, so that you can hang on to them (which is the object of your every exercise).

And what do you do when the more persistent of your heroes finally winkles you out? You lie there in a frenzy of passion-slaying worry: will the bed creak? Is that a tidal wave? Will I still love you tomorrow? Have I put the cat out? That's why you have to snap up admirers while they still see you as a moonlit enigma.

What kind of love rat are you?

The drowning kind: either you make yourself even grumpier, moodier and more depressive than usual (how can they tell?), so that any partner would rather go down with the ship than jump with you; or, more usually, you clamp your great pincer to the wreckage and cling on for dear life. Ex-partners have to emigrate, marry someone else and die before you accept that it's over (and even then you demand to see the death certificate).

Aries – hyperactive optimist meets paranoid pessimist.

Taurus – friends have to prize you apart, you are so possessive.

Gemini – you move sideways; they can always outswerve you.

Cancer – long, moody silences that only end when one of you dies (and maybe not even then)

Leo – they gleam and shine; you, serf, are a mere reflection.

Virgo – they insist on pouring bleach into your rockpool.

Libra – they live for pleasure, you exist because you must.

Scorpio – beadier eyes, a more wieldy shell; they make you feel even more worthless.

Sagittarius – will crush you and your shell without noticing.

Capricorn – they use your shell as a step up to higher things.

Aquarius – demystify your angst sessions by explaining the chemistry of light levels.

Pisces – slip out of your grasp to flirt with other shellfish.

RELATIONSHIPS

Feel the need

The thing is, you can only really relate to someone if you feel needed. Show you a mature, balanced, fully functioning, happy human being, and you stall, because there is nothing to get your claws into. (Mind you, as there are so few mature, balanced, etc., people on the planet, you're unlikely to stay lonely.) If you suspect you aren't being needed at some point in the relationship, you like to engineer a little side-swiping (pincers on stun, not kill), then pick up the pieces and help the loved one to convalesce.

Clingy and manipulative (although not in the Pisces class), you are a master of the 'mum manoeuvre': using long silences, suffocating devotion and stealth mood swings (no one ever sees them coming), you can make lovers and friends feel permanently guilty without them ever knowing why – ideal for getting them to do just what you want. You love helping your friends with their problems, but they'd rather you didn't, because they already have a mum, thanks, and when they want to feel 13 again, they'll go home.

What you like best is attaching yourself to someone who has made it quite clear that they are unavailable long-term (registered commitment-phobe/monk/nun/happily married), and then pining when they leave you. Crabs of all genders suffer from Mistress Syndrome: addiction to the aching poignancy of the lonely Christmas tree and the telephone that doesn't ring. When love dies, you don't mourn: you hook it onto a life-support system.

DREAM JOBS

The moon is full: you dream you are a superhero (cosmically empowered to infantilize the populace and save them from themselves, ensuring their eternal gratitude!); the moon is dark: you dream that no one needs you. Surely there is a middle way? Try these ...

Agony aunt

Spot on! All that vicarious suffering! All that transference! You get to hand out industrial amounts of compassion and motherly advice without even having to see the suckers, and they will all love you for it.

Hermit

It's a crying shame that wealthy landowners no longer employ hermits to accessorize their designer faux grottoes – grump in gloom all day, free hair shirt and all the hemlock you can drink: you'd walk it.

WORK

I could've been a contender

Let's face it, you shouldn't really be working, should you? Your ever-changing moods mean that whatever vocation you choose to devote your life to in one part of the month will be denigrated as a waste of your existence (pointless though that is) when the Moon changes a few days later. It's a Brightside cliché that you are well suited to the caring professions; of course you are, it means you are only competing with the halt, lame and underage.

After a month or so at work (you choose a desk in the dampest, darkest, most inconvenient corner, which will give you plenty of whinge-fuel), you notice that your colleagues are smuggling in Moon calendars and silver-tipped magic markers hidden under their cardigans, and approach you only in groups, when the sun is shining. It happens every time, and you don't understand why.

Bosses like you because you work hard (and your Eeyorish presence prevents outbreaks of unproductive *joie de vivre*). You like to work longer and harder than anyone else, because then you can feel hard done by and can bewail your lot whenever you manage to trap two or three colleagues in the lift. You also like a job for which you are overqualified so that you can feel superior and tell everybody else what to do (in a caring way, of course).

Whatever job you are in, you loathe it utterly until you leave it, when you immediately begin to look back in fond nostalgia at what fun it all was and how sad it is that all things must pass.

WHEN CRABS GO WRONG

Cancer could well be the criminal mastermind of the millennium, but who's to know, because you're stealthy, secretive and sneaky, do all your work behind closed doors or under cover of the night and very rarely get caught. These two professions are ideal.

Smuggler

Romance; history; dark waters; secret passages; success or failure turning on the tide; betrayed or protected by moonlight; no victims but the taxman. Even Brightside crabs might like to try this one.

Poisoner

Brightside you has a reasonable rep in the kitchen, so cooking up potions will be a breeze. It's non-violent, it's organic, it's non-confrontational and you work at home at your own pace. Don't forget to wash out the blender.

CRIMES AND MISDEMEANOURS

How bad could it get?

So what sort of crim would you be, if sociopathy became the new world order? How would you spend your days (or maybe nights) if you really lived on the Darkside? Well, you don't do confrontation, so hold-ups are out (unless you perfect the eyeless balaclava); and you are a very unconvincing liar (your shell goes puce), so it's no to fraud and deception. How about some lucrative anonymous stuff you can do from home? Poison-pen letters might suit your sharp tongue and your killer memory for the telling blackmailable detail. Kidnapping could be good; you'd enjoy having a captive victim to practise your caring skills on.

There is one particular international organization that would suit you down to the ground: a respectable family concern, run on traditional lines; where everyone is looked after unless they are very naughty boys, and where mum is king; where slights are taken seriously and properly punished. I think you know what I mean.

You accept the law as a fine historical artefact, something to be revered but scuttled around. If you are collared, you dread your day in court, because everyone will be looking at you; nasty, jibing barristers will upset you, and you will snap and call them names and be given extra time. It will cheer you up a bit if you are wrongly convicted, because you can get in some good martyring time and work up a fine set of grudges against the judge, lawyers, jury, police, media, system, etc. In prison, you'd soon become a trusty, and would try to escape only if your shell could easily fit sideways through the bars.

AT HOME

Dust to dust

When feng shui masters clear the clutter from their clients' homes, where do you think it all goes? *Chez* Cancer, that's where. Narrow, single crab-width passages thread around tottering piles of old Birmingham phone books (you live in Bognor Regis), 11-year-old calendars, graduation photographs of universities you didn't go to, and so on. Everything is in its place; just not in the place you'd think. You could dust, but it's taken years to get the layers so velvety smooth, and you would disturb your posse of elderly cats (some of them dead) and your windowsill collection of mummified bumblebees from summers past.

DOMESTIC DISHARMONY

Aries – they do mess; you do preserving for the nation.

Taurus – can't understand why all your biscuit tins only contain photographs of dead aunts.

Gemini – they lend you their antique collection while they go on holiday; you get arrested.

Cancer – they bring loads of old junk that gets in the way of your archived historical documents.

Leo – will be tempted to pay Aries to start a small fire.

Virgo – constantly tut-tut under their breath about something they call a vacuum cleaner.

Libra – they may be trapped in the upstairs bathroom, the one behind the Welsh dresser that you and Taurus found last year.

Scorpio – use their power-glare to make you throw things away!

Sagittarius – they kick aside your strategic piles of old utility bills as if they were unimportant.

Capricorn – they know where you have safely filed your bank statements, but won't tell you.

Aquarius – made a secret deal to sell some of your older collections to the British Museum.

Pisces – they contribute a rival hoard of corks and bottle tops.

Decor

There is no way to describe Cancer decor, because neither the walls nor the floor have been seen since you moved in, and most of the doors are blocked by old mangles and refrigerators. What windows? Brightside astros try to cover for you by enthusing about silvery, pearly, luminescent shades, but we all know that's just moonbeams bouncing off the cobwebs.

Sharing the Cancer museum

You often share your shell with lame ducks, political refugees, strays, misfits, the newly divorced — in short, the desperate whose life cannot get any worse. This is not because you are deeply caring, but because you don't notice them sobbing amid the bric-a-brac.

Cancer paint chart

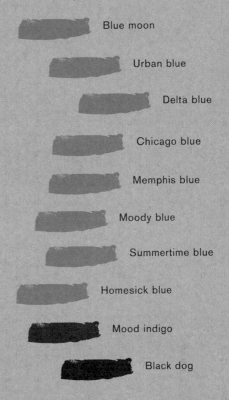

Blue moon

Urban blue

Delta blue

Chicago blue

Memphis blue

Moody blue

Summertime blue

Homesick blue

Mood indigo

Black dog

PLAYTIME

The darkside of fun

You don't of course deserve any fun, but if you're forced to take a break, then go alone, to spare us your filthy moods (always worse when you are at leisure and feeling guilty about all the downtrodden poor who are not); you'll be able to stare at lonely sunsets and pine exquisitely about things that were Not To Be. Try to move around, then you can feel homesick about the place you've just left.

And your gloom is catching: on any holiday beach, your beady little eyes look up, trying to pierce the cloudless blue skies to the endless black of the universe beyond; the futility of it all rains down on you and spreads to the luckless funsters on the next beachmat, who then have to slash their wrists and kill their families.

Go for a group self-catering deal, so that you can do all the cooking, cleaning and washing, and can beat yourself up with the belief that that's why they invited you. Everyone else gets to feel slightly guilty; you get to feel magnificently put-upon.

ZODIAC CULL

Suppose you were marooned on a desert island/up an alp/in a rainforest/ at sea with 11 others, each one a different star sign. Who would you eliminate in order to survive? Well, why should you survive? Perhaps it would be easier just to end it all and let the others hold a barbecue. Or you could rope everybody together with the apron strings you always carry, lead/steer them all to safety, then ostentatiously slip away before anyone could thank you, give you a medal or anything.

Holidays from hell

★ A month in appalling opulence with Leo and Taurus: your every whim catered for, no one you could put under emotional obligation by doing their washing when they're not looking; you'd be wretched.

★ A self-improving workshop course with Virgo. You might have to perform your new skill. In public. With everyone watching. Death won't come quick enough.

★ Anywhere with your entire family. How can you miss them, and moan about how much better it would be if they were there, if they *are* there?

Road rage

Once safely hidden in the extra shell of your own vehicle, you think no one can see you, and behave like the controlling mastermind you wish you were: you shout shocking abuse; you give the finger; you stick out your tongue; when challenged, of course, you back off instantly – if only there were a sideways gear. You read the map (but secretly and to yourself), then gripe and tetch when the driver can't read your mind and goes the wrong way.

Gamesmanship

You fear success and love to snatch defeat from the jaws of victory, so you set yourself up to lose. That way, you need not worry if you do lose; and if you win, well, that'll show them. If insulted, you stalk out, but leave your ball because it makes you feel good and martyred, and you think it will make ex-opponents feel ashamed and humble; it won't.

BAD COMPANY

Your hall of infamy

You may be feeling a bit emotionally fragile after a session on the Darkside, so to cheer the soul, let's look at a few of the famous, infamous, notorious and just plain bad Cancerians who might feel the same if they read this book. True, you're a bit low on world dictators or action villains, but you have plenty of in-your-dreams writers, artists and actors who like a wild side, but at once removed; you're in very good bad company. And, despite your formidable (though underpowered) Darkside, there are a number of people who appear to want to be you, but who have missed the tide. Think of any moody, insecure manipulators, low on self-esteem, but high on worry. All wannabe Cancerians. If they're not, someone's lying. Look at the panel below if you don't believe me.

WANNABES

Everybody's mum, all Russian novelists, all martyrs, everybody north of the Arctic Circle (and, to be hemispherically correct, 80 per cent of penguins), and most country-and-western singers are honorary Cancerians. Woody Allen, the gibbering genius, the neurotics' neurotic, the man whose entire career is built on middle-class white-boy urban angst and whose entire oeuvre twitches with restless paranoia – surely he must be at one with the crab? Sagittarius! (I know, I can't believe it either.) What of Thomas Hardy, 19th-century literary Eeyore, nihilist author of seminal gloomfests *Jude the Obscure* and *Tess of the d'Urbervilles*? Gemini. How about the eponymous Baron Leopold von Sacher-Masoch, insatiable lover of a bad time? Aquarius. And consider Mother Teresa, unstoppable carer of the poor and destitute? Virgo.

Henry VIII *28 June, 1491*

Shows what happens when crabs get their pincers on power. Tetchy, hard-arse, paranoid King of England; serially dissatisfied with his VI wives, none of whom gave him a viable son and heir; argued with everybody, even the Pope.

J.-J. Rousseau *28 June, 1712*

Bad-tempered, unsociable, misanthropic, quarrelsome, clinically paranoid French philosopher, who introduced the idea of the noble savage and the degeneracy of 'culture'; unabashed by contradiction, he championed the rights of children, but put his own five little bastards into an orphanage.

Marcel Proust *10 July, 1871*

Strange, wealthy, reclusive French writer who cocooned himself in a soundproof apartment in Paris, spent his days in bed and his nights working, and took 12 years to write a seven-volume novel all about retrieving the past.

Edward Hopper *22 July, 1882*

American artist (*Nighthawks*), who not only saw the infinite blackness that surrounds us and makes our every gesture futile, but also painted it. Angst on canvas.

Franz Kafka *3 July, 1883*

Czech insurance broker, better known as the author of celebrated works of fear, paranoia, alienation, hopelessness and nameless dread (*Metamorphosis* and *The Trial*). Chatting up a potential girlfriend, he winningly described himself as 'fretful, melancholy, untalkative, dissatisfied and sickly'. Now that's what I call true Darkside crab.

LEO

July 23 ~ August 22

Leo is a masculine, fixed Fire sign ruled by the Sun. It is the fifth sign on the zodiac wheel, directly opposite Aquarius, and is named after the constellation Leo (the lion), which roars and preens behind the Sun at this time of year.

On the Darkside, this makes you a vain, arrogant, condescending solipsist with imperial longings and an all-pervasive addiction to unconditional sycophancy.

ANNOYING HABITS

Punctuality

There must be some mistake. Of course you are never late. How could you be? No event would ever start until you and your entourage arrive, surely? If it did, you'd flounce off right away and have it cancelled

Toothpaste

Leos would not deign to behave inconsiderately around the toothpaste. You simply wouldn't know how to squeeze the tube from the middle; you have a little woman to do that for you

Temper gauge

0° to boiling point in a nanosacond. Dramatic solar flaring and flouncing, down a notch to murderous irritation, and then you allow yourself to be soothed by a meaty titbit thrown by a terrified acolyte

PERSONALITY

Bossy, boastful, bombastic

No doubt one of your lackeys has read to you all about astrology. (You may even have a court astrologer.) Your lackeys will have told you that, as a Leo, you are proud, loyal, courageous, generous, magnanimous, dignified, enthusiastic, splendid, bedazzling – all in all, a class act, Your Brightside Maj. Well, they would, wouldn't they? Don't you ever notice the fixed grins of your courtiers: the smile that doesn't quite reach their eyes? And the way they back out of your presence with pleasing abasement? You think this is reverential; they think they have hit upon an almost foolproof way to avoid a knife in the back.

History is benighted with dark lions – weak kings, bad kings, evil emperors, despotic tyrants. (And for the purposes of this book, all Leos are kings, in spite of the fact that large numbers of you are, technically and anatomically, queens.) Beneath the hollow crown, and deep within your roaring lion heart, you know that you are an arrogant, intolerant, patronizing, pompous, self-centred bully; but hey, keeping royal secrets is what you do.

You never really got beyond what child psychologists call the terrible twos, did you? And, just like the tyrant of the toyshop, you can't really believe you are getting away with it. You remember that scene in *The Wizard of Oz*, where the fearsome all-powerful wizard is revealed as an insignificant little old man behind a curtain, pulling on a vast array of levers? That's you, that is – scared that you will be found out and they will take away your crown.

You absolutely have to be adored; by everybody; all the time. It never occurs to you how boring this may be for the conscripted adorers; you do not see that they go through the motions (or perhaps you do, but you don't care – it's the motions you want). This lust for adoration is often your downfall because you are very easily flattered – you great, gorgeous, handsome, clever tawny thing, you – and you believe every word. You are too ready to roll over on your back and purr under the honeyed stream, and fail to notice that while you are blissing out, others (usually Scorpios, Taureans and Capricorns) are usurping your powers. You can't hear the whisper of plotting behind the roaring of the Hallelujah chorus, so you can be very easily manipulated.

You expect the world to revolve around you, and a surprising amount of it does: some of the other zodiac signs (they know who they are) have a positively craven attitude. When it doesn't, you plunge into grand imperial sulk mode (they call this dignified silence) until a little man comes to fix it. It has been reported to you that people think you have double standards; you can only shrug and agree. There is what you deserve by Divine Right, and what is good enough for everyone else. Is there a problem?

And you are never, ever wrong. Ever. Even when you are wrong, you have attentive people whose job it is to redefine wrong, or recalibrate the world so that you are right, looked at from a certain angle.

Bitch rating

B++. Why bitch? You are the king. You know that magnanimous praise – she does so well with what little she's got – can inflict just as much collateral damage as upfront abuse; but, of course, when you do condescend to go in for catty remarks, they are always big catty remarks.

Collective noun

A protocol tip for non-Leos. You may find yourself, for some bizarre zodiacal reason, in a grand salon full of Leos (and if you do, pause to wonder what an unranked nobody like you is doing there). The massed pools of limelight blind you, and a mistral of air-kisses musses your hair. You are privileged to be in the midst of a Royal Barge of Leos. Bow and grovel.

FAVE DEADLY SIN

And which deadly sin comes by royal appointment? All of them, is the republican response – they're practically a job description for successful monarchy. But your Number One sin has got to be Pride. For a start, it's the deadly sinners' deadly sin: it's known as the sin from which all others arise, and you just love to be up there with the top people. Pride is also known as Vanity, which as far as you're concerned is just as it should be: Vanity is your second favourite, and you get two sins for the price of one.

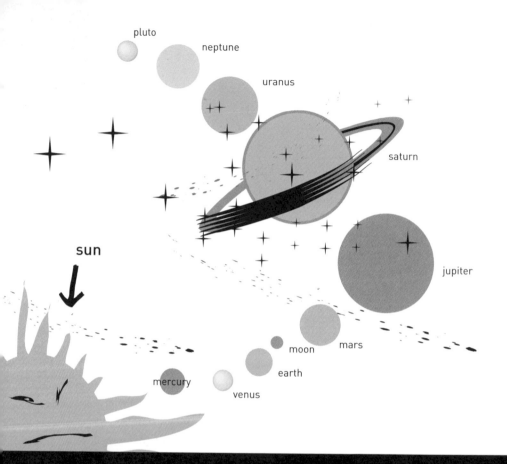

pluto

neptune

uranus

saturn

sun

jupiter

moon   mars

mercury   earth

venus

PLANET PLANET

Every sun sign has a planetary Godfather, whose job it is to establish respect and provide discreet muscle to ensure that it stays established. Before there were telescopes, astrologers could only see five planets in the sky, plus the Moon and Sun so they counted the two

as planetary rulers. It seemed a good idea at the time. Each planet babysat two zodiac signs – except for the Moon (Cancer's minder) and the Sun (which devoted itself to the comfort of Leo). Yes, your planetary ruler is the local star, centre of the solar system. Don't get overexcited

In cosmic terms, our little solar system (only nine-ish planets – call that a system?) is a very suburban number, on an outer arm of a flat, spiral galaxy and light years from celestial action of any kind. However, as Leos appreciate, better to be a small king than no king at all

BLAME YOUR PLANET

Big, bad and blazing

Even you think you have taken this Supreme Ruler business a bit too far, and your braver subjects are starting to call you Caligula. How can you regain your benign monarch status? Easy: blame your planet. In your case, it's the Sun.

Astrologers speak of the Sun moving in and out of the zodiacal signs; that's just the view from here. In astronomical reality, the Sun stands still and we all rush around it, helplessly captivated, in circles (or in some cases ellipses, but who's counting). Isn't that just SO, Leo? A ruling planet around which adoring satellites revolve: it's no more than you deserve. It even has a corona. Plus the Sun has always and everywhere been worshipped; there's not a culture on Earth that has not produced a sun god or goddess at some

point – the Greek Helios/Apollo rode the skies in a flaming golden chariot drawn by snow-white horses (nothing subtle about sun gods, and Leo wouldn't want it any other way).

Surely there can be no Darkside to the Sun? It may look like a benevolent disc (albeit with a penchant for cheap, tacky, retina-scorching sunsets); but up close, it's a scary great ball of gas, a giant nuclear reactor in the sky, gobbling up hydrogen and emitting all sorts of mysterious rays that it's just as well we don't know about. We think it eats itself for our warmth and benefit, but it would do this whether or not it was surrounded by dependent planets. It's the shining and stellar performance that counts. You can relate to that, can't you, Leo?

BAD MOON RISING

The darkside of Leo's darkside

It's not all sunshine on the Darkside. You know just how power-crazed and monomaniac your innermost thoughts and secret fantasies are, but where do you think they come from? The Moon, that's where – or whichever area of your birthchart the Moon was moodily plodding when you were born. The Sun is our daytime self; the Moon represents our inner psycho. The nippy little blighter rushes around, plunging in and out of signs every few days, so throughout Leo's month in the Sun, the lunar nuisance dodges around like a royal favourite in the face of unexpected regime change. That helps to explain why two Leos born only days apart draw up very different plans for world domination, depending on which sign the Moon was bothering at the time.

CATCHING THE MOON

That's all very well, you say, but how do I know where the Moon was when I was born? There are long, complicated (and, frankly, dull) tables called ephemerides that tell you where every planet (and for tedious astrological reasons, the Moon is an honorary planet) stood in the heavens, atmosphere bated, as you made your sorry debut. However, we have provided a Moon itinerary at the back of this book to enable you to get a rough idea. If that sounds like too much hard work, and you have the techno technique, then try visiting the following website: www.alabe.com/freechart. If you know where you were born, and when, they will produce, for *free*, a rough-cut birthchart that will pin your Moon on the zodiac wheel.

Lunatic combinations

Here's what happens to Leo when the Moon sets off on a royal progress.

Moon in Aries – more power, more leadership, more authority: the world is not enough!

Moon in Taurus – what you really like about this king business is the banqueting; and the palaces; and the banqueting; and the great frocks.

Moon in Gemini – you prefer the gypsy-king option, and fiddle your way around your domain.

Moon in Cancer – querulous grumping on your throne, dreaming of past slights to your authority.

Moon in Leo – instant upgrade from petty despot to full-on tyrant; twice as domineering, pompous and conceited.

Moon in Virgo – so busy fussing over details that you fail to notice barbarian hordes at the gate.

Moon in Libra – high-handed, patronizing, but diplomatic; you've got your eye on a Palais des Glaces of your very own.

Moon in Scorpio – power-crazed tyrant with actual power; the demon king.

Moon in Sagittarius – domineering, high-handed, but rash; you'd give your kingdom for a horse.

Moon in Capricorn – not a merry monarch; you hide the keys to the treasury from yourself.

Moon in Aquarius – obsessed with fairy palaces on inaccessible alps.

Moon in Pisces – easily swayed by unscrupulous favourites, but a mastermind at deploying the tyranny of the weak.

BORN UNDER A BAD SIGN

The scum also rises

And another thing. Your sun sign is modified by your rising sign. This is the zodiac sign that was skulking over the horizon at the very minute you were born. If your sun sign is your ego, then your rising sign gives you your public manners (such as they are), your Sunday worst. It's the painted smile behind which the real, disgusting you lurks. Some astrologers maintain that its malign influence affects what you look like. Be afraid.

You might like to know that, in the northern hemisphere, for tedious astronomical reasons, there are more people with Cancer and Leo rising than any other sign. You think this is just as it should be: the more Leos — however tangentially related — in your dynasty, the better. World domination just came one step nearer.

GOING UP

Now pay attention, because the following is quite brain-busting. There are 12 signs of the zodiac, and astrologers like to think of them as occupying a band of sky that spins around the Earth once every 24 hours. (This is a convention; it is not astronomically correct and you will not see the signs if you look up, so don't write in.) So, every two hours or so another sign hauls itself blearily over the eastern horizon. This is going on whatever time of the day or night you were born, and whichever benighted spot you chose to appear in. These astro-mechanics help to explain why lions born at either end of the same day toss their manes in a completely different way. There are long, nerdy and essentially tedious ways to discover your rising sign, but the easiest way is to get hold of a birthchart (see page 144).

Upwardly mobile

If your rising sign is Leo, then your public persona is a vain, snobby fashion victim who is obsessed with its hair. This is to distract the rest of us from your plans to rule the world. Here's what happens when other zodiacal upstarts rise above their station.

Aries rising

You love a uniform; and shouting; and being on the move; and even more shouting.

Taurus rising

Aren't you His/Her Royal Highness Solid and Respectable? What's going on below stairs?

Gemini rising

Rebel, rebel! Just as long as you are in charge when the dust settles.

Cancer rising

The people's princess (or prince), just as long as your subjects don't start to criticize you.

Virgo rising

Despotic ruler of the World of Neatness; what regal dirt can you be hiding?

Libra rising

Charlemagne of Charm; do your courtiers realize you don't mean what you say?

Scorpio rising

You appear darkly, hypnotically powerful; actually, you're just powerful.

Sagittarius rising

Absentee monarch; while you're on the crusades, lesser mortals seize your kingdom.

Capricorn rising

Uncanny ability to remove any concept of merriment from the state of monarchy.

Aquarius rising

A very chilly, sneering majesty; more at home (or palace?) on the chessboard.

Pisces rising

The Player King in person; you can't believe you are actually in charge.

DON'T YOU LOVE ME, BABY?

Venus and Leo

Just how much of a high-maintenance tease or bunny-boiler you are may depend on where the solar system's heartless tart (Venus) was blushingly dropping her handkerchief when you were born (*see below*). Oh, and Venus also has a say in how harmoniously you blend in with the rest of the world, but what do words like harmony have to do with the Darkside? Now, for astrological reasons that will fry your brain if I explain them here (basically, Venus is far too luxury-loving to move too far away from the Sun, and her orbital rate is in bed with Earth's), Venus only ever appears in your sun sign, or two signs on either side of it. In your case, lions, that means Venus will be in Leo, Gemini, Cancer, Virgo or Libra. And this is what it does to your love and lust life.

MAKE LOVE AND WAR

Venus is the girlie planet of lurve, right? And Mars is planet lad, the warlord. You may also have a sneaking feeling that men are from Mars and women are from Venus. Don't be upset if I tell you this is not true. All of us, of all genders, have a stake in both planets. Where they are in your birthchart has what I shall call consequences. You may think your sun sign makes you a born babe-magnet, but Venus in a chilly sign will cut you off at the knees; you may think that your sun sign means you are the twin soul of the dove of peace, but you may go red-eyed with bloodlust when beaten to a parking spot. Mars will be somewhere irascible. You'll need a birthchart (*see page 144*) to find out what Venus and Mars were getting up to when you were born. It is far too complicated – and, frankly, dull – to work out here

Venus in Leo

Imperious, demanding, expensive, impossible; the lightest touch of your velvet claw or silken whip keeps your love serfs in servile ecstasy.

Venus in Gemini

Nauseating, kittenish playfighting; toxic flirting levels; you just love to see handsome rivals duelling to the death over sweet little you.

Venus in Cancer

You like to keep your loves in a gilded cage, and so stuffed with delicious homemade birdseed that they never even rise from the perch. Just to make sure, you clip their wings with your golden scissors.

Venus in Virgo

You are the Virgin Queen. No one is good enough for you; the reckless (usually Sagittarians) who become your short-lived favourites die by a thousand cuts of your hypercritical tongue.

Venus in Libra

Darling, I was wonderful! Dramatic competitions to outperform each other; shameless upstagery in the intimate love scenes; and there are simply not enough mirrors in the cosmos for both of you.

ARE YOU LOOKING AT ME?

Mars and Leo

Leos do not do fisticuffs;, they have an army for that kind of thing. But just how confrontational, threatening, paranoid and gagging for a fight you are depends on which area of your birthchart the bruiser planet Mars is being held back in by his mates (leave it, Mars, he's not worth it). Mars is the next planet out from Earth, but paces its orbit rather more slowly (presumably to get some effective eyeballing in). It takes 2½ years for Mars to get around, and on the way it spends about two months of quality menacing time in each sign. As a Leo, of course, right is always on your side, so any fights you get into are always unprovoked. If you find your justifiable aggression comes out in a more cowardly lion mode, check out Mars' alibi at the time of your birth.

Mars in Aries
Just how many extra Y chromosomes do you actually have? You could start a fight on your own in an empty throne room.

Mars in Taurus
You can take a lot of flak, but are unstoppable when roused. Invariably you go for the throat. You are your own best royal bodyguard.

Mars in Gemini
Mouthy and quick on your feet, you love to provoke a fight with slow-witted lower orders, then dance around ribtickling them with your royal rapier.

Mars in Cancer
You don't do confrontation yourself (you're a sensitive monarch), but your discreet elite security guards do.

Mars in Leo

You are right; you are might; might is right. Does someone dare to look at you in a funny way? Or even just to look at you? Guards! Guards!

Mars in Virgo

Even if everything is right in your own kingdom, you can always find some slight laxity of protocol in another that demands military intervention.

Mars in Libra

Some days you roar like a tiger, other days you're just a pussycat. In tiger mode, you'll take anyone on, but not without backup; you only like victory.

Mars in Scorpio

Everyone knows who you are, Mr Big. Nobody would dare look at you unless ordered to, so you are never bothered, not even in the meanest streets.

Mars in Sagittarius

What you love best is throwing off the royal robes and getting down to a really exhilarating bar-room brawl, back to back with your drinking mate from the other side of the tracks.

Mars in Capricorn

Assassin.

Mars in Aquarius

Fighting is so uncool; but when it comes down to it, you have quick reactions and some extremely unexpected moves picked up from a very obscure (but aristocratic) form of martial arts.

Mars in Pisces

Grant us all a favour; don't fight. You're such a muddled mover that you always get a bloody nose and your crown slips. But then, part of you enjoys being beaten to a martyred pulp.

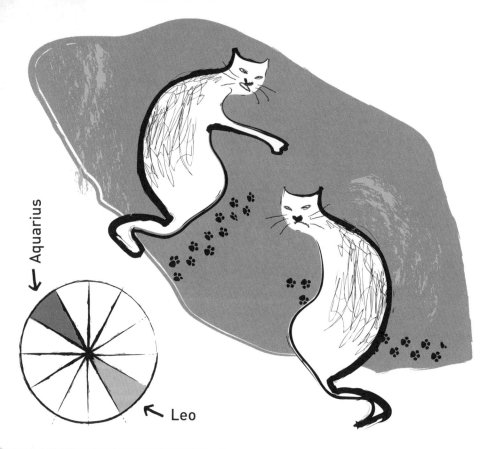

Aquarius

Leo

POLAR BEARS

Your polar sign sits on the opposite side of the zodiac wheel, six signs away, giving you knowing looks. You have a dark umbilical link with it. If Darkside you is your evil twin, then your polar sign is your evil twin's evil twin. It's got your number – but then you've got its, so that's alright, isn't it? Brightside astrologers maintain that there is a strong complementary relationship between you and your polar sign, and that this relationship is positive and fruitful, especially at work, because you share the same energy quality (fixed). Well excuse me; on the Darkside it's more like the tension between two torn-eared tomcats meeting on alien territory; lots of pointless posturing, standing at insolent angles and waiting for the other to spit first; but they both want the same thing: world domination.

WHO'S GOT YOUR NUMBER?

check out the opposition

Your polar opposite sign is Aquarius: aloof, standoffish, mad, bad and dangerous to know. (For more about your darkly fascinating opposite number, *see pages 328–359.*) What would a drama queen like you want with a celebrity-phobe loner like your average Aquarian? How do you have this – shall we say – understanding? Well, like good cop and bad cop, or arch villain and superhero, you need each other to make the Darkside work for you. It's all about elements (undesirable ones, of course). You are Fire; Aquarius is Air. Fire needs oxygen to burn, just as you need the oxygen of adoration to show how gorgeously you can light up any event.

You are a creature of bombast and histrionics, but can't you feel, deep down,

the chilly, insolent Mr Cool, watching you flouncing around issuing your impossible orders and demanding instant grovel? Ever wonder how you can order three executions and a public flogging and still play with sweet little kittens? Or how a vain, self-deluded egocentrist like you can muster the detachment to compile an effective long-term masterplan?

Respect your inner Aquarian; it provides a small (but potent) sliver of icy detachment that cools the furnace of your raging self-regard, separating your inner self from the consequences of your actions, so that your soul can sleep at night. It is the little spot of head-ruled yin in the swirl of your heart-ruled yang. Of course, if it gets too icy in there, you graduate from king to evil emperor.

DARKSIDE DATE

There is no possibility that you will not get a date. You know you are handsome, noble and irresistible. Plus there is always *droit de seigneur* (the king gets to date whomever he wants, or the peasants will pay – it works for both sexes). You love the chase and the pouncing, and

can wait for days behind an acacia bush for a particularly doe-eyed young gazelle. But dates have to remember that it is all about you. You have got to be adored. The more dependent and servile they are, the more you love them. Your ideal date is with a poor and impressionable

(but beautiful – you are a total lookist) beggar maid (or boy) whom you can smother with condescending luxury, put on a pedestal (you don't hear the protests), demand undying love from, and then despise and discard when they cannot deliver, or when you get bored

SEX

Powerful, professional, performance

What your lovely assistants have to realize is that Leo sex is all about performance and applause. Just because you're experiencing intimate passion, does it mean you have to be alone? (Your definition of intimate, in any case, is just you, your partner, your hairdresser, your caterer, your aromatherapist, your fitness coach and a few gofers.) Basic requirements are a hall of mirrors and a satellite uplink to global TV. To be fair, you take your part seriously, buffing the bod and practising hip grinds and pelvic thrusts to the Jagger standard, but then you focus so hard on style, posturing and execution that you fail to notice your partner has gone to sleep. This makes you angry, for he or she (or they) will not then be able to give you marks out of 10 with the special numbered cards you have prepared, or offer a round of wild applause and scream for an encore.

Because you need so much adoration, many of you go for the harem (or 'pride') option. This is quite unusually sympathetic and thoughtful of you, for no individual human can grind out as much unconditional attention as you need.

What kind of love rat are you?

Once your ardour has cooled and the thrill has gone, you can't be bothered to tell your ex that they are an ex. However, if you need the ex for some reason – perhaps your wardrobe needs shifting or you're feeling suddenly lonely at the top – then you just lift your little despotic digit and reel them back in.

Aries – bitter confrontations over who is to wear the Pants of Dominance.

Taurus – you flash your claws; they dig in their hooves.

Gemini – is it you they love or your penumbra of celebrity?

Cancer – when you're in a royal

Leo – serious strategy defect; who will do the adoring?

Virgo – they don't eat meat!

Libra – synchronized charm offensives; but their magic mirror is incompatible with yours.

Scorpio – you suspect they may be secretly in control. You'd

Sagittarius – 'nuff respect? Well, no, actually.

Capricorn – cramp your style by hiding your Gold Card.

Aquarius – rational, reticent and republican – yet fascinating.

Pisces – pleasingly servile, but always run away with Guinevere

RELATIONSHIPS

Kiss my royal paw

Relate is probably the wrong word. Leos condescend; or form alliances; or allow themselves to be worshipped. You don't need to network. At a party you are the one in the middle, either radiating charm and loveliness or in a histrionic fit so mighty that no one can fail to notice.

A fearful snob (and what's wrong with that?), you prefer to ally yourself with people who will make you look good – the powerful, important, influential or just plain rich (bedazzled beggars are best kept for bed). However, they must not be more handsome, successful, powerful and rich than you. If people displease you (perhaps your royal radar detects a slight dimming in the sycophantic wattage), you drop them instantly; it never crosses your mind that they deserve an explanation.

Anyone with even the most tenuous grip on the psychology of the individual can easily crash the Leo magic circle: all they have to do is fawn, bow and scrape. The brighter among them realize that you need them – or at least the oxygen of their esteem – just as much as they need you; is a king still a king when he has no subjects? The rest of us have often seen haughty, handsome Leos accompanied (one pace behind) by inconspicuous mousy spouses and wondered why; now we know: they give great grovel.

In any romance, you initiate the game (and heaven help any Chosen One who does not respond). The 'relationship' is conducted at your command; everything will be fine as long your partner realizes that you rule, in all senses of the word.

DREAM JOBS

Most of you are already in your dream job (any job with you in it must by definition be a dream), but even you may take a break from bossing to scratch beneath the crown and wonder if perhaps you are hiding your glorious light under a bushel. I so superjobs include:

Monarch

What better way to express regal longings than through the proper channels? All you have to do is either marry an existing royal or maul your way through the existing heirs. How hard can that be?

Megastar

Bathe in the hot white limelight, hear the roar of the crowd, feel the love of the little people! But move into a gated compound and drive everywhere in a sealed limo – you don't want to bump into the sweaty little oiks.

WORK

You're the boss

It will all be OK as long as you are in charge. Clearly, your way is the only way. Why don't people know what's good for them? The actual job is a teensy bit irrelevant. You must: a) be in charge; b) be seen to be in charge; c) be paid in gold; d) have an admiring horde of slavish acolytes (minimum number: three) to do the heavy work and the fawning.

Your strategy in any work situation is to sweep in, with or without a retinue, impose your rule and punish treasonable behaviour. You can do this with a clear conscience because you are king. That's why astute employers often take you on as a hatchet person: it costs only a big desk and an imposing title. As for working your way up the workplace hierarchy, excuse me? Whatever your position, you are, in your eyes, the boss. Officially you do not do office gossip; unofficially, of course, you have organized a posse of sycophantic informers whose balls you have in a vice and who report to you at noon. And if you are any good at kingship, you dress down every now and then and mingle with the common people around the water cooler (but be warned: your disguise may not be as good as you think it is).

You may appear to be a workaholic, but really you are only good at face time; you (and I) know that you can be titanically lazy. (Have you seen what male lions do all day?) Lolling on velvet divans being fed peeled grapes and watching the workforce sweat is part of the job description, isn't it?

WHEN LIONS GO WRONG

Leo crimes are always on the large scale; there will always be an Organization (all Leos want to be the Godfather, if they aren't already) and you avoid carrying out the actual work. You like the purry white cat on your lap, and giving orders as you savour your hand-rolled cigar.

Bullion thief

Think Auric Goldfinger, but with style. Repatriating obscene amounts of gold (all gold is yours, by Divine Right) cannot be wrong, can it? It has to be solid gold, in bars; silver is so bourgeois, and cash is common

Grand scammer

Great! Dress up as Crown Prince Leopold of Ruritania and strip-mine the assets of impressionable social climbers. If that doesn't work, you're just as impressive as a televangelist or snake-oil salesman

CRIMES AND MISDEMEANOURS

How bad could it get?

So what sort of crim would you be, if sociopathy became the new world order? How would you spend your days (or maybe your nights) if you really lived on the Darkside? Petty larceny is below you – you have other people to do that kind of thing. What you like best is the big job: stealing countries, for example. Anything involving bullion (in huge amounts) is good. You are also adept at high-society confidence trickery, fraudulent behaviour that involves dressing up and suckering Joe Public. Being a Fire sign, you are very attracted to arson, especially the kind that yields fat insurance payouts.

Of course you respect the law; you *are* the law after all (it's the law of the jungle of which you are king); but the rest of us have to understand that what is the law for us simply does not apply to you, because you have diplomatic immunity and the Divine Right of Kings on your side. If your subjects insist that you have transgressed, you insist right back on being tried by your peers – that is, a team of other royals who will understand. Mind you, you just love a day in court – what a supremely regal word that is. Even if it's only a question of non-returned library books, you will take it all the way to the High Court of Appeal, because then you can give your star turn in the dock. An audience is an audience is an audience.

And if it all goes slammer-shaped and you are locked up, you do at least get a captive audience, peasants to patronize and your very own guards, and pretty soon you seize the throne as the King of the Cooler.

AT HOME

Palace, sweet palace

On the whole, you welcome visitors to your royal enclosure (as long as they take their shoes off and leave backwards) since even the most irascible lions among you want to show off your dazzling array of trophies and spare crowns, and how tastefully you can pay someone else to decorate your lovely home. And since few of us can resist rubbernecking around a mansion, we flock (taking our desert-gauge sunglasses with us, of course). Occasionally, we find a Miss Havisham lion in there, slumped in dusty finery on a grimy, gilded throne, garlanded with cobwebs, dreaming of former glories.

DOMESTIC DISHARMONY

Aries – your meat shelf in the fridge will always be empty.

Taurus – territorial standoffs in the kitchen; they are stubborn, you are resolute.

Gemini – they laugh in the face of protocol and will borrow your crown without asking!

Cancer – they are always adding inappropriate homely touches to the state rooms.

Leo – twin thrones; no room for both sets of courtiers.

Virgo – constantly tut-tutting under their breath about something they call extravagance.

Libra – serious bathroom gridlock, and they may well have more self-portraits than you.

Scorpio – they're the power, you're the glory; the only palace mate you can't intimidate.

Sagittarius – they will use your coronation robes for bathmats and forget to turn the tap off.

Capricorn – forever switching off the lights so no one can see you properly.

Aquarius – cool brains; they will outwit you when it's bill-paying time.

Pisces – pleasingly slavish, but unreliable around corkscrews.

Decor

You think Neuschwanstein and Versailles are just a shade too restrained. What exactly is wrong with leopardskin *chaise-longues*, ruby-dusted lampshades and a solid gold catflap? And you have just commissioned a swimming pool with your portrait in gilded tiles at the bottom. What could be more tasteful?

Sharing the Leo palace

Sometimes, when the royal coffers are a few gold bars short of a banquet, you deign to fling open the palace gates and allow the little people to come in. It'll be a bit smelly, of course, but remember that not only do they pay hard cash and give good grovel, they can also be made to do all the chores.

Leo paint chart

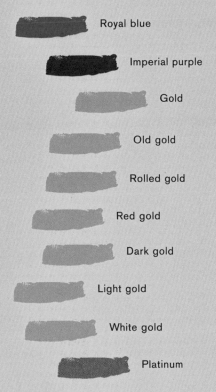

Royal blue

Imperial purple

Gold

Old gold

Rolled gold

Red gold

Dark gold

Light gold

White gold

Platinum

PLAYTIME

The darkside of fun

You are unbearable anywhere the Sun don't shine. (You are a Fire sign, don't forget.) Avoid anywhere with world-class attractions that divert attention from your own glory – Rome, Uluru, the Taj Mahal, the Grand Canyon, the Great Wall of China. Don't go camping: you know you are strictly a hotel and hairdryers person. Don't go on adventure holidays unless you have a very large number of intrepid servants, diplomatic immunity and a bulletproof sedan chair. And never, ever go anywhere on your own. You may begin to believe you don't exist.

Remember, however, that anywhere with a population of sycophantic locals (preferably poor, pathetically grateful and used to worshipping their superiors) will soothe your soul – it's always good to know that somewhere in the world, someone is admiring you. Group holidays (with a carefully vetted membership) can be extremely satisfying – an instant captive audience.

ZODIAC CULL

Suppose you were marooned on a desert island/up an alp/in a rainforest/ at sea with 11 others, each one a different star sign. Who would you eliminate in order to survive? Well, you would of course have to leave a quorum to do the admiring, but you would have to get rid of Gemini (no respect for your leadership), Sagittarius (thinks he or she knows better), Aries (wants to kill you and take over the leadership), Virgo (criticizes your every move) and Taurus (eats all the food).

Holidays from hell

★ An adrenaline-packed adventure holiday with Gemini and Sagittarius; you will ruin your hair.

★ A far-from-the-madding crowd holiday with Aquarius and Scorpio; madding crowds are exactly what you live for – there'll be no one to impress.

★ Going camping in North Wales with parsimonious Virgo and Capricorn; you cannot cope with anything less than five-star luxury.

Road rage

Either you are the one being driven in the big, purring stretch-limo and have a chauffeur to do road rage for you; or you are the one driving the gas-guzzling SUV (a lion's got to have room for the retinue and regalia) that takes up the whole motorway; you don't understand why anyone else is on the road, because you did not declare the day a public holiday. You do the map reading, perfectly; you do the driving, perfectly; you decide where to go. You hear no complaints. Likelihood of you being the trudging peasant? Zero.

Gamesmanship

If it's a team game, you must be captain, regardless of your qualifications. You know exactly how great you are; therefore you resent any criticism – and any praise, because no one should presume that they can appreciate you as well as you do. You always play to win; if you don't win, you sulk and order a lackey to take your ball home.

BAD COMPANY

Your hall of infamy

You may be feeling a bit emotionally fragile after a session on the Darkside, so to cheer the soul, let's look at a few of the famous, infamous, notorious and just plain bad Leos who might feel the same if they read this book. You will be impressed by the number of megastars and world leaders/dictators/emperors; you're in very good bad company. And, despite your formidable (though somehow magnificent) Darkside, there are a number of people who appear to want to be you, but who have missed the royal yacht. Think of anyone with an unjustifiably high opinion of themselves, big hair, an unfundable love of luxury and a pathological inability to play follow my leader. All wannabe Leos. If they're not, someone's lying. Look at the panel below if you don't believe me.

WANNABES

Take John McEnroe. (I do NOT have to tell you who he is.) Archetypal Leo, wouldn't you say? King of the Court? Nope. Aquarian (but then, you now know that Aquarius is your opposite sign, so you can see where he is getting his Leo chops from). Or Elvis, the

King himself: glitter, limelight, sparkly stuff, wealth and *still worshipped even though he is dead*? Capricorn. And you'd think, would you not, that Leo would bag a fair number of royals – but not so. Henry VIII of England: bombastic, dynastic, made himself head of his own

Church? Cancerian. Richard the Lionheart, the Crusader king? Name a bit of a giveaway? Virgo. William the Conqueror? Libra. Louis XIV, the Sun King of France, creator of Versailles, the ultimate gilded lion cage? Virgo. Disappointing for all of them, isn't it?

Napoleon Bonaparte
15 August, 1769

Top Leo badboy. From a standing start as a tiny Corsican nobody, Napoleon clawed his way to the top to become emperor of France; he really did have a plan for world domination.

Benito Mussolini *29 July, 1883*

Proclaimed himself *Il Duce* (leader) of the one-party Fascist government in Italy in 1922. Democracy – who needs it! But it all ended in tears in 1945, at the end of World War II, when he was murdered by his own countrymen. See what happens when bigger lions muscle in…

Fidel Castro *13 August, 1926*

Premier of Cuba, which he kept an iron grip on from 1959 until 2008, when he handed over to his brother Raul. Often described as a revolutionary, when he was really just an old-fashioned king (and what's wrong with that?), ruling by divine (all right, Marxist) right.

Andy Warhol *6 August, 1928*

Conceptual artist (which means that he had the idea, while everyone else did all the hard work); coiner of the phrase 'Famous for 15 minutes' (excepting of course A. Warhol; so everlasting fame for him, stale cake for the rest of us).

Madonna *16 August, 1958*

Globally worshipped international superstar, film star, style icon, children's author and hard-nosed businessperson, Madonna is the epitome of Blonde Ambition, the queen of the showbiz jungle.

VIRGO

23 August ~ 22 September

Virgo is a feminine, mutable Earth sign ruled by Mercury. It is the sixth sign on the zodiac wheel, directly opposite Pisces, and is named after the constellation Virgo (the virgin), which carps and nitpicks behind the Sun at this time of year.

On the Darkside, this makes you a peevish, hypercritical anal-retentive, with an obsession for sterile perfectionism and a pedantic fetish for detail.

Punctuality

You are never, ever late; or early, for that matter. You are always exactly on time – it's not difficult. If only they'd let you run the world, you'd make sure that DBL (Deliberately Being Late) was a criminal offence.

Toothpaste

In a time-locked closet in your bathroom are 3 x 365 individual prewrapped disposable toothbrushes, each loaded with the precise amount of toothpaste needed for one cleaning. Only you have the key.

Temper gauge

In your case, the gauge has to be recalibrated, as you maintain the constant inner seethe-rate you were born with. Although you can reach boiling point instantly if your patterns are disturbed, you never return to 0°.

PERSONALITY

Peevish, pedantic, perfectionist

OK, Virgo, you are famous for telling it like it is, so let's see if you can take what you dish out. Brightside apologists claim that, disabled by chronic perfectionism, you are just as laceratingly tough on yourself as you are on the rest of us – only on the inside, where we can't see. Yeah, right. Let's do a test: all Virgos are negative, tiny-hearted fusspots obsessed with detail, who do nothing but carp and criticize. What is your response? You carp and criticize (I rest my case), letting loose with that spiteful tongue, saying: a) that all Virgos are loyal, hard-working and kind (unlike any other sun sign); and b) what is wrong with criticism anyway? And you will not be a prisoner to cant and hypocrisy. Where are those legendary analytical skills that you apply to everything but your own inner self? Can't you see the simple logical contradiction in b)? I'd let it go, but then you file another defence – viz, that you have a Zany Sense of Humour; and we all know what that means.

When you are hot on the anti-hypocrisy crusade, the first casualties are diplomacy, tact and basic manners. If asked a simple question that anticipates the answer 'No' (e.g. 'Does my bum look big in this?'), not only do you reply, 'Well, sure it does, lardarse', but you kindly go on to give your estimate of exactly how much bigger than the norm it looks, in both metric and imperial measurements. After a couple of bruising encounters like this, few people ask your advice about anything; that doesn't stop you giving it.

You are never wrong; but you aren't not wrong like Leo (who just isn't, end of story); you secretly fear the possibility that you might be wrong, but will kill your firstborn rather than admit it, because you despise the weak. This means, among other things, that your first impressions are cast in stone. If you met the Boston Strangler on a good day, you'd maintain that he was a great guy, right up until they threw Old Smokey's switch; if you got off on the wrong foot with, say, St Francis of Assisi, you'd maintain acidly and forever that he was nothing but a molester of fluffy kittens.

Possibly because no one will talk to you, and you spend a lot of time on your own you obsess about your health. Considering the tanker loads of bleach and pallets of rubber gloves you get through, it's amazing how many diseases you contract (they're all listed in your bedside copy of *The Big Book of Scary Diseases You Might Have*). There is no healing therapy that you haven't tried, except maybe Western scientific medicine – mainly because you suspect it might cure you, and then where would you be? You are also a sucker for cults (you've been reprogrammed six times), faux gurus (where did all your money go?) and food fads (you've tested allergic to everything except polystyrene).

For all that, you've got no soul; show you a sublime moment, and you kill it stone-dead with trivia. You don't see the rainbow because you are fretting about who's borrowed your umbrella.

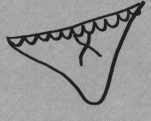

Bitch rating

A+. Not quite in Gemini's class, but a worthy silver medallist. *Premier cru* spite is let down by lumpy delivery; even slow bitchees can't fail to get the point and are liable to deck you, especially if they are Aries; the trick is to slash and run, but you always stick around to make sure the finer points have been rammed home.

Collective noun

A point of order for non-Virgos. You may find yourself, for some bizarre zodiacal reason, in a utility room full of Virgos (are you wearing clean underwear?). Bleach-fumes sear your mucous membranes, and eyes narrow as Virgos bring each other's attention to contentious subclauses. This is a Nitpick of Virgos. Look busy.

FAVE DEADLY SIN

Don't cast your eyes down modestly, shuffle your feet and pretend you don't know what I'm talking about. Oh, sin is such a filthy word it could never pass your lips, let alone cross your mind. You are the zodiac's Mary Poppins (the harpy in the books, not the sugarplum in the film): insufferably pleased with yourself, but cruelly critical of everybody else. Your sin is Vanity, the lighter side of Pride. And you do something clever with Gluttony, reversing it to make a homely little nameless sin of sucking all the joy, taste and mouth-feel out of food.

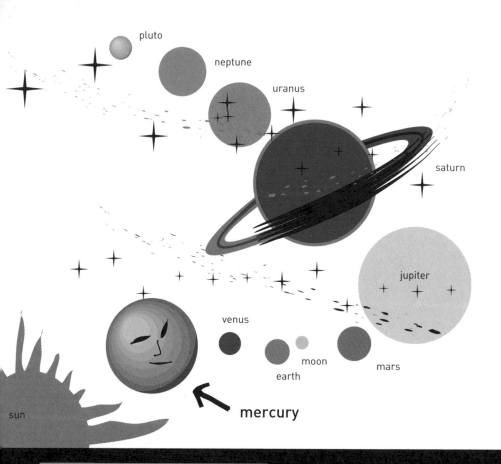

pluto

neptune

uranus

saturn

jupiter

venus

moon

earth

mars

sun

mercury

PLANET PLANET

Every sun sign has a caretaker, someone to keep it spick and span, go around picking up everybody's litter, mop up after parties to which you were invited but didn't go and keep keys safe in your key cupboard, because no one else can be trusted not to lose them.

Before there were telescopes, astrologers could only see five planets in the sky, plus the Moon and Sun, so they counted these two as planetary rulers. It seemed a good idea at the time. Each planet babysat two zodiac signs – except for the Moon (Cancer's minder) and the Sun

(which allows Leo to rule). Your planetary ruler is Mercury, which you have to share with that dirty, no-good, thieving low-life, Gemini; some of you have put in a bid for a nice clean, quiet, ruler of your own, an asteroid called Chiron, but you haven't quite finalized the paperwork.

BLAME YOUR PLANET

Busybody of the gods

You spent the whole of your honeymoon cleaning the 10-star hotel's lavatories to your exacting standards; friends invite you around for a relaxing evening listening to their favourite sounds, and you spend three hours recataloguing their entire CD collection in an impenetrably complex system of your own devising (involving alphabetical, chronological, biorhythmical and colour-coded matrices); people all around you freely discuss obsessive-compulsive behaviour. Is it your fault you're the only one with any idea of order in this zodiac? Not entirely; you can blame your planet. In your case: Mercury, small but neat, and nearest to the Sun.

It's a zodiacal outrage that you have to share this with Gemini; but you are not one to complain, you have never made a fuss in your life, so you just buckle down and get on with it, unlike some other star signs you could mention.

As I told Geminis (*see page 79*), Mercury is a tricksy planet, and one of its more tricksy tricks is to be whatever will get its feet under the table. When it's with you, Virgo, Mercury comes on as a hard-working communicator, tirelessly and thanklessly serving the universe, even when specifically asked not to. It's named after the workaholic Roman god (Hermes in Greek), the one who takes on all those extra responsibilities (healing, cattle, marketplaces) because, frankly, no one else cares; he is run off his feet at the beck and call of bigger gods, especially Zeus, who couldn't tie his own shoelaces without Mercury's assistance. Sniff.

BAD MOON RISING

The darkside of Virgo's darkside

It's not all sunshine on the Darkside. You know just how power-crazed and monomaniac your innermost thoughts and secret fantasies are, but where do you think they come from? The Moon, that's where – or whichever area of your birthchart the Moon was moodily plodding when you were born. The Sun is our daytime self; the Moon represents our inner psycho. The nippy little blighter rushes around, plunging in and out of signs every few days, so throughout Virgo's month in the Sun, the lunar nuisance dodges around like a hypochondriac at an Alternative Healing Festival. That helps to explain why two Virgos born only days apart reorganize other people's sock drawers using completely different systems, depending on which sign the Moon was bothering at the time.

CATCHING THE MOON

That's all very well, you say, but how do I know where the Moon was when I was born? There are long, complicated (and, frankly, dull) tables called ephemerides that tell you where every planet (and for tedious astrological reasons, the Moon is an honorary planet) stood in the heavens, atmosphere bated, as you made your sorry debut. However, we have provided a Moon itinerary at the back of this book to enable you to get a rough idea. If that sounds like too much hard work, and you have the techno technique, then try visiting the following website: www.alabe.com/freechart. If you know where you were born, and when, they will produce, for *free*, a rough-cut birthchart that will pin your Moon on the zodiac wheel.

Lunatic combinations

Here's what happens to Virgo when the Moon sets off on a dust inspection.

Moon in Aries – when you are world dictator, you will impose vegetarianism by martial law, and levy a fun tax.

Moon in Taurus – you plan to start an upmarket company specializing in designer bathrooms with extremely powerful showers.

Moon in Gemini – maybe it wouldn't matter this once if you left the dirty dishes and just partied.

Moon in Cancer – if you thought you could dodge the germs, you'd be a lot clingier than you are.

Moon in Leo – sometimes you feel like a drama queen trapped in the body of an assistant stage manager.

Moon in Virgo – you lie awake at night, listening to the dust accumulating and planning new ways to destroy it.

Moon in Libra – you don't think it's fair only to criticize your partner, so you nag all your other lovers at the same time.

Moon in Scorpio – you occasionally think there's such a thing as being too neat.

Moon in Sagittarius – sometimes you don't tidy thoroughly, just stuff everything in cupboards and ram the doors shut.

Moon in Capricorn – outside you appear cautious; inside you are overcautious.

Moon in Aquarius – you suspect you may be a changeling, since you don't give a damn about detail.

Moon in Pisces – gullible virgin chained to a rock, just asking to be rescued by a superhero you can belittle.

BORN UNDER A BAD SIGN

The scum also rises

And another thing. Your sun sign is modified by your rising sign. This is the zodiac sign that was skulking over the horizon at the very minute you were born. If your sun sign is your ego, then your rising sign gives you your public manners (such as they are), your Sunday worst. It's the painted smile behind which the real, disgusting you lurks. Some astrologers maintain that its malign influence affects what you look like. Be afraid.

It would not surprise you one bit to know that, in the southern hemisphere, for tedious astronomical reasons, there are fewer people with Virgo (and Libra) rising than any other sign. Typical! You have to work twice as hard to keep the place looking half decent, because you're the only one who can be bothered – and no one even thanks you.

GOING UP

Now pay attention, because the following is quite brain-busting. There are 12 signs of the zodiac, and astrologers like to think of them as occupying a band of sky that spins around the Earth once every 24 hours. (This is a convention; it is not astronomically correct and you will not see the signs if you look up, so don't write in.) So, every two hours or so another sign hauls itself blearily over the eastern horizon. This is going on whatever time of the day or night you were born, and whichever benighted spot on the globe you chose to appear in. These astro-mechanics help to explain why virgins born at either end of the same day turn up their noses at the rest of us at a slightly different angle. There are long, nerdy ways to discover your rising sign, but the easiest way is to get hold of a birthchart (see page 176)

Upwardly mobile

If your rising sign is Virgo, then your public persona is an irritating, plain-speaking perfectionist, never seen without rubber gloves. This is to distract the rest of us from your plans to reorganize the world. Here's what happens when other zodiacal upstarts rise above their station.

Aries rising

Militant eco warrior; you don't take any prisoners – you just recycle them.

Taurus rising

Respectable virgin of wealth and means. What would the neighbours think, if only they knew?

Gemini rising

Independent virgin, with a sharp tongue, a sharper mind and a very convincing Remote Psychic Healing scam on the go.

Cancer rising

Caring virgin, who talks soothingly to everyone until they tell all their secrets.

Leo rising

Royal virgin; surrounded by lust-crazed princelings panting for dragons to slay.

Libra rising

Professional virgin.

Scorpio rising

You appear darkly, hypnotically fastidious; actually you're just faddy.

Sagittarius rising

Rash virgin, gallops off with the gypsies without taking precautions.

Capricorn rising

Thrifty, cautious virgin who knows how much he/she is worth.

Aquarius rising

Enigmatic virgin – no one is sure if you're for real, or a replicant.

Pisces rising

Wet virgin, constantly being taken advantage of, but still keeps coming back for more.

DON'T YOU LOVE ME, BABY?

Venus and Virgo

Just how much of a high-maintenance tease or bunny-boiler you are may depend on where the solar system's heartless tart (Venus) was blushingly dropping her handkerchief when you were born (*see below*). Oh, and Venus also has a say in how harmoniously you blend in with the rest of the world, but what do words like harmony have to do with the Darkside? Now, for astrological reasons that will fry your brain if I explain them here (basically, Venus is far too luxury-loving to move too far away from the Sun, and her orbital rate is in bed with Earth's), Venus only ever appears in your sun sign, or two signs on either side of it. In your case, virgins, that means Venus will be in Virgo, Cancer, Leo, Libra or Scorpio. And this is what it does to your love and lust life.

MAKE LOVE AND WAR

Venus is the girlie planet of lurve, right? And Mars is planet lad, the warlord. You may also have a sneaking feeling that men are from Mars and women are from Venus. Don't be upset if I tell you this is not true. All of us, of all genders, have a stake in both planets. Where they are in your birthchart has what I shall call consequences. You may think your sun sign makes you a born babe-magnet, but Venus in a chilly sign will cut you off at the knees; you may think that your sun sign means you are the twin soul of the dove of peace, but you may go red-eyed with bloodlust when beaten to a parking spot. Mars will be somewhere irascible. You'll need a birthchart (*see page 176*) to find out what Venus and Mars were playing at when you were born. It is far too complicated – and, frankly, dull – to work out here.

Venus in Virgo

You slip into your latex catsuit, invite your lover around for an intimate tongue-lashing and spend a happy evening pointing out that every little thing they do is not good enough.

Venus in Cancer

You cling to your lover as they try to leave in the morning, brushing specks of dust from their collar, retying their shoelaces, inspecting their fingernails and packing them a nourishing five-beanburger lunch, then spend the day wondering why they never call.

Venus in Leo

You hand-carve a pedestal for your beloved, insist they take their shoes off

before you put them on it, then prowl around them with a duster and a giant can of spray polish.

Venus in Libra

Your boudoir has two en-suite bathrooms, one of which is for ardent incoming lovers, and the other one for sorrowful outgoing exes. You keep a neat, detailed rota under your pillow.

Venus in Scorpio

You see nothing wrong with a little depravity, as long as it is properly scrubbed. You keep your shiny black PVC hotpants and tall stiletto-heeled boots neat and tidy in their special closet, and your whips are a pleasure to be chastised with.

ARE YOU LOOKING AT ME?

Mars and Virgo

Virgos are reluctant to fight, because it makes such a mess, and physical contact can give you germs. Just how threatening, paranoid and gagging for a fight you are depends on which area of your birthchart the bruiser planet Mars is being held back in by his mates (leave it, Mars, he's not worth it). Mars is the next planet out from Earth, but paces its orbit rather more slowly (presumably to get some effective eyeballing in). It takes 2½ years for Mars to get around, and on the way it spends about two months of quality menacing time in each sign. As a Virgo, you find that people are always attacking you just because you are a plain speaker. If you find that your justified reaction expresses itself in a less than hygienic manner, check out Mars' alibi at the time of your birth.

Mars in Aries
Not only can you strip a Bofors gun in 20 seconds, but you can also name all the parts and their serial numbers; not that you're obsessive, or anything.

Mars in Taurus
You escalate from your usual seethe-mode to code-red alert and meltdown if anyone moves your piggy bank.

Mars in Gemini
You suffer fools ungladly; in fact, you're likely to make clever cutting remarks to get them off-balance, and then throw rotten (but organic) veg at them.

Mars in Cancer
Ferocious cleaning of the home from top to bottom in the mistaken belief that a filthy temper can be washed clean.

Mars in Leo
You're always ready to send in the army if enemies sully your royal flag.

Mars in Virgo
While the battle for civilization rages all around, you concentrate your firepower on a remote latrine whose soap dispensers, you observe, have not been filled to regulation level.

Mars in Libra
It has taken you simply ages to hand-launder these divine silk camo combats, and you are not about to go out there and get them muddy all over again.

Mars in Scorpio
No one would ever dare spill Bordeaux down your Armani, or rearrange your fine display of antique edged weapons, or move the sugar bowl, because they know you will get your revenge.

Mars in Sagittarius
So keen to get in on the action that you fail to read the small print and charge into the fray of the completely wrong war.

Mars in Capricorn
Easily needled by trivia, and given to shameless fantasizing about what you will do to litter louts when you rule.

Mars in Aquarius
A squaddy you're not – that would be far too engagé; you're happier locked in your laboratory devising hideous virus strains to destroy the enemy's immune and/or computer systems.

Mars in Pisces
You're always ready with a great show of resentful peevishness over minor matters, but hold back from major confrontations because you are feeling a little fragile – probably a fantasy war wound playing up.

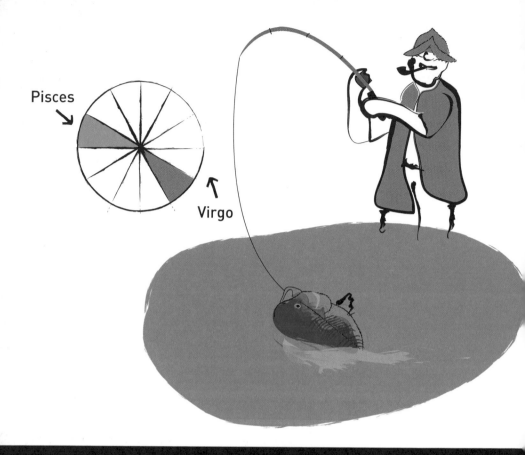

Pisces

Virgo

POLAR BEARS

Your polar sign sits on the opposite side of the zodiac wheel, six signs away, giving you knowing looks. You have a dark umbilical link with it. If Darkside you is your evil twin, then your polar sign is your evil twin's evil twin. It's got your number – but then you've got its, so that's alright, isn't it? Brightside astrologers maintain that there is a strong complementary relationship between you and your polar sign, and that this relationship is positive and fruitful, especially at work, because you share the same energy quality (mutable). Well, excuse me; on the Darkside it's more like the tension between an irate angler and a recalcitrant 20-pound cod; both pull, struggle, flail and writhe, trying to get one over on the other; neither will give in, but both want the same thing: to triumph over the other.

148

WHO'S GOT YOUR NUMBER?

check out the opposition

Your polar opposite sign is Pisces: weak, confused, disorganized and shiftless. (For more about your darkly fascinating opposite number, *see pages 360–391.*) What would a tiny-hearted, tight-sphinctered control queen like you want with a slippery, inconsistent drifter like your average Piscean? How do you have this – shall we say – understanding? Well, like good cop and bad cop, or arch villain and superhero, you need each other to make the Darkside work for you. It's all about elements (undesirable ones, of course). You are Earth; Pisces is Water. And together they make mud, which is great for slinging at the neighbours (although you have a problem with the mess).

Don't you get tired of being organized, right and respectable all the time? Of constantly trying to hold the whole world together (because if you don't, who will)? Don't you suspect that having everything neat and tidy, done and dusted, over with before anyone's had a chance to live in the moment, is not the only way to do it? Close your eyes and be one with the zodiac's fishy duo, chilling out under a rocky ledge, their tiny attention spans caught by drifting weed, glittery insects, anything that moves.

Respect your inner Piscean; it's what makes you let go every now and then, put Mr Fussy on hold, have a beer and rock on the turn of life's tides. People start to think you're not such a pain in the bum after all. So do you. Don't overdo it, though (those great, glassy eyes are very hypnotic); someone's got to run the world.

DARKSIDE DATE

You have to ask yourself: is there anyone good enough for you out there? There probably isn't. Just as well, really; if there were, you'd have nothing to be picky about, which would really frazzle your circuitry. The most practical solution would be another Virgo; you can easily

track one down through an online dating agency (to avoid loitering in the social arena, where you might catch germs). You will recognize each other easily by your cold, standoffish manner; if the chemistry kicks in, this will soon thaw into a cool, standoffish manner. Your

ideal date, set up after mutual negotiations since no one wants any sudden surprises, would be an afternoon surfing the Public Records Office, followed by an early supper at your favourite vegan hotspot, then on for some hardcore data-merging at the Obsessive-Compulsive café.

SEX

A *full service*

Contrary to popular opinion, you don't not like sex, do you? In fact, there are some bits of it that give you a strange, not unpleasant damp feeling. We all know you don't wear that black rubber all-in-one just to protect yourself from intimate squidginess and alien bodily fluids.

Just like you service the car, you do sex by the manual, which you read to your partner beforehand, bookmarking the more complicated passages for ease of on-the-job reference, and making sure that all the necessary tools are in good working order. Of course, you leave the lights on (why strain your eyes?); you may even video the event, as a teaching aid, so that you can show your lover precisely what they did wrong during that tricky three-point turn. In the afterglow, when you've both been through the antibac shower (separately), you issue a consumer response form to fill in, then you run a quick statistical analysis on your laptop to see how it compares with previous sessions. When asked how it was for you, you deliver a comprehensive report with synopsis and bibliography.

What kind of love rat are you?

You never dump; it's worse than that. You always want to talk about it. You look forward to the bad times, so that you can point out how your partner has reneged on the secret, unilateral pre-nup you carry in your head, and you never accept their resignation. Hag-ridden exes who try to escape are nagged to death long-distance, by text, e-mail, phone and letter.

Aries – you make constructive critical remarks; they slug you.

Taurus – you say austerity; they say I don't think so.

Gemini – they outbitch you and laugh at your clumsy retorts.

Cancer – will always be able to worry on a more cosmic scale than you ever can.

Leo – despise you for having no grip on pomp and pageantry.

Virgo – knick-knack overload.

Libra – you think they are insincere hypocrites; they think you are tactless curmudgeons.

Scorpio – you suspect you will never be able to obsess to their benchmark standard.

Sagittarius – you speak as you find; they are tactless oafs.

Capricorn – your rival in the local austerity drive.

Aquarius – ships that pass in the night, on different oceans.

Pisces – appear tempting as punchbags, but always manage to dodge the knockout blow.

RELATIONSHIPS

You're on your own

No one can live up to your fusspot perfectionism, not even you, so relating on any level is very fraught, and living with you is far too irritating. Once, you tried to make it work by targeting people dimmer than you, because you thought you could impose your system on them without them noticing. Now you realize that you are better off stalking around alone with your tail in the air – except, of course, for the other 46 cats who share your basket and who understand about addictive grooming and looking superior.

You want to know how you alienate people so thoroughly? It's the little things that do it (and how ironic is that?). At a party, you are the one sneering at the aubergine dip (not organic) and running a fastidious digit over the top of the door frame; or you are the one blind-drunk under the host, because the drink is free. In the days when you had friends, your posse used to plan nice simple nights out: a couple of beers, maybe a pizza; but your faddy food fascism meant that evenings always ended early in a dank, beige-walled, alcohol-free, macrobiotic restaurant, with them watching tight-lipped as you toyed with your *miso royale;* then they had to wait 45 minutes while you scrupulously divided the bill.

What you really want from a friend, lover or partner is a punchbag; someone who will just twist slowly and passively in the air while you hurl critical right hooks, snide uppercuts and scathing straight lefts, followed by a pummelling of general put-downs: a real nitpicker's workout.

DREAM JOBS

Let's make this quite clear, you are *far too busy* to idle away your employer's precious time fantasizing about dream jobs, and if you catch anyone else doing so, you will only be doing your duty if you shop them to the boss. However, on your tofu break, consider:

Forensic accountant

Long, hot days at your desk spent nitpicking through ancient records, tracing ingenious patterns of creative fraudulence made by people whose attention to detail was impressive, but can't touch yours.

Censor

Mixes prudery, perversion (your very secret vice), grading and telling others what they should think, in one absorbing activity. And don't you just love the patterns the blue pencil makes on a virgin manuscript.

WORK

You don't want to do it like that

You love work, because if it wasn't for work, you would have to talk to your family and get a life. And bosses love you (at least to begin with): you are the perfect lackey, always ready at a moment's notice to put in extra weekends or cancel the luxury holiday of a lifetime, for which you have saved for years, to sort out an urgent logistical problem in the stationery cupboard. You love to serve somebody. It's your way of controlling the hideous randomness of the universe.

It's not the money, it's the status and respect you crave. And if you don't feel valued, you avenge yourself with spite, sarcasm, bitchery, backbiting, gossipmongering, petty politicking and snitching on juniors who use the photocopier for non-work-related purposes.

Colleagues can't believe their luck when you first show up, because you can be counted on to do all the dull, boring routine jobs (you think they are exciting, stimulating routine jobs). They are soon turned off you, though, because your abject slavishness makes them look slack, and nobody loves a smart-arse.

Eventually, bosses realize that you put in long hours not because you are forging ahead and taking the company with you, but because you are mired in detail: you spend at least an hour every morning colour-coding your files. But they can't sack you: you have made yourself indispensable, because you are the only one who understands the database, which you set up, since you were the only one who could be bothered to read the manual.

You lack the overview to be a criminal mastermind, but you are great at detailed planning and all the dull bits that masterminds don't bother with; however, you have a fatal tendency, when you have James Bond cornered, to stop and explain your entire evil plan, instead of just getting away.

Forger

A job that requires no imagination but meticulous attention to detail, working slowly and methodically to recreate perfect but illegitimate versions of notes, coins, great art, etc.; it's what you were born for.

Serial killer

It's not bloodlust, it's the pattern, you see; the victims are an irrelevance, for your thrill comes from devising an MO and a sequence so complex and baffling that no police force can crack it. Ha!

CRIMES AND MISDEMEANOURS

How bad could it get?

So what sort of crim would you be, if sociopathy became the new world order? How would you spend your days (or maybe your nights) if you really lived on the Darkside? Very successfully: you are neat, clever with your hands and can be relied on never to leave clues behind. You'd make an excellent lock pick, and an even better non-explosive safe-cracker (all those combinations to untangle). And you are, of course, in demand as a clean-up man/woman, sent round to retrieve the situation when hits go wrong.

You wear gloves as a matter of course, and would never leave a fingerprint in the dust because you would never leave any dust (even if the slobs whose place it is haven't cleaned): you always pack a telescopic feather duster.

You respect the law because you respect any attempt to bring order from chaos, but feel that it should concentrate on the things that really matter, such as littering and playing loud music.

In court you conduct your own defence (you're not paying those lawyers' fees); you drone on about precedents, torts and stuff, until judge and jury are so ground down they let you off. But you often get let off earlier on, because you look so well presented (but then, so did the Nazis). On the rare occasions you are locked up, prison staff dread it, because you know your rights and cause endless paperwork demanding them. You quite like doing solitary – just as well, since the warders don't take kindly to you pointing out each time they bend a regulation.

AT HOME

Isolation ward

You are rarely troubled by visitors – at least, not more than once. Some people find the decontamination chamber on your porch a bit difficult to operate; or perhaps it's the fitted plastic covers on the furniture, or the clingfilm stretched hygienically across the lavatory or the sight of your minivac snug in its holster on your hip, ready to waste any speck. Which is a shame, because you are nearly always pleased to receive guests (by prior appointment) – even dinner guests, as long as they eat up their *lentilles marinières* as soon as they hit the plate, and then leave, because you need to get everything into the sterilizer a.s.a.p.

DOMESTIC DISHARMONY

Aries – they refuse point-blank to keep their meat rations out in the garden shed.

Taurus – think it's perfectly normal to eat three times a day, rather than just the once.

Gemini – they hide the manuals to all your electronic goods.

Cancer – whenever you throw anything away, they bring it back in for their collection.

Leo – 'no faith in your cleaning skills, so they bring in a pro.

Virgo – constantly tut-tutting under their breath about your filing system not being compatible with theirs.

Libra – spend hours in the bathroom, but never take the bleach in with them.

Scorpio – secretly destroy your more pointless knick-knackery.

Sagittarius – they invite all their mates round and accidentally trample all your footstools.

Capricorn – you both sit in the cold, unwilling to be the first to switch the heating on.

Aquarius – study your habits as if you were an alien life form.

Pisces – make a terrible mess, but get around you by pretending to listen to your advice.

Decor

As you have a morbid fear of bright colours, including magnolia, all the walls in your house are white. That way you can spot the minute they get dirty. You don't hang things on the walls, because it might make marks, but create plenty of interest with your sea of low-level footstools and occasional tables (many of them covered in small, ugly ornaments) arranged in that special configuration of yours.

Sharing the Virgo enclave

Few make it past the compulsory 30-page questionnaire; and you find that those who do are often reluctant to submit to the twice-daily room inspection, or try to refuse to take their turn at the weekly regrouting of the bathroom tiles.

Virgo paint chart

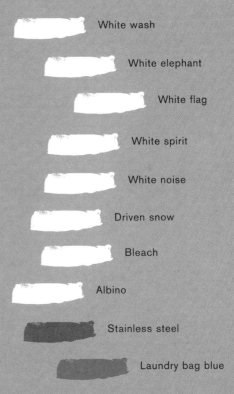

White wash

White elephant

White flag

White spirit

White noise

Driven snow

Bleach

Albino

Stainless steel

Laundry bag blue

PLAYTIME

The darkside of fun

As far as you're concerned, the best bit about any holiday – if you must take one – is planning how you are going to fly goat-class, take enough chickpea sandwiches to last for 10 days and spend

even less than you did last year, when you gleefully brought back all your spending money untouched, mostly because you bumped into an old Taurean friend. But you acknowledge that there are advantages to an all-in package, preferably somewhere damp: while the family is at the beach, you can spend quality time calculating whether you are getting your money's worth, and if you're not (oh joy), you can have satisfactory complaining sessions with the rep.

What would really suit you is a trip somewhere you can pick up a couple of unusual foreign diseases: something recurrent and comfortably incurable, preferably with a distinctive rash, so that you can get in with the in-crowd down at Hypochondriacs Anonymous.

ZODIAC CULL

Suppose you were marooned on a desert island/up an alp/in a rainforest/ at sea with 11 others, each one a different star sign. Who would you eliminate in order to survive? You may not have to; at least half the zodiac signs will run away to another part of the desert/alp/forest/boat and form a breakaway group, rather than listen to you telling them how to do things a minute longer; the gloomier ones may set up suicide pacts, or simply walk out into the howling blizzard.

Holidays from hell

★ Chilling out at a faraway retreat where you cannot plug in a laptop, alongside laid-back Libra; you don't do relaxing and you know the office would fall apart without your daily data input.

★ Rio at carnival time with Leo and Gemini; noise, bright colours, fun, potential adventures – far too disorganized.

★ Anywhere sunny (it brings out the colour in everything) or cheap (no scope for cunning, creative budgetry).

Road rage

You have memorized all the Highway Code, including all the updates, and will not hesitate to advise other motorists where they are going wrong and which bylaw they are breaking. Some of you have got a removable flashing blue light that you put on your car roof to make it easier to flag them down. You are hurt and upset when they give you the finger or ram you, or when you are arrested for impersonating a police officer. You always memorize the route, and a few possible alternatives in case of unforeseen hold-ups, but bring the map anyway, folded and stored in a plastic, wipeable wallet.

Gamesmanship

You know all the rules to every known game, and frequently hold up play while you explain them to the ref, umpire and teammates. You never let anyone play with your ball in case it gets dirty, so you always take it home with you in the plastic bag in which you brought it.

BAD COMPANY

Your hall of infamy

You may be feeling a bit emotionally fragile after a session on the Darkside, so to cheer the soul, let's look at a few of the famous, infamous, notorious and just plain bad Virgos who might feel the same if they read this book. You will be impressed by the number of world-class obsessives and hypercritical handwashers who share your sign; you're in very good bad company. And, despite your formidable (though somehow small-minded) Darkside, there are a number of people who appear to want to be you, but who have failed to fill in the paperwork correctly. Think of any picky, self-righteous perfectionists with no social life but always ready to tell everyone else how to live. All wannabe Virgos. If they're not, someone's lying. Look at the panel below if you don't believe me.

WANNABES

Surely Howard Hughes, near-legendary engineer, aviator and dirt-fearing adventurer, is a prime candidate – a career recluse who wouldn't shake hands unless everybody was wearing rubber gloves, and who always put a sheet of Kleenex between him and the world?

No, Libra; but only just (24/9) and we can't be sure of that, because mystery surrounds his birth. How about William Gladstone (1809–1898), English Prime Minister who used to prowl the late-night streets of London looking for fallen women to save? He'd take them home,

read the Bible at them and beat himself pure afterwards. No, Aquarian. But all homeopaths are honorary Virgos: have you seen the endless list of symptoms to be correlated with the endless list of possible remedies? People recover just watching you work it all out.

Ivan the Terrible
25 August, 1530

First ever Tsar of Russia; a martyr to chronic ill health, Ivan is famous for his progressive administrative policies, which unified Russia into a powerful country, and infamous for his repressive peasant policies, which killed or enslaved a large proportion of its inhabitants.

Cardinal Richelieu
9 September, 1585

First Minister of France and top-class lackey to the king, Louis XIII, whose status and power he improved by an integrated programme of political repression and force. Celebrated safely in retrospect for his powerful analytical intellect, Richelieu believed that small crimes should be harshly punished, to discourage bigger ones – it's all in the detail, you see.

D. H. Lawrence
11 September, 1885

English author of the infamous *Lady Chatterley's Lover* (among other works), Lawrence was plagued by ill health (which made him peevish), and simultaneously obsessed with and repelled by earth-shaking sex, which he appears neither to have experienced directly nor to be able to describe without making readers laugh uncontrollably.

Greta Garbo
18 September, 1905

Reclusive Swedish-born Hollywood star, who conducted many love affairs with members of all sexes, but never committed to anyone. Famous for wanting to be alone, she managed to be so for almost 40 years after retiring from the silver screen at the age of 36.

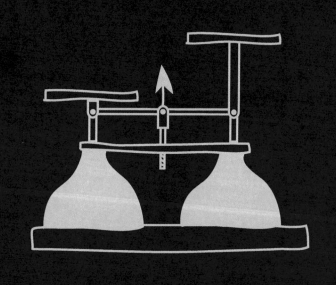

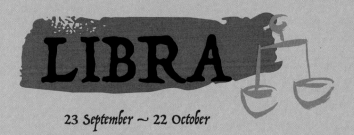

LIBRA

23 September ~ 22 October

Libra is a masculine, cardinal Air sign ruled by Venus. It is the seventh sign on the zodiac wheel, directly opposite Aries, and is named after the constellation Libra (the scales), which flirts and vacillates behind the Sun at this time of year.

On the Darkside, this makes you a vain, shallow, petulant spendthrift with an unerring eye for style over substance and a lifelong dedication to the quest for an easy meal ticket.

ANNOYING HABITS

Punctuality

You're always late because you take so long to decide what to wear (and to tear yourself away from the mirror), but look so gorgeous, and are so limpidly, charmingly abject when you do show, that you are forgiven.

Toothpaste

You don't have toothpaste in tubes, since squeezing involves effort. You have three kinds of pump-action dispenser instead, and there is always an intimate friend around to help you choose which flavour you want.

Temper gauge

0° to boiling point in 20 seconds, but rarely, and only if you think appearing to have lost your cool will get you what you want. You pout, flounce, toss your curls and stamp your little foot; it always works.

PERSONALITY

Shallow, superficial, shrewd

Vanity, fickleness, idleness, extremes, follies, whims and inconsistencies – that's what little Librans are made of. You can switch from Jerry Springer to Mother Teresa, Che Guevara to Attila the Hun, Einstein to Homer Simpson without missing a beat. People say: inconsistent; you say: what? Brightsiders leap gallantly to your defence (you skewered them with a spare cupid's dart millennia ago), claiming that this is a symptom of your endless cosmic quest for equilibrium. Rubbish – it's a sign of a shallow mind trying to fill an empty vessel.

You may smile for the cameras, but underneath you are an antsy malcontent, restlessly searching for satiation. Whenever you get what you want, you don't want it. It happens every time, but being an airhead's airhead, you never learn. As you can't fill the void with stuff, you turn to a cheap and renewable resource: other people. Sometimes a little empathy tourism is all you need (hey, guys, let's go see the poor!); at other times it's out with your My Little Emotional Vampire suit. You simply can't help using people – and they do fall over themselves to let you, but as an accomplished parasite, you know better than to kill the host. The only pain you are likely to suffer is RSI of the pinkie, from too many willing fools winding around it.

Of course you could have been a contender, but you couldn't be bothered – why work when you can sip mint juleps and watch other people's muscles ripple? You can look after yourself, though;

underneath that ditzy surface is a double-entry bookkeeper trained by Capricorn; there is a column for favours out (what you do for other people), and one for favours in (what they do for you). You always balance the books at the end of trading every day and are quick to send round the bailiffs if anyone owes you.

You're not the sweet, helpless little cupcake you want us to think you are, are you? You love the feeling of power you get when you bunch your iron fist in its velvety glove. You're the zodiac's drag queen, a masculine sign that outclasses its inner girlie when it comes to frocking up and what were once known as feminine wiles.

And now let's examine your Unique Selling Point: your inability to make a decision. Oh, how you can faff. It's true you are in danger of starving in the midst of plenty; confronted by heaps of goodies (lovers, diamonds, etc.), you can't bring yourself to choose one, because that would mean forfeiting all the others. What you'd like best is to have your cake and eat it – and own the cake shop, to ensure a reliable supply. But then you're not really hesitating, are you? You're playing for time; gathering data, like the wily probability theorist you are, computing the odds on the best possible outcome (for you). Don't think we haven't noticed that when you dither deliciously with admirers over two gorgeous gifts, you're always in Tiffany's (never in Tesco's); and we know you think that, if you dither long enough, you'll get both.

Bitch rating

A+ or D. Depends on where you're standing, really. You'd never dream of saying anything nasty to anyone's face (they might slap you and leave an ugly mark). Instead, you whisper poisonous remarks behind your fan or victim's back, about their bad hair or unsightly shoes.

Collective noun

A diplomatic word in the ear for non-Librans. You may find yourself, for some bizarre zodiacal reason, at a masked ball thronged with Librans. Operatives insert discreet carbon rods to prevent charm levels reaching critical mass; eyelash flutter-speed registers Force 9 and rising. You are enmeshed in a Flirtation of Librans. Lash yourself to a handy mast.

FAVE DEADLY SIN

'Oh dear', you dither winsomely, 'how can you possibly ask me to choose just one deadly sin, when they are all so rich and charming and handsome?' In the interest of finishing the book, let's offer you a choice of three. After some soul searching (like you've got a soul?) you go for Vanity, Greed and Sloth (but you hedge your bets by writing pretty apologies on scented notepaper to the other four). Why are we not surprised? We're just grateful that your main motivator is Sloth, which means that you rarely act on your worst impulses.

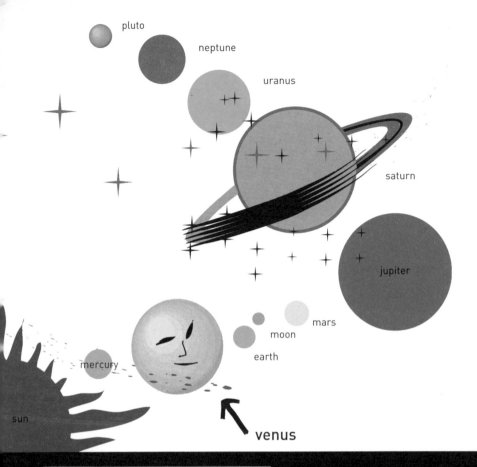

pluto

neptune

uranus

saturn

jupiter

mars

moon

earth

mercury

sun

venus

PLANET PLANET

Every sun sign has a planetary sugar daddy, whose job it is to provide treats and discreet apartments, and platinum cards and sporty little vehicles, and to take care of boring things like bills. Before there were telescopes, astrologers could only see five planets in the sky

plus the Moon and Sun, so they counted these two as planetary rulers. It seemed a good idea at the time. Each planet babysat two zodiac signs – except for the Moon (Cancer's minder) and the Sun (which allows Leo to rule). Your planet is Venus. You have to share it with Taurus, but

frankly, darling, you don't care because they are so deliciously rich: they pay the maintenance and the rent; all you have to do is turn up and look gorgeous at those tedious AGMs. Plus, it's good to have an admirer to practise flirting moves on during the slack season.

BLAME YOUR PLANET

Idle, vain and heartless

Besotted admirers, bloated with your signature dish of full-fat flattery, darken the skies as they hover in stacking formation over airstrip Libra; you've already maxed your credit card (and everybody else's within melting-glance range) and it's only the second of the month; you've changed your shoes (and your mind) 49 times today. Surely this can't be all down to sweet little you? Of course it isn't – you didn't get where you are today by carrying your share of any load, so blame your planet; in your case, Venus.

As I told Taurus (*see page 47*), it's named after the goddess Venus, the saccharine Roman version of the Greek Aphrodite, the flint-hearted tease who went through lovers (gods and human) like a stiletto through crème fraîche, and who just loved stirring (she started the Trojan Wars on a whim). Her attributes (that's just god-speak for accessories) are mirrors, and a girdle that makes the wearer irresistible. You like her already.

Venus is the second rock from the Sun, Earth's nearest neighbour, and the planet most like us (see – mirrors again). Astros often call it our sister planet and bang on about how harmonious and lovely it is, gliding along with us in almost twin orbits. Obviously these are astros without sisters of their own. And it has the slowest rotation rate in the solar system: it takes 243 Earth days for Venus to make one languorous twirl on its own axis. Supermodels won't get out of bed for less than £10K; Venus won't even get out of bed. That's power-sloth.

BAD MOON RISING

The darkside of Libra's darkside

It's not all sunshine on the Darkside. You know just how power-crazed and monomaniac your innermost thoughts and secret fantasies are, but where do you think they come from? The Moon, that's where – or whichever area of your birthchart the Moon was moodily plodding when you were born. The Sun is our daytime self; the Moon represents our inner psycho. The nippy little blighter rushes around, plunging in and out of signs every few days, so throughout Libra's month in the Sun, the lunar nuisance dashes in and out of signs like a retail slut in a Harvey Nick's changing room. That helps to explain why two Librans born only days apart accessorize basic black in completely different styles, depending on which sign the Moon was bothering at the time.

CATCHING THE MOON

That's all very well, you say, but how do I know where the Moon was when I was born? There are long, complicated (and, frankly, dull) tables called ephemerides that tell you where every planet (and for tedious astrological reasons, the Moon is an honorary planet) stood in the heavens, atmosphere bated, as you made your sorry debut. However, we have provided a Moon itinerary at the back of this book to enable you to get a rough idea. If that sounds like too much hard work, and you have the techno technique, then try visiting the following website: www.alabe.com/freechart. If you know where you were born, and when, they will produce, for free, a rough-cut birthchart that will pin your Moon on the zodiac wheel.

Lunatic combinations

Here's what happens to Libra when the Moon steps out for a little retail therapy.

Moon in Aries – you have been known to make a decision in less than two days.

Moon in Taurus – you suspect love may not be all you need, unless it comes with a steady income and property portfolio.

Moon in Gemini – you appear frivolous and superficial, but just below the surface lies a creature of hidden shallows.

Moon in Cancer – surrounded by 999 besotted fools, you brood, fret and sulk about the one that got away.

Moon in Leo – inside every dancing princess there's a drama queen trying to flounce her way out.

Moon in Virgo – you secretly scrub under the *chaise-longue* when no one's looking.

Moon in Libra – industrial-strength charm and sycophancy corrode all rational judgement within a seven-mile radius.

Moon in Scorpio – Mr or Ms Whiplash.

Moon in Sagittarius – after a couple of sweet Martinis at the embassy, your inner tactless oaf overpowers your outer diplomat, which is why you are only sent to countries that we want to destabilize.

Moon in Capricorn – constantly fighting uncontrollable inner urges to get a real job and take responsibility for your life.

Moon in Aquarius – once a month you try to make radio contact with the mothership to report that you have been trapped in an Earthling love machine.

Moon in Pisces – you get hammered on Southern Comfort and put too much reliance on the kindness of strangers.

BORN UNDER A BAD SIGN

The scum also rises

And another thing. Your sun sign is modified by your rising sign. This is the zodiac sign that was skulking over the horizon at the very minute you were born. If your sun sign is your ego, then your rising sign gives you your public manners (such as they are), your Sunday worst. It's the painted smile behind which the real, disgusting you lurks. Some astrologers maintain that its malign influence affects what you look like. Be afraid.

In the southern hemisphere, for tedious astronomical reasons, Libra is a sign of short ascension, and there are fewer people with Libra (and Virgo) rising than any other sign. Delicious! You just love being part of an exclusive group (the Rich List, for example), and it must mean you don't have to get up unpleasantly early or stay off the sofa for long.

GOING UP

Now pay attention, because the following is quite brain-busting. There are 12 signs of the zodiac, and astrologers like to think of them as occupying a band of sky that spins around the Earth once every 24 hours. (This is a convention; it is not astronomically correct and you will not see the signs if you look up, so don't write in.) So, every two hours or so another sign hauls itself blearily over the eastern horizon. This is going on whatever time of the day or night you were born, and whichever benighted spot on the globe you chose to appear in. These astro-mechanics help to explain why scales trying to balance at either end of the same day use a totally different measuring system. There are long, nerdy ways to discover your rising sign, but the easiest way is to get hold of a birthchart (see page 208).

Upwardly mobile

If your rising sign is Libra, your public persona is an irresistible, handsome charmer who has unfortunately just mislaid their wallet. This is to distract the rest of us from your plans to wind the world around your little finger. Here's what happens when other zodiacal upstarts rise above their station.

Aries rising

Too impatient to put your diplomat disguise on properly, so everybody can see the magnum in your pants.

Taurus rising

You move slowly, at a pace compatible with the average ground speed of unattached octogenarian billionaires.

Gemini rising

So unfeasibly charming that even a gullible Piscean can hear warning bells.

Cancer rising

You have just found out what MILF means and you can't believe your luck.

Leo rising

Prince Charming? Or King Midas?

Virgo rising

The red(dish) lamp outside your door is so neat and discreet that the neighbours had not noticed it until last night's police raid.

Scorpio rising

You appear darkly, hypnotically seductive; actually, you're just a small-town flirt.

Sagittarius rising

Love makes the world go around; you go around the world making love.

Capricorn rising

It's a business doing pleasure with you.

Aquarius rising

You inadvertently enslave Arien admirers, who see your natural cool detachment as a challenging hard-to-get come-on.

Pisces rising

Ickle me? I can't decide which luxury yacht I need; you must do it for me.

DON'T YOU LOVE ME, BABY?

Venus and Libra

Libra and Venus have an arrangement anyway (*see page 207*), but just how much of a high-maintenance tease or bunny-boiler you are may depend on where the solar system's heartless tart (Venus) was blushingly dropping her handkerchief when you were born (*see below*). Oh, and Venus also has a say in how harmoniously you blend in with the rest of the world. Now, for astrological reasons that will fry your brain if I explain them here (basically, Venus is far too luxury-loving to move too far away from the Sun, and her orbital rate is in bed with Earth's), Venus only ever appears in your sun sign, or two signs on either side of it. In your case, scales, that means Venus will be in Libra, Leo, Virgo, Scorpio or Sagittarius. And this is what it does to your love and lust life.

MAKE LOVE AND WAR

Venus is the girlie planet of lurve, right? And Mars is planet lad, the warlord. You may also have a sneaking feeling that men are from Mars and women are from Venus. Don't be upset if I tell you this is not true. All of us, of all genders, have a stake in both planets. Where they are in your birthchart has what I shall call consequences. You may think your sun sign makes you a born babe-magnet, but Venus in a chilly sign will cut you off at the knees; you may think that your sun sign means you are the twin soul of the dove of peace, but you may go red-eyed with bloodlust when beaten to a parking space. Mars will be somewhere irascible. You'll need a birthchart (*see page 208*) to find out what Venus and Mars were playing at when you were born. It is far too complicated – and, frankly, dull – to work out here.

Venus in Libra

You murmur soothing sweet nothings as you spoon warm, clear, quick-setting honey over the beloved so that when you throw yourself at them, nothing can prize you off. If they object, threaten to call in your little friends, the ants.

Venus in Leo

Queen of Hearts; you pounce on your lovers, bat them playfully with your velvety paws and adore them fiercely until they wilt. When crossed, you order their beheading.

Venus in Virgo

You love your beloved to pieces – which you then sweep up carefully, categorize and label in your best calligraphy, and pin out in neat, regimented rows in your specimen case.

Venus in Scorpio

Permanently hot and lecherous, you are always up for dirtying the satin sheets in glossy hotels, preferably with someone illicit and unsuitable, because after sex you love a long, indulgent soak in muddy emotional waters.

Venus in Sagittarius

You swing into the love object's boudoir at midnight on a velvet rope, make passionate and almost energetic love, then dash off into the dawn, leaving only your hoof-prints on their bed and heart.

ARE YOU LOOKING AT ME?

Mars and Libra

Librans might rip their Armani in an affray, so they tend to stand back and hold the coats. But just how confrontational, threatening, paranoid and gagging for a fight you are depends on which area of your birthchart the bruiser planet Mars is being held back in by his mates (leave it, Mars, he's not worth it). Mars is the next planet out from Earth, but paces its orbit rather more slowly (presumably to get some effective eyeballing in). It takes 2½ years for Mars to get around, and on the way it spends about two months of quality menacing time in each sign. As a Libran, you are never sure which side it is to your advantage to be on, so you always wait to see who's won. If you find yourself being unexpectedly gung-ho or partisan, check out Mars' alibi at the time of your birth.

Mars in Aries

You refuse to put on the velvet gloves, even though you know that exposed iron fists are just asking for trouble. That is because you like trouble.

Mars in Taurus

You glower at everybody since you can't work out who the enemy is, then side with whoever offers the most cattle cake.

Mars in Gemini

Lots of spectacular swordsmanship, blades and teeth glinting in the sun, impressive feints, and handsome manoeuvres, but no actual action.

Mars in Cancer

Luckily you've got your own portable bunker to hide in until it's all over, then you can come out and seduce the victor.

Mars in Leo

You always like to lead your troops to war (you look so cute and stylish in uniform), but get proles to do the dirty work.

Mars in Virgo

Your platoon never quite make it into combat, because you have put most of them on a charge for not polishing their buttons to the required mirror brightness.

Mars in Libra

Even though you claim to have no conception of that time of day, if anybody comes between you and what you want, it's handbags at dawn.

Mars in Scorpio

Your emissaries make it known that you are not happy about certain aspects of some people's behaviour and may have to withdraw privileges. There is never any trouble after that.

Mars in Sagittarius

You charge enthusiastically into battle, fighting for both sides at once; you either die from self-inflicted wounds or get sent to trial by both sides for war crimes.

Mars in Capricorn

How dare they call you an arms dealer; you only sell to both sides to maintain a peace-inducing balance of power.

Mars in Aquarius

You want to do your bit, so sign up as *Vogue*'s war correspondent (conflict is so now), filing dispassionate dispatches on strategy, tactics, morale and combat chic.

Mars in Pisces

You deploy a really effective guerrilla defence manoeuvre that involves you sliding out of sight when the going gets tough, to re-emerge – when it's over – at the other end of the pond, scales untarnished.

Aries

← Libra

POLAR BEARS

Your polar sign sits on the opposite side of the zodiac wheel, six signs away, giving you knowing looks. You have a dark umbilical link with it. If Darkside you is your evil twin, then your polar sign is your evil twin's evil twin. It's got your number – but then

you've got its, so that's alright, isn't it? Brightside astrologers maintain that there is a strong complementary relationship between you and your polar sign, and that this relationship is positive and fruitful, especially at work, because you share the same energy quality

(cardinal). Well, excuse me; on the Darkside it's more like the tension between two party guests who arrive in great style but exactly the same outfit. You outstare each other like very chic gun-slingers; both of you want the same thing: the other one to leave, preferably in tears

WHO'S GOT YOUR NUMBER?

check out the opposition

Your polar opposite sign is Aries: the zodiac's incoherent, inconsiderate, mad axe person. (For more about your darkly fascinating opposite number, *see pages 8–39*.) What would a mellowed-out slacker like you want with a short-fused loose cannon like your average Arien? How do you have this – shall we say – understanding? Well, like good cop and bad cop, or arch villain and superhero, you need each other to make the Darkside work for you. It's all about elements (undesirable ones, of course). You are Air; Aries is Fire. Together you make towering infernos – but while you appreciate the flame aesthetic, Aries just loves the smell of burned boats in the morning.

As you toss restlessly on your lounger, immobilized by all those life-changing decisions (Apple or Android? Brad or Angelina? Killer heels or Mary-Janes? Chocolate chip or raspberry sorbet? Champagne, mojito or chocolate malt?), don't you hear, deep inside, the sound of the zodiac's drill sergeant ordering you to quit stalling, move your arse and just get on with it? Do you ever wonder where your celebrated whim of iron comes from? Or why you don't dissolve in a sea of indecision more often than you do?

Respect your inner Arien; it provides a nano-nugget of resolve, with just enough critical mass to tip the scales in favour of a decision, finally. Alright, it may not mean equilibrium, but it does allow forward motion; take it slowly – if you're too dynamic, you may have to get out of bed.

DARKSIDE DATE

As your default mode is gigaflirt, you can get a date while you're asleep or dead. Supply is never a problem; but your demands are, since you only want datees if they are beautiful and come in batches. This is because you simply cannot choose, although you have enough spare charm to fuel a rewarding evening with half a dozen lovesick saps (they all bring gifts) and make them all believe you are their soulmate (you work out who's most cost-effective later).

Your ideal date is with a sugar daddy/mummy, handsome, well-dressed and loaded; you don't care that they have the wit, wisdom and conversational skills of a carpet tile. You go somewhere obscenely luxurious (you're not paying), where you can be seen and snapped by the paparazzi. What's the point of being gorgeous and lovely if no one sees you at it?

SEX

Easy, teasy

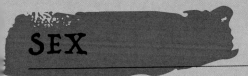

At first provocative glance, you are sex on a stick (well, you've got the Brightsiders fooled). Hmmm. You flatter and flirt, fondle and kiss, and make boudoir eyes at your prey; but you don't do unbridled lust because that would make you sweaty and out of control. When you look deeply into your lover's (or lovers') eyes, it's because in those dark pupils, made huge by desire, all you can see are the reflections of two perfect little yous. So let's be frank, you are in it for the money or the sports car or the Rolex; you do sex because it's better than working, not because you can't help yourself.

And no one could say you don't do a professional job; you know everything there is to know about seduction, deferred gratification and teasing, and you've got a very naughty toy box; but by the time you have adjusted the mirrors, lit enough candles to constitute a fire hazard, slipped in and out of something more comfortable several times and several times again, and reconfigured the satin cushions and velvet throws, your partner has usually fallen asleep. You don't mind: less mess and more beauty-sleep for you.

What kind of love rat are you?

You couldn't call it ratting – it's more like plate spinning. Ersatz affection comes easily to you, so it's not hard to keep the more lucrative of your lovers hanging on (you get more goodies that way, and they may come in useful); you just do a weekly round of flattery and ego massaging to keep them all sweet.

INCOMPATIBILITY RATING

Aries – too much action and not enough lights and cameras.

Taurus – they trample and gore anyone you smile at.

Gemini – same games, same tactics, same scams: stalemate.

Cancer – they indulge you, accept your alibis, wait up for you with hot chocolate; hi, Mum!

Leo – they expect unconditional adoration; so do you …

Virgo – macrobiotic love potion?

Libra – you know how magnets with the same polarity repel each other? Well …

Scorpio – they know you know that they know that you are a tease and a day-tripper.

Sagittarius – when you are prettily piqued, they don't notice.

Capricorn – they buy you diamond earrings, but keep them in their own safe.

Aquarius – you are from Venus, they are from another galaxy.

Pisces – their scales are a lot more slippery than yours.

RELATIONSHIPS

Love the one you're with

You meet, you greet, you smile, you do eye contact and call people by their first names – you're just as good at this relating business as the Brightsiders say you are; but out of sight is out of mind capacity, so you have to dump regularly. So when you meet again the people you just met, you simply don't remember them and redeliver your charm schtick. Great for you; Groundhog Day for them.

At your weekly *salon*, you are the *grande horizontale*, stretched benign and slothlike on the only sofa, receiving gifts and *billets doux* with unaffected grace and charm from your admiring horde. But you can adapt; if cosmic circumstances conspire and you are faced with a single scruffy, graceless Z-lister, you simply make them over to suit: if you can't be

with the one you love, love the one you're with, as they say in the song. But actually, you are always with the one you love, because the love of your life is *you*. It's rubbish about you looking for a soulmate to achieve cosmic balance – you've already got one; it lives in your mirror.

They say you are in love with love, but what you are really in love with is the power of love, and all the things it can get you. You are a great one for marriages of convenience (especially yours) and will ensnare a plain but loaded supermarket heiress or software Übernerd before the mousse has settled on the Veuve Clicquot. Nor can you see anything wrong with bigamy, trigamy or infinitigamy – after all making a final choice is always so dull and limiting.

221

DREAM JOBS

As we all know, you are allergic to the words 'work' and 'job', so while you are blagging your way to promotion, you dream of painless careers – in which you get shedloads of cash and your picture in all the best mags, while doing something you'd do anyway for fun. Here are two:

Fashion maven

Achingly chic in head-to-toe black (black is the new black), you dictate what everyone else should wear, which means that you get to make people who are more successful than you look ugly and foolish, ha-ha.

Spin doctor

It's the old-straw-into-gold routine: take any piece of info, especially the dull or damaging kind, and spin it in a web of silken verbiage until it gleams. You make Rumpelstiltskin look like an amateur.

WORK

A *four-letter word*

An active connoisseur of leisure like you should not really be made to work, should you? You adore luxury and lovely things, but feel sure there must be easier ways to get them than by the sweat (yuck!) of your beautifully Botoxed brow. If you haven't inherited or married money, there is the courtesan/gigolo/mistress/toyboy option; OK while you're young and fit, but not very secure, and you love security.

So you go for 'work' that suits your style; it doesn't matter what you do, as long as it doesn't involve actual work, ugly clothes or unpleasant locations, and there are enough people to make up a quorum of admirers. You were teacher's pet at school, and it doesn't take you more than a toss of your curls to be the boss's pet at work. (You have never seen anything wrong with the casting-couch system.) Once embedded, your work tools of choice are lethal charm, power flirting (with all genders) and high-calibre manipulation. You look soft and easy (a big girl's blouse is a great disguise), but in any situation you are always working out what's in it for you; you constantly flutter your long, Hollywood eyelashes so that rivals don't get a chance to look into your cold, calculating eyes.

What you are really good at is looking busy, while doing nothing but surfing for your next city break; you're equally skilled at gliding serenely across the treacherous lake of office politics while paddling like fury below the surface. Surely they don't expect you to put in all that effort and get some work done as well, do they?

WHEN SCALES GO WRONG

Libran misdemeanours are *la crème de la crime*; they are designed to replace work (nasty cold word) and capitalize on Libra's many natural assets – calm, poise, discretion: so no violence, adrenaline or tight corners, and always some poor devoted sap to take the rap.

Credit-card fraudster

Ideal for the bored shopaholic; you know exactly what to buy for quick and easy disposal, and your charm so enchants the sales staff that they truly believe you are Kate Moss incognito, like it says on your card.

Fence

Paradise! You get to look at, handle and fantasize about luxury goods, art, antiques and jewellery, then you get to manipulate rival buyers; no one threatens you because you've got the goods on everyone.

CRIMES AND MISDEMEANOURS

How bad could it get?

So what sort of crim would you be, if sociopathy became the new world order? How would you spend your days (or maybe your nights) if you really lived on the Darkside? Well, they do say that the Devil makes work for idle hands, and few mitts are more idle than yours, Libra, so you should slide effortlessly into a life of crime – but of the deluxe variety: casino heists, an audacious art scam (with you as the gorgeous, pouting, bent insurance investigator), smuggling rubies on a luxury yacht, VIP identity theft, celebrity phone cloning. With your persuasive flirt power, you'd make a creditable industrial spy. It might be an idea to avoid upmarket jewel theft – you'd still be dithering over whether to snatch the emeralds or the sapphires while the alarm bells yammered. And you always avoid doing anything that involves violence to the person (especially your own).

Of course you respect the law; the scales of justice belong to Libra, after all; maybe, because they do, you believe you know exactly how to tip them in your favour. While you might privately admit to a fair cop if you really have done the dirty, you will be outraged if mistakenly charged for the one crime you did not actually commit. You are very at home in court, radiating innocence and rueful charm in the dock so that impressionable jury members (and some judges) fall in love with you and let you off.

If your charm stalls, and you are locked away, the screws just dust out your usual cozy cell and compete with each other to bring your early morning tea.

AT HOME

Love shack

You live in a darling little cottage or a stylish loft, in a *bijou* townhouse or the penthouse suite of a cosmopolitan hotel, depending on the wallet size of whichever dear friend (usually Taurus) is footing the bill. Between essential frock shopping and agonizing over what flavour cheesecake to order in from the deli (or room service), you fidget constantly with the decor and the soft furnishings. You adore visitors as long as they come in braces or trios, so that you can group them at certain angles for exquisite symmetry, but will send them out of the room if their clothes clash with the curtains.

DOMESTIC DISHARMONY

Aries – they lock you out of the bathroom while they strip down a vintage V8 they got on eBay.

Taurus – they refuse to let you rearrange their cushions.

Gemini – they blackmail any influential people they bump into outside your boudoir.

Cancer – they fill the fridge shelves with food so there is no room for your make-up.

Leo – they expect to be waited on hand and foot; so do you.

Virgo – constantly tut-tutting under their breath about something they call the rent.

Libra – no *chaise* is *longue* enough to accommodate both of you at the same time.

Scorpio – they throw out the flowers you kindly arranged to soften the angles of their room.

Sagittarius – they bring their mates round and practice drop-kicks with your raw-silk cushions.

Capricorn – they blow out all your scented candles, claiming they are a fire hazard.

Aquarius – their overstuffed bookshelves ruin your feng shui.

Pisces – they fill up their fish bowl with the pink champagne you keep for special guests.

Decor

Tasteful yet restless; one tiny patch of wall is pockmarked with paint samples of previous seasons ~ *les beiges d'antan*, a fossil record of your chameleon taste. Guests often get the unnerving feeling that there are more of them than actually came in: that'll be the multi-mirror effect.

Sharing the Libra lovenest

As long as they are babes, new batches of sacrificial maidens and youths are always welcome *chez* Libra (you can always use the extra cash, even though you're not actually paying the rent). Naturally they have to bring their own mirrors, stick to your bathroom rota and be prepared to move on quickly when you fire the current meal ticket.

Libra paint chart

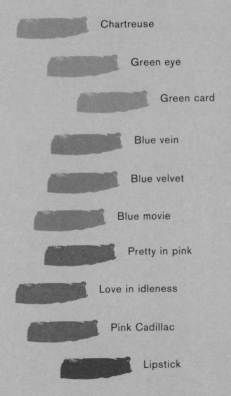

Chartreuse

Green eye

Green card

Blue vein

Blue velvet

Blue movie

Pretty in pink

Love in idleness

Pink Cadillac

Lipstick

PLAYTIME

The darkside of fun

Your many holidays are designed to let the rest of the world watch you doing what you do best – nothing, but with style. And though you don't like to blow your own trumpet (mainly because it ruins your bridge-work), you would like to point out that, were it not for you, entire economies would crash. You would never dream of self-catering when you can support whole villages by staying in multistar hotels and ordering room service every hour. And how could you refuse to support local shops, fascinating markets and megastores by selflessly burning plastic throughout your waking hours? Where would the indigenous hammock and cocktail-umbrella industries be without your unflinching dedication to idle pleasure? And how would the more attractive young locals learn a second language, and so improve their prospects, if you weren't as admirably assiduous as you are in the holiday romance arena? And they say Librans don't work hard!

ZODIAC CULL

Suppose you were marooned on a desert island/up an alp/in a rainforest/at sea with 11 others, each one a different star sign. Who would you eliminate in order to survive? A routine operation for you: engineer alliances, establish rivalries and wait for them all to destroy each other; make sure you keep two (Taurus and Leo) to hunt for food; set them up to duel over you, if you get bored or they get stroppy. When rescued, seduce the winchman on the way up to the helicopter.

Holidays from hell

★ Anything with Sagittarius or Gemini that involves walking further than from the lobby to the pool, or carrying anything heavier than your make-up bag.

★ A wilderness adventure; there are no shops, and there won't be anyone to flirt with once you've seduced your companions, Aquarius and Scorpio.

★ A working holiday cleaning up the environment with anal-retentive Virgo; you might sweat, break a nail or look slightly unattractive in overalls.

Road rage

Driving is a bit too much like hard work, so you avoid it, relying instead on the kindness of strangers, your account with a taxi company (funded by a dear friend)

or a limo-hire firm (funded by an even dearer friend). When an incredibly dear friend gives you a car of your own, you very sweetly exchange it for an automatic, or hire a young chauffeur. People don't let you have maps, not after they have experienced one of your 48-hour which-route-is-best sessions.

Gamesmanship

You don't like games that make you sweaty, so you persuade everyone else to play something you know you can win. This is usually Monopoly. If you do lose, you sulk petulantly (but prettily) until the other players bend the rules to let you back into the game. If you had anything so uncouth as a ball, you would take it home only if it hadn't got dirty.

BAD COMPANY

Your hall of infamy

You may be feeling a bit emotionally fragile after a session on the Darkside, so to cheer the soul, let's look at a few of the famous, infamous, notorious and just plain bad Librans who might feel the same if they read this book. You will be impressed by the number of world-stage strutters and self-indulgent artists there are; you're in very good bad company. And, despite your formidable (though somehow charming) Darkside, there are a number of people who appear to want to be you, but who have lost their balance. Think of any gullible, narcissistic style victims with a penchant for procrastination and a pathological inability to get off the *chaise-longue*? All wannabe Librans. If they're not, someone's lying. Look at the panel below if you don't believe me.

WANNABES

Let's start by putting in a claim for honorary Libradom for the entire French nation (pragmatic luxury lovers to a *personne*). Plus all judges, of course. Oh, and all those chatshow hosts who don't aspire to Gemini (because they think it's too intellectual) and who glow with

that strange pink light of fake sincerity onscreen and blank their guests in the aftershow hospitality room. What about the night they invented champagne, a quintessential Libra moment, *n'est-ce pas?* Apparently it was 8 April, 1693, which makes it Aries – so no, but

close, because Aries is Libra's opposite sign. Marlon Brando, you'd think, a man of extremes, unafraid of indulgences of the flesh? No, but he's Aries too, so getting warm. Well then, what about Coco Chanel, pioneer of effortless chic for lazy style queens? 'Fraid not – Gemini

Oscar Wilde *16 October, 1854*

Flamboyant writer, dandy and wit, famous for being able to resist anything but temptation. His works, especially *The Picture of Dorian Gray*, dwelt on the folly of judging a book by its cover and on the downside of a life of indulgence and devotion to pleasure alone.

Arthur Rimbaud *20 October, 1854*

French *vers libre* poet who wrote all his poetry in the five hot years between the ages of 15 and 20, when he was shot and wounded by his lover, Paul Verlaine. Then he gave up *la vie bohème* to become a trader in Africa. Extremes, see.

Alfred Nobel *21 October, 1883*

Swedish chemist who invented dynamite, one of the first of many man-made weapons of mass destruction, and who then, to balance things up, used the profits to endow international prizes for contributions to 'the good of humanity'. It didn't work, but nice try, Alfred.

F. Scott Fitzgerald *24 September, 1896*

Great American novelist, chronicler of the lives of the beautiful and the damned and no stranger to indulgence himself.

Margaret Thatcher *13 October, 1925*

First British woman Prime Minister (1979–1990): an iron fist clutching a velvet handbag (she transformed the word 'handbag' from noun to verb). Memorably described by French leader François Mitterand as having 'the eyes of Caligula, but the mouth of Monroe'.

SCORPIO

23 October ~ 22 November

Scorpio is a feminine, fixed Water sign ruled by Pluto. It is the eighth sign on the zodiac wheel, directly opposite Taurus, and is named after the constellation Scorpio (the scorpion), which broods and plots behind the Sun at this time of year.

On the Darkside, this makes you an obsessive, possessive manipulator with an unquenchable lust for power and a penchant for degradation.

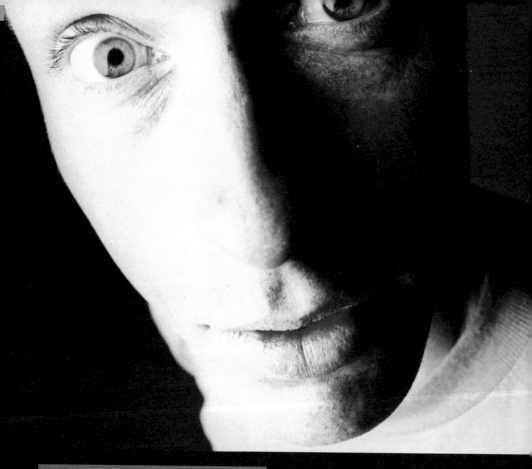

Punctuality

Scorpios are never late. It's
tactically unsound. You like to
get there a bit early so that you
can observe your victim arrive;
then you calculate an angle of
approach that ensures the sun
shines directly into their eyes

Toothpaste

You neither leave the lid off the
toothpaste nor squeeze from
the middle of the tube; you
either use rock salt and a twig,
or minimalist Japanese designer
devices that disgorge paste in
precise, bead-shaped portions.

Temper gauge

0° to boiling point in 10 seconds,
or several days, just to unnerve
the guilty. You don't shout. What
would be cool about that? You
stare intimidatingly and speak
with ominous quiet, to summon
your henchmen.

PERSONALITY

Intense, ruthless, domineering

Power-crazed, brooding, obsessional, ruthless, intense, sexy sadists with a cake habit, you Scorpios have a heavy rep. and have successfully convinced the rest of the zodiac that: a) you are sex on a very big stick; and b) no one messes with you. And that's just your Brightside.

The Scorpio Darkside is darker than the rest – almost out of the Dark into a whole other dimension, a kind of soul-sucking meta-dark, where suddenly the words 'evil' and 'mastermind' seem inadequate. There is no sin, depravity, perversion, cruelty, degradation or villainy you wouldn't consider, is there? You know it, I know it and the rest of the zodiac has a strong suspicion. You may never actually carry any of them out, of course – you are, after all, a control supremo, and

sometimes it's even more exquisite and refined to deny yourself than to indulge. You find it easy to contemplate turpitude, since you never fear dissolution of the self, but you really enjoy watching other, weaker beings drowning in your lake of iniquity. The rest of the zodiac crouches cravenly in the hypnotic beam of your trademark power-glare: you can do what you like with us.

Old-school astrologers considered that the star group Scorpio represented an eagle. Didn't you always know, deep inside your secret dark heart, that devouring the weak was your birthright, because you despise them – along with all whingers and non-copers – and when you are world dictator (if you aren't already), they will be ruthlessly put down.

Brightsiders praise your analytical skills (they have to do something to distract you from stapling them to the floorboards); you may spit upon their fawning cowardice, but you acknowledge that they are right. (Scorpion comes from a Greek word meaning 'to cut to pieces'.) It's such a blast to dissect small animals and see how they run, or to probe, poke and interrogate until you have unearthed everybody else's secrets (while keeping all your own, of course).

Your favourite sport is competitive mind-gaming (you are a Fifth Dan); you play long after everyone else has gone home for their supper, and you have to have the last spiteful word, or your day is just ruined. You have never been known to apologize for anything, since it would make you look weak; nor do you grant second chances – if people let you down, they are non-persons. You shun them (and their friends, relations, birthplace, residence, hometown, state and country). You are up there with the Amish on shunning, only you'd throw in hanging, drawing and quartering as well, just to see your betrayers writhe.

In fact, if it wasn't for your self-destructive streak and obsession with sex, the rest of us would be in deep doo-doo, for you will stop at nothing to get what you want, even if it means global meltdown. Fortunately, you are often so fixed on taking things to the edge that you fall off; and you can always be distracted by lust, at least long enough for the rest of us to run away.

Bitch rating

A+. People are so frightened of you that you don't have to bother much, but what's the point of a sting in the tail if you don't use it? You study the psychology of the individual, can pinpoint all those tectonic weaknesses where reality meets ego and self-loathing runs near the surface; that's where you make your surgical strikes.

Collective noun

A piece of advice for non-Scorpios, with Mr Big's compliments. You may find yourself, for some bizarre zodiacal reason, in a sleazy bar full of Scorpios (perhaps the Inquisitors Reunited annual bash). The air crackles with magnetism as power-glares collide. This is a Menace of Scorpios. Don't look at the eyes.

FAVE DEADLY SIN

You know them as the Seven Surefire Methods of Manipulation, for there will always be one that pushes the buttons of the most incorruptible. So, which is your favourite? Of course, you have dabbled stylishly with all seven, and enjoyed some vintage lost weekends with Greed and Envy, but you always come back to Lust: lust for power, lust for money, lust for status, lust for revenge, lust for other bodies, lust for your own. But don't you secretly wish that Total Control was a deadly sin, so that you could enjoy it even more?

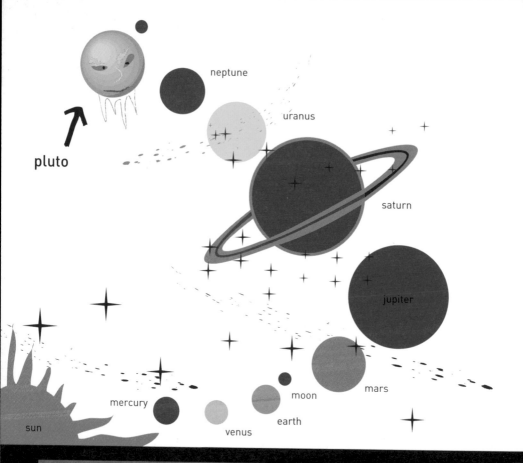

pluto

neptune

uranus

saturn

jupiter

mars

mercury

moon

earth

venus

sun

PLANET PLANET

Every sun sign has a planetary secret police sergeant whose job it is to seek and destroy dissent, foil plots before they've been hatched and ensure that everyone thinks Correct Thoughts. Before there were telescopes, astrologers could only see five planets in the sky, plus the Moon and Sun, so they counted these two as planetary rulers. It seemed a good idea at the time. Each planet babysat two zodiac signs – except for the Moon (Cancer's minder) and the Sun (which allows Leo to rule). Your ruler is Pluto. You once had a 50 per cent share with Aries in Mars (a useful, if loud, bit of muscle, but with very little brain and even less style), and you occasionally go back to check on your investment. But when Clyde W. Tombaugh discovered Pluto in 1930, you realized at once that it was the Master you had been seeking.

BLAME YOUR PLANET

Icy, remote, mysterious

When Pluto was discovered, planet buffs hurled their astrolabes in the air for sheer *joie d'étoile*. Mars (*see opposite*) never really fitted Scorpio (far too obvious, although it does explain the aggression, determination, iron will, cruelty, etc.) and here was a prime source for manipulation, mystery and masochism. So if complete strangers look into your eyes and lose the will to live, or you have pulled the wings off so many flies that the flypaper industry has complained of falling sales, you know who to blame (because it's not your fault, nothing is your fault, ever): Pluto.

Pluto is a mysterious loner, a planet in a poncho who rides down from the sierra at unexpected angles, a kind of celestial Clint Eastwood. A small, dense iceberg, it moves with menacing, thorough slowness through the void. A day on Pluto is like an Earth week and it takes almost 248 years to orbit the Sun. It's named after Pluto, King of the Underworld and everything in it: oil, diamonds, dead people. It goes everywhere with a giant henchmoon, called Charon (the guy who ferried the dead across the Styx) – your kind of planet.

Or is it? In 2015, Earthlings finally got a good look at Pluto. With a suicidal disregard for the glare of a Scorpio scorned, they decided to downgrade it to Dwarf Planet. Before you could nail them to their own Very Large Array for disrespect, they also revealed that it has an icy exterior but a red-hot, molten inner core (maybe) and that they don't know what it is made of. So, still an enigma. You're OK with that: size isn't everything.

BAD MOON RISING

The darkside of Scorpio's darkside

It's not all sunshine on the Darkside. You know just how power-crazed and monomaniac your innermost thoughts and secret fantasies are, but where do you think they come from? The Moon, that's where – or whichever area of your birthchart the Moon was moodily plodding when you were born. The Sun is our daytime self; the Moon represents our inner psycho. The nippy little blighter rushes around, plunging in and out of signs every few days, so throughout Scorpio's month in the Sun, the lunar nuisance dodges around like an undercover double agent trying to sell the plans to a third party. That helps to explain why two Scorpios born only days apart control their environments in completely different ways, depending on which sign the Moon was bothering at the time.

CATCHING THE MOON

That's all very well, you say, but how do I know where the Moon was when I was born? There are long, complicated (and, frankly, dull) tables called ephemerides that tell you where every planet (and for tedious astrological reasons, the Moon is an honorary planet) stood in the heavens, atmosphere bated, as you made your sorry debut. However, we have provided a Moon itinerary at the back of this book to enable you to get a rough idea. If that sounds like too much hard work, and you have the techno technique, then try visiting the following website: www.alabe.com/freechart. If you know where you were born, and when, they will produce, for *free*, a rough-cut birthchart that will pin your Moon on the zodiac wheel.

Lunatic combinations

Here's what happens to Scorpio when the moon sets off on a power walkabout.

Moon in Aries – activates your Martian sleeper; aggressive, cruel, ruthless, resentful, but short on subtlety, finesse, imagination or long-term strategy.

Moon in Taurus – double-strength obstinacy, possessiveness, jealousy and greed, but also double servings of cake.

Moon in Gemini – obsessive, possessive, etc., but light-minded; extreme shopping rather than world domination.

Moon in Cancer – power-grumping, continent-shifting mood swings and an endless list of grudges to settle.

Moon in Leo – you brood darkly on the throne as you draw up plans to neutralize little princes, heirs apparent, pretenders.

Moon in Virgo – you keep back-up hard copy of your Other People's Secrets database in pristine black filing cabinets.

Moon in Libra – jealous, possessive, etc., but with a secret addiction to trivia.

Moon in Scorpio – you avoid mirrors; either you will have no reflection, or you will be in danger of mesmerizing yourself.

Moon in Sagittarius – you are passionate, but not quite able to hack brooding.

Moon in Capricorn – obsessive desire for money; often to be found burying treasure at crossroads.

Moon in Aquarius – dark, powerful, brooding, obsessive, cruel, harsh and alien … Good evening, Lord Vader.

Moon in Pisces – dark, brooding, etc., but wet; you think dark, damp thoughts but never actually get around to action.

BORN UNDER A BAD SIGN

The scum also rises

And another thing. Your sun sign is modified by your rising sign. This is the zodiac sign that was skulking over the horizon at the very minute you were born. If your sun sign is your ego, then your rising sign gives you your public manners (such as they are), your Sunday worst. It's the painted smile behind which the real, disgusting you lurks. Some astrologers maintain that its malign influence affects what you look like. Be afraid.

If you were born around dawn (unlikely, because you prefer to operate under cover of the night, or in the hour before dawn when it's darkest), your rising sign will almost certainly be the same as your sun sign. This means your image is only a slight spin away from the scary actuality beneath the mask. People can feel your shadow coming. Gulp!

GOING UP

Now pay attention, because the following is quite brain-busting. There are 12 signs of the zodiac, and astrologers like to think of them as occupying a band of sky that spins around the Earth once every 24 hours. (This is a convention; it is not astronomically correct and you will not see the signs if you look up, so don't write in.) So, every two hours or so another sign hauls itself blearily over the eastern horizon. This is going on whatever time of the day or night you were born, and whichever benighted spot on the globe you chose to appear in. These astro-mechanics help to explain why scorpions born at either end of the same day plug into entirely different electrical outlet. There are long, nerdy ways to discover your rising sign, but the easiest way is to get hold of a birthchart (*see page 240*).

Upwardly mobile

If your rising sign is Scorpio, your public persona is a dark, hypnotic, powerful Überbeing who won't need to distract the rest of us, since we will already do anything you say and hand you the world on a plate. Here's what happens when other zodiacal upstarts rise above their station.

Aries rising

Rogue scorpion with short-fuse sting and defective control system.

Taurus rising

Wear thick enough tweed and your tight leather thong won't show through.

Gemini rising

Stage hypnotist who secretly programs the audience to hack into GCHQ.

Cancer rising

Norman Bates.

Leo rising

Being secretly in control doesn't mean you shouldn't ride around in a gold coach.

Virgo rising

Your burnished iron maiden won best in show for neatness and presentation, and your truth serum is 100 per cent organic.

Libra rising

Your diplomatic smile may be on full beam, but so are your mad, staring eyes.

Sagittarius rising

Who would have thought a simple, meathead rugger-bugger like you would be MI5's most effective hooker?

Capricorn rising

Thanks to expensive tailoring, your lethal tail sting is hardly noticeable under your impeccable business suit.

Aquarius rising

You find that if you behave like an absent-minded professor, you get away with all kinds of sinister experiments.

Pisces rising

Splash about helplessly out of your depth, hiding your dorsal fin until rescuers come.

DON'T YOU LOVE ME, BABY?

Venus and Scorpio

Just how much of a high-maintenance tease or bunny-boiler you are may depend on where the solar system's heartless tart (Venus) was blushingly dropping her handkerchief when you were born (*see below*). Oh, and Venus also has a say in how harmoniously you blend in with the rest of the world, but what do words like harmony have to do with the Darkside? Now, for astrological reasons that will fry your brain if I explain them here (basically, Venus is far too luxury-loving to move too far away from the Sun, and her orbital rate is in bed with Earth's), Venus only ever appears in your sun sign, or two signs on either side of it. In your case, scorpions, that means Venus will be in Scorpio, Virgo, Libra, Sagittarius or Capricorn. And this is what it does to your love and lust life.

MAKE LOVE AND WAR

Venus is the girlie planet of lurve, right? And Mars is planet lad, the warlord. You may also have a sneaking feeling that men are from Mars and women are from Venus. Don't be upset if I tell you this is not true. All of us, of all genders, have a stake in both planets. Where they are in your birthchart has what I shall call consequences. You may think your sun sign makes you a born babe-magnet, but Venus in a chilly sign will cut you off at the knees; you may think that your sun sign means you are the twin soul of the dove of peace, but you may go red-eyed with bloodlust when beaten to a parking space. Mars will be somewhere irascible. You'll need a birthchart (*see page 240*) to find out what Venus and Mars were getting up to when you were born. It is far too complicated – and, frankly, dull – to work out here.

Venus in Scorpio

Intense, obsessive, relentless, steaming, get-a-room sex anytime, anyplace, anywhere. It would be a crime of passion to diminish your magnificent obsession with flattery, flirting or foreplay, and your lust-slaves know better than to ask.

Venus in Virgo

You dress up as doctors and nurses and have lots of strenuous, bracing, physical sex (with regular shower breaks) on orthopaedic beds, with rubber sheets tightly tucked in with hospital corners.

Venus in Libra

Intense, languid, romantic sex, with slidey satin sheets and pretty acolytes (you'll get to them later) strewing rose petals and mint leaves. If there are enough mirrors, you don't even need a partner.

Venus in Sagittarius

A dark sweaty horse, you like your sex intense, competitive, athletic and adventurous, with lots of chandelier swinging, strange exotic positions and lustathons you can place bets on – fastest gallop through the entire *Kama Sutra*, the four-minute orgasm and so on.

Venus in Capricorn

Unbutton that three-piece suit, take off your specs, and get down to some intense, powerful and serious sex on the solid mahogany boardroom table of an old established merchant bank, with an old, established merchant banker.

ARE YOU LOOKING AT ME?

Mars and Scorpio

Scorpios and Mars go way back (*see page 238*), and you always fight to the death anyway, but just how confrontational, threatening, paranoid and gagging for a fight you are depends on which area of your birthchart the bruiser planet Mars is being held back in by his mates (leave it, Mars, he's not worth it). Mars is the next planet out from Earth, but paces its orbit rather more slowly (presumably to get some effective eyeballing in). It takes 2½ years for Mars to get around, and on the way it spends about two months of quality menacing time in each sign. As a Scorpio, you get very little trouble, because only berserkers or ignorant new kids on the block usually call you out. If you find yourself considering retreat or surrender, check out Mars' alibi at the time of your birth.

Mars in Aries
Artemis (Greek goddess of hunting) once ordered a tiny scorpion to attack the giant Orion; and it did. That's you, that is.

Mars in Taurus
No Pasaràn! Once roused, you continue to fight even when you have no more troops, no more weapons, there is no more point and the ceasefire has been signed.

Mars in Gemini
The verbal sting is your preferred weapon because words can break the spirit, which you know is more important than bones.

Mars in Cancer
If even vaguely slighted, you take class-action revenge against the enemy, their families, friends, ancestors, dependants, future generations, acquaintances, pets ...

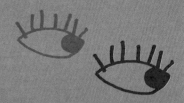

Mars in Leo

Of course you have a Royal Torturer, but you'd much prefer to do the job yourself, and so you have ordered the royal jeweller to create your own set of crested thumbscrews, racks and hot irons.

Mars in Virgo

By the time you have lovingly unwrapped and assembled (in the correct sequence) all the gleaming parts of your long-range sniper rifle (with silencer), your victim has left town; you don't mind, because it's disassembling it all again that you enjoy.

Mars in Libra

You resent expending valuable sexual energy on common violence, but are always ready to get out your weapon in the defence of love.

Mars in Scorpio

Homicidal maniac.

Mars in Sagittarius

You are the intense, brooding lone gunslinger who rides into town with the tumbleweed, shoots the sheriff and rides out again before you can be lynched.

Mars in Capricorn

You know the pen is mightier than the sword, so you get yourself a desk job drawing up the execution lists and watch your enemies die a little every day.

Mars in Aquarius

Cool, detached tactic-*meister* who flies high over the battlefield before deciding which of your crack battalions should be sacrificed to gain a famous victory.

Mars in Pisces

You wave your stinger around, but lack verve of execution and wander off across the desert, where you get lost. Then you accidentally maim the rescue party.

Scorpio

Taurus

POLAR BEARS

Your polar sign sits on the opposite side of the zodiac wheel, six signs away, giving you knowing looks. You have a dark umbilical link with it. If Darkside you is your evil twin, then your polar sign is your evil twin's evil twin. It's got your number – but then you've got its, so that's alright, isn't it? Brightside astrologers maintain that there is a strong complementary relationship between you and your polar sign, and that this relationship is positive and fruitful, especially at work, because you share the same energy quality (fixed). Well, excuse me; on the Darkside it's more like the tension between disputing eagles, grimly locked onto each other's talons as they spiral downwards into Death Valley. First to let go is a sissy. Neither looks down, and both want the other one to let go. No chance!

WHO'S GOT YOUR NUMBER?

check out the opposition

Your polar opposite sign is Taurus: the placid plodder with the turning circle of a grain tanker. (For more about your darkly fascinating opposite number, *see pages 40–71.*) What would a subtle, suspicious, sophisticate like you want with a slow-minded stodgeasaurus like your average Taurean? How do you have this – shall we say – understanding? Well, like good cop and bad cop, or arch villain and superhero, you need each other to make the Darkside work for you. It's all about elements (undesirable ones, of course). You are Water; Taurus is Earth. And together you make mud – excellent for getting stuck in, or for constructing golem henchpersons.

You pass your mornings discreetly analyzing all around you, identifying their psychological springs and triggers so that you can orchestrate their behaviour at a time convenient to your masterplan; you spend your nights wide-eyed in the dark on a cold, hard, narrow bed, perfecting a political manoeuvre that depends on two triple agents double-crossing each other, then one of them reneging on the deal. Can't you hear a tiny, plaintive inner bellowing, begging you to keep it all a bit simpler and more practical? Haven't you ever wondered about your completely out-of-character cake obsession?

Respect your inner Taurean; it provides something solid to cling to, when raging passion threatens to flush you away, as well as a sensible old-age pension. Of course, if it gets too solid and respectable in there, you lose your edge and are eaten alive by other Scorpios.

DARKSIDE DATE

You may look like a love god, a cave troll or a slant-shouldered librarian – it really doesn't matter, because Scorpio magnetism has nothing to do with looks. You will always get a date. You become one with the tomcat, stand at certain indefinably arousing angles, your ears go back your eyes go black and you focus on the love object, who becomes a rigid rabbit in the glare of your headlights. You don't bother with all that romance and flirting and bower-building McGuffin – you just walk away, and your date, overcome by your pheromones, trails after you. You like drawn curtains, beat-up shades, and hot rooms in the afternoon – illicit action with people you shouldn't be with, in places you shouldn't be, at times when you should be somewhere else. Your ideal date is a midweek hotel room with the wife of a close friend.

SEX

Obsessive, relentless, illicit

Admit it, there's nothing you won't try, is there? Brightside and Darkside, you are the zodiac's Lizard King. You just love sex – lots of it, at any time, anywhere; straight, deviant and downright weird – because you know that sex is power. Your tuning fork is in permanent harmony with the bat's squeak of desire that you know drives the world, and a serious seeing-to recharges your batteries and plugs you into the power source of the universe.

Sex with Scorpios is intense, passionate, erotic (alright, alright, it's hard to see the Darkside here), but the rest of us should be warned: you are just the same when you're on your own. It's the sex you love, not the one you're with. Of course, while you are often almost blind with lust, you are always in control in any relationship, and sex is on your terms. You might want serial one-night stands. You might want intense, constant, obsessional sex with a single lust-slave. You might even want to show how in control of control you are and give up sex altogether for a life of hot-eyed celibacy (sweetened by delicious daily sessions with your personally designed nettle flail).

What kind of love rat are you?

You are well aware of the difference between love and sex (which is why you make really hot sex-workers and bonk-buddies), but you don't care if others aren't. The world is littered with Scorpio discards (usually Pisceans) who believed that a 12-hour lustfest meant it was time to start choosing curtains.

INCOMPATIBILITY RATING

Aries – you want total control; they never listen to you.

Taurus – you want total control; they do what they always do.

Gemini – you want total control; they mock and jeer.

Cancer – you want total control; they say you will have to learn to share like the other children.

Leo – you want total control; they overrule you.

Virgo – you want total control; they introduce sub-clauses.

Libra – you want total control; they let you think you've got it, but seduce your henchmen.

Scorpio – you want total control; they want total control.

Sagittarius – you want total control; they bolt in the night.

Capricorn – you want total control; they engineer a corporate buyout and fire you.

Aquarius – you want total control; they beam up.

Pisces – you want total control; they drip through your fingers.

RELATIONSHIPS

Remote controller

I'm not sure if you can call a one-way power bond a relationship. Most people are so scared of you, they just do what you say. You decide on a friend? They will be your friend. You want a lover? Oh, please. At a party you are the fascinating one in the corner, saying nothing but establishing a little power base; any group with you in the centre always looks like a conspiracy, and mostly it is.

As in all other aspects of your life, you have to be in control. Not a natural socializer, you have lots of acquaintances (too scared not to grovel white-lipped as you pass), but only a clawful of close friends, whom you have chosen because they are loyal and non-competitive, respect your superiority, freely admit that they don't know as much as you do and

don't object to giving up all their secrets any time you turn your hypnotic gaze on them. They also have to know about the thin line between love and hate that you have scratched around yourself in the black sand; there are broken men and women languishing in the world's rehab clinics and bankruptcy courts because they unwittingly transgressed your unwritten law. You never forget or forgive, but unlike Cancer, who just moons about, you plot and execute meticulous revenge.

You can do long-haul (it means you always have someone to manipulate), but are jealous and possessive and always read secret diaries. You must be the dominant partner, although, as you are ultra-cunning, you can do subordinate if it will benefit your overall masterplan.

DREAM JOBS

What am I saying? You are already in your dream job, because: 1) you willed your way there; 2) you own the company; or 3) no one who values their sanity and/or gonads would dare send you a rejection letter. So the following info is just for non-Scorpio reference.

Secret agent

Secret power, mysterious code names, *carte blanche* (*noire?*) to do anything to anybody, an arsenal of gadgets and a car that transforms into a Stealth bomber; and by day you are mild-mannered Kent Clark ...

City analyst

You get paid to spend all day playing with other people's money, second-guessing trends, setting up slick moves that will come to bonus-laden fruition in four weeks' time and drinking your weight in Roederer Cristal.

WORK

Competitive spirit

You have a big brightside rep. as a workaholic, because you never let anything get in the way of your career path, and you spend 26 hours a day at the workplace, either actually working or retrieving staff e-mails, shredding secret plans, changing your passwords and those of your enemies, and devising whole new, more efficient ways of making money.

Because, let's face it, you are not a very good employee, since you can't stand not being in total control. Bosses notice that your less robust colleagues tremble when you are around, as they do themselves. You aren't always as good at cloaking your raging competitiveness as you think you are. Ruthless but cowardly bosses who employ you as the office Doberman often live to regret it. So you do your job, don't tread on any toes (you like revenge served cold), keep your ears open and your eyes down, pick up all the contacts, techniques and inside info you need, then go off and set up an evil empire of your own.

(An alternative Scorpio solution is to drift off into a career of drinking and debauchery, to which, it must be said, you bring all the focus, determination and willpower that you do to any enterprise.)

Perversely, when you have trashed the opposition and your empire is at its glorious height, you like to destroy it, cackling maniacally, partly to show the world just how hard you are, but mostly because you are now cosmically bored. Then you start all over again.

WHEN SCORPIONS GO WRONG

Crime is a serious business, but it's just a business, and you are a professional. Other people are lazy, greedy, weak and deserve exploitation; if you act polite, dress immaculately and stay on top of the detail, you can get away with anything and turn a handsome untaxable profit.

Mr Big

Your will, imagination, nerve and attention to detail mean you can run any number of operations simultaneously, while planning the next audacious job and ordering a cull of weaker vessels in the organization.

Assassin

You leave the bread-and-butter intra-organization contract killing to dull cousin Taurus. You prefer the edgy intrigue, secrecy and political overtones of a top-class assassination; so much more stylish and much better paid.

CRIMES AND MISDEMEANOURS

How *bad* could it get?

So what sort of crim would you be, if sociopathy became the new world order? How would you spend your days (or maybe your nights) if you really lived on the Darkside? Well – large numbers of you are already reputable crooks. The most upright and respectable Brightsiders point out daringly that you make good criminals because you are amoral, focused and cruel (then they change their names and run away to Rio). There's no 'if' about it; you probably already control the southside.

So how best to capitalize on your criminal genius? Well, how to choose: Murder Inc.? Grand theft? Property scams? Money laundering? Global drug dealing? Internet piracy? Something that generates a larger GNP than a small country (in fact your business often provides the GNP of a small country). Yet you live austerely and are never seen dripping in gold – you're more of a felonious monk (I'm sorry, it just came out).

Of course you respect the law; control is always good. You can afford to, as you are unlikely to be caught. In court you are immaculate and scary, glaring at judge and jury in a way that makes it clear that not only do you know where they all live, but where their dear white-haired old mothers live as well. And *their* mothers.

But if judges retain enough control of their own minds to lock you up, you either laser through the bars with your bare eyes or hypnotize the governor and get a luxury cell (with shower), gourmet food and pole dancers bussed in. Other inmates never menace you.

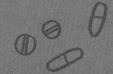

AT HOME

Black hole

You don't encourage visitors; you prefer to visit others, especially when they least expect it. Your own nest is menacingly tidy; just the one scrubbed table, two bum-numbing stools, a bare-bulb lamp and obscenely expensive black-lacquered cabinets that look as if they might house a well-oiled collection of inquisitional instruments. Or perhaps it's part of your cover story to live in squalor; not just mess – full-on, call-in-the-ratcatchers squalor (except that you don't call them in). And sometimes it suits you to retire to a monk's cell in the desert, with a stone slab for a bed and a single nail to hang your flagellation device on.

DOMESTIC DISHARMONY

Aries – think the black granite bath is an ox-roasting pit.

Taurus – their desire for your well-hidden cake will always overwhelm their fear of you.

Gemini – they unscramble all your encrypted phone lines.

Cancer – they find the designer kitchen items you store in the garage (in the original packing) and actually cook with them.

Leo – upholster your stainless-steel armchairs in gold lamé.

Virgo – constantly tut-tut under their breath, but not too loudly in case your supersensitive bugging devices pick up on it.

Libra – they know about the two-way mirrors, but think they are just for sex games.

Scorpio – people will be too scared to visit; fine by you.

Sagittarius – use your genuine 16th-century Spanish eye gouge to change their oil filter.

Capricorn – align their cutlery at different angles to yours.

Aquarius – they won't tell you what they are up to in the shed.

Pisces – never remember the door security code, so you have to get up to let them in after midnight; night after night.

Decor

Minimalism made your day, especially those concrete baths, but you find it a little overexuberant now. Restraint, precision, lines and alignments are what you use to articulate the void in your controlled environment. Style victims will soon follow. Your favourite colours are black. And black.

Sharing the Scorpio nest

Anyone allowed to intrude on your space will have been selected by you (although they don't know this) for their readiness to give up their own rituals and routines to follow yours. They may notice that the cleaning rota you circulate does not include your name, but will be too scared to mention it. You despise them for it.

Scorpio paint chart

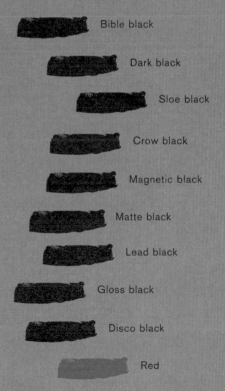

Bible black

Dark black

Sloe black

Crow black

Magnetic black

Matte black

Lead black

Gloss black

Disco black

Red

PLAYTIME

The darkside of fun

You resist holidays because it means you have to trust strangers (at least until you have subdued them to your will); although you did once have a blissful break in Vienna, following the sewer trail of the fascinating and amoral Harry Lime (The Third Man), and stuffing yourself with *Sachertorte*, the Austrian drug of choice, and a chocolate Übercake devised by a descendant of Baron von Sacher-Masoch, inventor of your favourite -ism.

If you are wrenched from your home power base, you could hang around in dubious bars with the locals so that you can discover, infiltrate and take over a power base abroad. Or what about a retreat with other Scorpios, including degradation by consent and an enticing list of luxuries you can deny yourself?

If your lust-slaves are clever, you may not notice you are on holiday at all, for you will be going at it 24/7, and never emerge from the tent/Winnebago/luxury villa/cabin/cheap hotel room.

ZODIAC CULL

Suppose you were marooned on a desert island/up an alp/in a rainforest/ at sea with 11 others, each one a different star sign. Who would you eliminate in order to survive? You'd have to find them first. They may not be as powerful as you, but their survival instinct is, so they'll all run away and band together to kill you. You'll find out – there's always one weak-willed Gollum (Pisces, precious) in your power, but delay revenge until everybody's safely back home, with their family.

Holidays from hell

★ An all-inclusive, fun-for-all-the-family package holiday where you might have to join in, dress up and look ridiculous.

★ Spiritual detox at an Indian ashram where you have to surrender control to a guru (unless on a field trip to pick up hints for a guru-ing career of your own).

★ 'Murder Weekend'; you will know whodunnit in 10 seconds and there's not a minibar in the world big enough to get you through the following 48 hours.

Road rage

You are doing business in a big, powerful black car with fogged windows and a disgraced Formula One driver at the wheel; or a big, black etc., which you are driving yourself, at 110 m.p.h. Any weak, incompetent motorists you force off the road shouldn't be on it in the first place, but you find that any dispute resolves itself as soon as you take off your shades and look meaningful, or your colleague, Mr Black, steps out of the vehicle. Maps don't give you enough control; you have a military-standard GPS uplink.

Gamesmanship

Whatever the game is, you will win. No one will let you not win because of what happened to poor Mr Frobisher last time. If you don't win, you don't speak, but control your terrible temper, then wait in a dark alley for the victorious fools, their friends and people with names slightly like theirs. You always take home your ball, and any fingers stuck to it.

BAD COMPANY

Your hall of infamy

You may be feeling a bit emotionally fragile after a session on the Darkside, so to cheer the soul, let's look at a few of the famous, infamous, notorious and just plain bad Scorpios who might feel the same if they read this book. You will be impressed by the number of dark, brooding manipulators and merchants of excess who scuttle across the black desert sands with you; you're in very good bad company. And, despite your formidable (though magnificently obsessive) Darkside, there are a number of people who appear to want to be you, but are just a little bit too scared. Think of any jealous control-freaks with piercing eyes, an unstoppable sex drive and a worrying collection of black leather. All wannabe Scorpions. If they're not, someone's lying. Look at the panel below if you don't believe me.

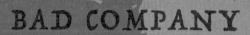

WANNABES

Think broody, intense, violent, sexy, secretive – who springs to mind? James Bond, of course, in his Sean Connery avatar. Hold on to your Walther PPKs: Connery is Virgo! No, I hear you cry; but it's true – I suppose all that nitpickery with the shaken-not-stirred vodka Martini is a bit of a giveaway; a true Scorpio drinks any old *rotgut du pays*. Well then, consider Niccolò Machiavelli, the deep, dark and treacherous political guru to the Borgias, author of *The Prince* (1513) – top manipulator's manual and still walking off the Ruthless Business Management bookshelves? Taurus; but as you know, Taurus is Scorpio's opposite sign, so a small cigar. Honorary Scorpionship definitely goes to all spies, criminal masterminds, City analysts, the Spanish Inquisition and, of course, dark overlords (Voldemort, Sauron, Vader, etc).

Fyodor Dostoevsky
11 November, 1821

Dark, brooding Russian writer, military engineer and gambling addict, who was sentenced to death, but reprieved. Author of *Crime and Punishment* (1866), a study in sociopathic homicide, and *The Brothers Karamazov* (1880) about three dark, brooding brothers.

Bram Stoker *8 November, 1847*

Dark, brooding Irish civil servant, theatrical impresario, writer and creator of *Dracula* (1897), a fable of blood, obsession, sex, lust, evil, death and un-death.

Pablo Picasso *25 October, 1881*

Dark, brooding Spanish artist, the passionate, prolific, seminal shaping spirit of the 20th-century who considered art to be 'an instrument of war against brutality and darkness'. His powerful genius lay in his ability to analyze and synthesize form (Cubism), yet his work was all about humanity's cruelty, folly and love; also an indefatigable womanizer.

Dylan Thomas *27 October, 1914*

Dark, brooding Welsh poet, permanently steeped in alcohol; his most famous work, the verse drama *Under Milk Wood* (1953), was published a year after Thomas slipped, raging, into the crow-black, sloe-black night.

Larry Flynt *1 November, 1942*

Not so dark, brooding American 'pornographer, pundit and social outcast' (his own words), begetter of *Hustler*, a magazine devoted to mindless sex, and an obsessive defender of free speech and civil liberties.

SAGITTARIUS

23 November ~ 21 December

Sagittarius is a masculine, mutable Fire sign ruled by Jupiter. It is the ninth sign on the zodiac wheel, directly opposite Gemini, and is named after the constellation Sagittarius (the archer), which crashes and burns behind the Sun at this time of year.

On the Darkside, this makes you a reckless, tactless, obnoxious oaf, with a morbid fear of restraint and an addiction to losing your shirt.

ANNOYING HABITS

Punctuality

Never knowingly on time; you are either four hours late and covered in scorchmarks, two days late because you fought the law and the law won or don't show up at all because

Toothpaste

Grab the nearest tube and squeeze in the middle until the cap pings off and toothpaste haemorrhages out and hits the ceiling; catch some on its way down, hurl tube aside, clean

Temper gauge

0° to boiling point in a nanosecond. Red mist, loud shouting, violent rampage, possibly with weapons (which include your bare hands), then you canter off in a different

PERSONALITY

Brash, crass and tactless

Do not think that you are getting away with your 'Oh, whoops, I'm just one big clumsy clot, but I mean well' routine here. This is me you are talking to. You may be brash, crass, loudmouthed and impetuous, but you aren't stupid, and you know that you should at least look a bit remorseful when caught with the smoking gun, the bloodstained hammer or the empty safe. That does not mean you didn't do it, or that you won't do it again, because you just love the unholy thrill and the pant-dampening rush of it all, the anarchic joy of sheer naughtiness; no, you have learned that looking rueful just increases your chances (and no one is hotter than you at calculating the odds) of getting away with it next time – and the one after that.

You are the zodiac's mindless hooligan and Überlad (or ladette), game for anything mindlessly risky, violent and pointless. So, Russian roulette? Pass the Kalashnikov. No one keeps you on a tight rein, or any rein at all; you crash your way through any barriers, even those set up for your safety (especially those set up for your safety). If you see a commitment in the distance, you vanish like a gambler's lucky streak. The slings and arrows of outrageous fortune bounce off your thick skin (although it must be said that you shot most of the arrows yourself). And tactless? Virgo may tell it like it is when asked, but you don't wait to be asked. Your best friend loses a leg in a terrible accident (probably caused by you). You immediately ask if you can have their

vintage Air Jordan IVs. What do you mean insensitive? They're not going to need them now, are they?

You have never had any truck with this only living once business – you're here to live twice, and then some. I wish I could say that you spent all this cosmic energy on exploring ways to improve the human condition, but that would never occur to Darkside you. Largeing it is your idiom; whatever you do, you take it to the limit and push it over the edge. An early evening drink? Get sodden, then bet on who can drink a shot from every bottle in the bar without going blind. Dinner? La Grande Bouffe, with a free pass to the executive vomitorium. Show you a Class A restricted substance, and you stuff it into your nearest orifice without blinking.

Then of course there's the gambling; Brightside you loves a flutter at the track; Darkside you will bet the farm, your firstborn, your best friend's firstborn and Grandpa's pacemaker on which will be the first raindrop to make it to the bottom of the windowpane.

Your zodiac animal is the centaur, a mythical beast, half human, half horse, armed to the scarily large strong teeth (no one else on this zodiac carries a weapon they weren't born wearing) with a bow and arrows. So, on the one hand, you are a human with an uncontrollable urge to gallop and frisk and kick things over; on the other, you are a horse trying to do up its buttons without the benefit of opposable thumbs. And on the Darkside, you are the worst half of both.

Bitch rating

D-. But it's difficult: you don't bitch within the meaning of the term, but what you lack in subtlety and finesse you make up for in crudity and bluntness, blurting out jaw-droppingly rude remarks 'without thinking' (oh yeah?), so the end result is still someone sobbing in the toilets.

Collective noun

A tip from the horse's mouth for non-Sagittarians. You may find yourself, for some bizarre zodiacal reason, starfished against the cliff wall of a narrow ledge thronged with Sagittarians. Hooves clatter impatiently against rock, as bets are placed and safety harnesses shrugged off. This is Basejump of Sagittarians. Don't look down.

FAVE DEADLY SIN

What? All of them of course – what would be the point of not savouring the experience of every available combination of moral, physical and spiritual degradation? You're only young once. So you gallop along, snatching a few mouthfuls from each, but if you're honest (!), the simple, obvious stuff like Lust, Greed and Gluttony does it for you – because you can't resist indulgence and extremism – and just a slick of Vanity to create that naughty, devil-may-care, messed-up look. And Sloth? What's that all about?

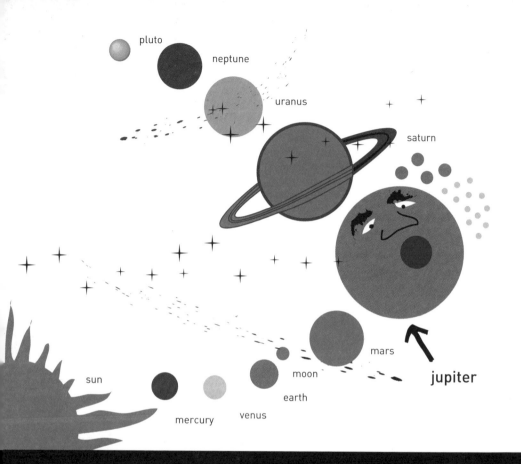

pluto

neptune

uranus

saturn

jupiter

mars

moon

earth

venus

mercury

sun

Every sun sign has a planetary M.C., whose job it is to provide non-stop fun, issue whoopee cushions, sparkle relentlessly with bonhomie, keep the sunny side up and always look on the bright side. Before there were telescopes, astrologers could only see five planets in the sky

plus the Moon and Sun, so they counted these two as planetary rulers. It seemed a good idea at the time. Each planet babysat two zodiac signs – except for the Moon (Cancer's minder) and the Sun (which allows Leo to rule). Your ruler is Jupiter, the biggest planet in the entire solar system

the jolly gas giant, ho-ho-ho (most of Jupiter is hot air), which gallops across the void, flanked by 16 or so moon outriders (it can never recall exactly). You can tell it's Young at Heart, because it sports a Giant Red Spot. You used to share Jupiter with Pisces, but they drifted off

BLAME YOUR PLANET

Large, loud, ludicrous

It's your great-granddaddy's 100th birthday party. You have drunk all his rubbing alcohol, told the same joke 20 times (and still can't remember the punchline), jeered at the carer's facial hair, dropped and trampled on the commemorative plaque; and the strobe effect generated by your revolving bow tie has set off the epileptics. Everybody seems hacked off at you (they are just no fun), but how can it be your fault? Blame your planet. In your case, Jupiter.

Jupiter, fifth rock from the sun, is called the planet of expansion by Brightsiders, but is known to us as planet crass. It's 480 million miles away, but we can still see it. Enormous and unmissable, it bowls around its orbital path like a hippo in a hamster ball, well over the speed limit, getting around in 12 years, when it appears in your birthchart in exactly the same position it did when you were born. Brightsiders claim this is significant, but it's more like one of those people you meet on holiday when your guard is down; you invite them to drop in, and they do; a day on Jupiter lasts just under 10 hours, but probably feels longer.

It's named after Jupiter, the Roman version of Zeus, life and soul of the Greek pantheon. Though king of the gods, he was never at home ruling, but was always gadding about manifesting himself in places where he wasn't welcome, in amusing shapes he thought would make nymphs, minor goddesses and prettier mortals come across (e.g. swans, bulls, showers of gold); an Olympic-class twit.

BAD MOON RISING

The darkside of Sagittarius's darkside

It's not all sunshine on the Darkside. You know just how power-crazed and monomaniac your innermost thoughts and secret fantasies are, but where do you think they come from? The Moon, that's where – or whichever area of your birthchart the Moon was moodily plodding when you were born. The Sun is our daytime self; the Moon represents our inner psycho. The nippy little blighter rushes around, plunging in and out of signs every few days, so throughout Sagittarius's month in the Sun, the lunar nuisance dodges around like a bottom-dealing cardsharp avoiding irate punters in a frontier town. That helps to explain why two Sagittarians born only days apart charge off in entirely different directions, depending on which sign the Moon was bothering at the time.

CATCHING THE MOON

That's all very well, you say, but how do I know where the Moon was when I was born? There are long, complicated (and, frankly, dull) tables called ephemerides that tell you where every planet (and for tedious astrological reasons, the Moon is an honorary planet) stood in the heavens, atmosphere bated, as you made your sorry debut. However, we have provided a Moon itinerary at the back of this book to enable you to get a rough idea. If that sounds like too much hard work, and you have the techno technique, then try visiting the following website: www.alabe.com/freechart. If you know where you were born, and when, they will produce, for *free*, a rough-cut birthchart that will pin your Moon on the zodiac wheel.

Lunatic combinations

Here's what happens to Sagittarius when the Moon bolts off into the blue.

Moon in Aries – you waste more energy drumming your hooves, impatient for the off, than you use running the entire race.

Moon in Taurus – you sometimes wonder whether the world really would come to an end if you just stood still for a bit and digested your oats properly for once.

Moon in Gemini – people who take you for a one-trick pony go away with egg on their face and nothing in their wallets.

Moon in Cancer – you always turn back to look wistfully at the bright little lighted windows in the houses as you and the herd gallop past late at night.

Moon in Leo – undisputed king of the road, permanently on your high horse.

Moon in Virgo – best not to tell the rest of the herd about the top-of-the-line first-aid kit you keep in your saddlebag.

Moon in Libra – a beautiful carousel horse; gorgeously painted, always on the move, but just going around in circles.

Moon in Scorpio – you like to unnerve punters by playing poker with the tarot cards you won off Aleister Crowley.

Moon in Sagittarius – when people call you crazy horse, it's not because they think you are leader of the Sioux nation.

Moon in Capricorn – always look at your insurance policies before you leap.

Moon in Aquarius – not as mindless as you appear; *alpha centauri*, in fact.

Moon in Pisces – always secretly cast a shoe or two so that you can limp pitifully with stones wedged in your hooves.

BORN UNDER A BAD SIGN

The scum also rises

And another thing. Your sun sign is modified by your rising sign. This is the zodiac sign that was skulking over the horizon at the very minute you were born. If your sun sign is your ego, then your rising sign gives you your public manners (such as they are), your Sunday worst. It's the painted smile behind which the real, disgusting you lurks. Some astrologers maintain that its malign influence affects what you look like. Be afraid.

If you were born around dawn (and I bet you did spring from the traps as soon as starter's orders were called, trying to make for the hills before the midwife could throw and brand you), your rising sign will almost certainly be the same as your sun sign. This means your image is only a slight spin away from the scary actuality beneath the mask.

GOING UP

Now pay attention, because the following is quite brain-busting. There are 12 signs of the zodiac, and astrologers like to think of them as occupying a band of sky that spins around the Earth once every 24 hours. (This is a convention; it is not astronomically correct and you will not see the signs if you look up, so don't write in.) So, every two hours or so another sign hauls itself blearily over the eastern horizon. This is going on whatever time of the day or night you were born, and whichever benighted spot on the globe you chose to appear in. These astro-mechanics help to explain why archers born at either end of the same day never place-bet the farm on the same horse. There are long, nerdy ways to discover your rising sign, but the easiest way is to get hold of a birthchart (*see page 272*).

Upwardly mobile

If your rising sign is Sagittarius, your public persona is a tiresomely jovial mindless extrovert, game for anything. This is to distract the rest of us from your plans to free the world from restrictive regulation, such as the law of gravity. Here's what happens when other zodiacal upstarts rise above their station.

Aries rising

Outwardly a grumpy, tactless, impatient hothead; inwardly an amiable, tactless, impatient hothead.

Taurus rising

Always the tortoise, never the hare.

Gemini rising

Glossy plausible favourite in the inspection paddock; you blunder into the third fence in the big race and ruin thousands.

Cancer rising

Who'd have thought that a loving parent of seven like you would run off to Vegas with the Child Benefit?

Leo rising

Casino royale.

Virgo rising

Your state-of-the-art filing system is full of incoherent notes scribbled on the back of old betting slips.

Libra rising

Flirting, eyelash-fluttering and pretty dithering make great diversionary tactics at your high-roller poker soirées.

Scorpio rising

You appear darkly, hypnotically driven; actually, you're just impetuous.

Capricorn rising

You look so businesslike in that pinstripe poncho; surely you have a plan?

Aquarius rising

They call you Cool Hand Luke.

Pisces rising

Gallop carelessly in the seaside shallows, disregarding the incoming tsunami.

DON'T YOU LOVE ME, BABY?

Venus and Sagittarius

Just how much of a high-maintenance tease or bunny-boiler you are may depend on where the solar system's heartless tart (Venus) was blushingly dropping her handkerchief when you were born (*see below*). Oh, and Venus also has a say in how harmoniously you blend in with the rest of the world, but what do words like harmony have to do with the Darkside? Now, for astrological reasons that will fry your brain if I explain them here (basically, Venus is far too luxury-loving to move too far away from the Sun, and her orbital rate is in bed with Earth's), Venus only ever appears in your sun sign, or two signs on either side of it. In your case, archers, that means Venus will be in Sagittarius, Libra, Scorpio, Capricorn or Aquarius. And this is what it does to your love and lust life.

MAKE LOVE AND WAR

Venus is the girlie planet of lurve, right? And Mars is planet lad, the warlord. You may also have a sneaking feeling that men are from Mars and women are from Venus. Don't be upset if I tell you this is not true. All of us, of all genders, have a stake in both planets. Where they are in your birthchart has what I shall call consequences. You may think your sun sign makes you a born babe-magnet, but Venus in a chilly sign will cut you off at the knees; you may think that your sun sign means you are the twin soul of the dove of peace, but you may go red-eyed with bloodlust when beaten to a parking space. Mars will be somewhere irascible. You'll need a birthchart (*see page 272*) to find out what Venus and Mars were getting up to when you were born. It is far too complicated – and, frankly, dull – to work out here

Venus in Sagittarius

Mug Cupid, steal an arrow or five and fire them at random. Swoop down on the wounded like an Arab steed, whisk them away to an exotic faraway oasis, feed them grapes and palm wine and roger them senseless. As the sun rises over the purple desert sands, gallop off alone.

Venus in Libra

You toss your silky mane and swing your hindquarters provocatively until you have gathered together an admiring herd, then run away with the one who offers the most sugar lumps and the biggest stable.

Venus in Scorpio

Saddle up your lover, add a tight leather bridle and whip them (and yourself) to

ecstasy with your riding crop. Don't forget to negotiate good odds beforehand on who comes first and how many times.

Venus in Capricorn

Mating is serious business, so before you do anything rash, you send off for the relevant stud books to compare form. Then you do something rash.

Venus in Aquarius

You stand enigmatically against the skyline at dusk or dawn (but not for too long or you will be signed up by a fourth-rate ad agency) until you intrigue a soulful lover. You gallop off with them into the black-velvet night, get out your enormous telescope and show them the glories of the horsehead nebula.

ARE YOU LOOKING AT ME?

Mars and Sagittarius

Sagittarians love scrapping, preferably in a large crowd. But just how confrontational, threatening, paranoid and gagging for a fight you are depends on which area of your birthchart the bruiser planet Mars is being held back in by his mates (leave it, Mars, he's not worth it). Mars is the next planet out from Earth, but paces its orbit rather more slowly (presumably to get some effective eyeballing in). It takes 2½ years for Mars to get around, and on the way it spends about two months of quality menacing time in each sign. As a Sagittarian, the zodiac's hooligan, you often find yourself fighting, although you don't always know why. If your aggressive tendencies only happen in response to a rational cause or coherent plan, check out Mars' alibi at the time of your birth.

Mars in Aries

War horse. Permanently at action stations, loaded with weapons and ready to blunder unstoppably into the valley of death.

Mars in Taurus

You are the big one drinking quietly in the corner while the brawl rages, and only step into the fray after you've been hit by three flying bottles and a chair.

Mars in Gemini

You frisk about the crowd with a little kick here, a bit of tale-telling there, some light rumourmongering, *et voilà*, you have an enjoyable ruckus to play in.

Mars in Cancer

You roam the home beach with a phalanx of armoured mates, clicking your great claws rhythmically, to provoke an attack.

Mars in Leo

You personally patrol the frontiers of the kingdom in the hope that wild hill tribes might be invading, so you can enjoy some border skirmishing unfettered by protocol.

Mars in Virgo

You love close-in hand-to-hand combat, so you always pack your customized reinforced rubber gloves, for extra grip and protection against bodily fluids.

Mars in Libra

You like a scrap to have some style and elegance, so have signed up for a course of *capoeira* (that Brazilian dancey martial arts where all the guys have great buns).

Mars in Scorpio

'You talkin' to me? You talkin' to me? Then who the hell are you talkin' to? You're talkin' to me? Well, I'm the only one here'. Whatever you say, Travis.

Mars in Sagittarius

A hooligan's hooligan; while waiting for your posse to show up, you start fights with yourself in the bar-room mirror and regularly put yourself in casualty.

Mars in Capricorn

You stand in the correct position to deliver perfect jabs and upper cuts, but are left bruised, black-eyed and winded by street fighters who don't do rules.

Mars in Aquarius

You just love joining in these primitive yet exhilarating Earthling fighting rituals, which have an energy about them that is missing on your home planet of Pfnrdxx.

Mars in Pisces

Swagger around shouting the odds about fighting them on the beaches, but slide away to hide behind a rock when it looks like your side might end up as fish pâté.

Sagittarius

Gemini

POLAR BEARS

Your polar sign sits on the opposite side of the zodiac wheel, six signs away, giving you knowing looks. You have a dark umbilical link with it. If Darkside you is your evil twin, then your polar sign is your evil twin's evil twin. It's got your number – but then you've got its, so that's alright, isn't it? Brightside astrologers maintain that there is a strong complementary relationship between you and your polar sign, and that this relationship is positive and fruitful, especially at work, because you share the same energy quality (mutable). Well, excuse me; on the Darkside it's more like incurable gamblers betting the kids' university fees on a best-of-three arm-wrestling match in a seedy pub. Hands grip, eyes and muscles lock, sinews strain, neither gives an inch; both want the same thing: another drink.

WHO'S GOT YOUR NUMBER?

check out the opposition

Your polar opposite sign is Gemini: the scheming, sophisticated, seditious two-timer with a price for everything and a value for nothing. (For more about your darkly fascinating opposite number, *see pages 72–103*.) What would a gaff-blowing, tact-free loose cannon like you want with a subtle, devious grifter like your average Gemini? How do you have this – shall we say – understanding? Well, like good cop and bad cop, or arch villain and superhero, you need each other to make the Darkside work for you. It's all about elements (undesirable ones, of course). You are Fire; Gemini is Air. Together you can set the world alight and burn down the *ancien régime*; won't that be fun?

Unlike any other polar pairings, you two have a relationship that shows up above the subatomic particle level. (Take a look at page 89 if you don't believe me.) It's the Darkside's dynamic duo. You are the dark horse, and Gemini is the smart jockey; together you conspire to throw the race, or come up unexpectedly from behind and blow the favourite off course. Gemini always gets to take home the money, but you don't care as long as you get plenty of top-grade oats, and hay to roll around in.

Respect your inner Gemini; it provides that little spark of nous that stops you from leaping high buildings without at least hedging your bets, and contains the worst of your foot-in-mouth outbreaks; but don't get too devious in there – you will confuse yourself, lose your animal instinct and end up as pet food.

DARKSIDE DATE

You are a dead cert for a date, for you are convinced you have the pulling power of a shire horse on steroids. You just know that everyone fancies you for the big race, and that one flash of your handsome teeth, a coltish wriggle of your fetlocks (whatever they are) and you will be the instant favourite. If turned down, you don't retire to your stable with your fragile ego in pieces; you just don't take no for an answer, at least not until the chosen one calls in the law. Datees are bafflingly upset that you are going out with them as a result of a bet with friends; a result of a bet with friends;

you don't know why, you got great odds. Your ideal date (anybody will do) starts with a bracing high-speed police chase (you win), followed by a Japanese meal which includes that fish that might kill you if not prepared properly, and ends with moonlit bungee jumping

SEX

Rigorous, adventurous, energetic

No one could accuse you of lacking enthusiasm; you love sex, it's such fun – but not everybody can swing from a trapeze by their ankles in that nonchalant way you have, and not everybody wants to be somebody else's bench-press buddy. You may pride yourself on leaving 'em breathless, but fail to grasp that partners should be à bout de souffle with all passion spent, not just puffed out.

It's not the case that you are a heartless jackhammer – you always give your partner a friendly slap on the haunches while you are doing your post-coital cool-down stretches. And every statement of love you make is true at the time you make it; being a rather good philosopher of semantics, you point out that the expression of a sentiment in a statement does not imply that the sentiment per se continues for longer than the duration of the statement – but usually on your way out because you have learnt that it upsets some people.

You can't bear the idea of not having sexual adventures with as many people as possible; or the idea of them not experiencing the adventure that is you.

What kind of love rat are you?

Frankly, anyone who thinks they have got you tethered is a category-A self-deluder. You will always slip away in the night, no matter how many natty bowlines your partners tie, because you don't do routine and boredom. If the rest of the zodiac cannot read body language that simply screams 'bolter', that's their problem.

INCOMPATIBILITY RATING

Aries – often a bit overcautious and faint-hearted for you.

Taurus – they want to settle down; you want to settle up and get the hell out.

Gemini – lead you astray, but you were going there anyway.

Cancer – bring you down with a bola made of apron strings.

Leo – they like to lay down the law; you like to jump over it.

Virgo – they whine that you never remember trivia, like their name.

Libra – you play the field; they play My Little Pony.

Scorpio – get incandescent when that controlling with the eyes thing just doesn't work.

Sagittarius – dead cert for a death-by-misadventure pact.

Capricorn – they have developed a foolproof casino system; where's the fun in that?

Aquarius – intellectual anti-hero meets anti-intellectual stuntman.

Pisces – wet and clingy, so they cramp your skydiving style.

RELATIONSHIPS

Don't fence me in

Even dark horses like to run with the herd, and you love to range freely, galloping impetuously over the prairie, or clustered in a cozy group around a camp-fire in the Arizona desert, while your family in Chingford put your dinner in the dog and wonder where you are. And parties? You are the official (and relentless) life and soul, unless prevented. Ever wondered why cerebral archers (Brightside you is famous for its philosophers) spend such a lot of time at intellectual get-togethers they call symposiums? Because it's ancient Greek for drinks bash, that's why.

Careless and indiscriminate (you prefer to call it open and spontaneous), you will relate to anybody, but not for long or too deeply, because they might tie you down. If anyone starts building darling little picket fences around you, being jealous or possessive, or even asks if you are going to be around for lunch, you shy and bolt. And the rest of the zodiac should know by now not to tell you any secrets, because you will blurt them all out at the next inappropriate moment, for you believe knowledge should be free.

You are always having affairs, not because you fall in and out of love, but because you can't resist adventures; even if supplied with regular oats at home, you will still stick your nose into exotic foreign nosebags, just for a new taste experience. You willingly get engaged and married because you want to see what it's like; then you get divorced and remarried to see what that's like as well.

DREAM JOBS

What you'd really like to be is a wild horse with no name, so that no one can pin you down and make you re-key all that timetabling data you carelessly wiped when your TGIF tequila slammed a little harder than everybody else's. But you can't

Stunt supremo

Yeee-ha! Hang one-handed from a helicopter! Drive high-performance cars into brick walls! Crash through plate-glass windows! Throw punches in a bar-room brawl! Dowse yourself

Mercenary

When government agencies want a diehard danger lover ready to slash through hostile terrain, live on dung beetles and recycled body fluids, then kill complete strangers in a strange

WORK

Risky business

No one could say you were lazy; you'll do anything, anywhere, but not for long. You usually run three or four jobs at once, all of them erratically; office temping by day, bartending by night, moonlighting as a minicab driver on the weekend, all done with what you consider to be verve and style. To begin with, employers love what they call your get-up-and-go and can-do attitude; but then they don't usually have to sit in the same office with you and your relentless pranks, unhilarious jokes and tedious hoax e-mails. If the minutes begin to drag, you organize paperclip racing, inter-departmental chair-spinning contests or wastebin infernos (you bet on whose burns longest before the sprinklers go on and the whole office closes down for the day). You are also the indefatigable organizer of those bonding weekends and training days, when you get to yomp around a muddy plain at dawn with the accounts department re-enacting the Tet offensive; you are the one, rather endearingly, who does not understand that you do not paintball the boss.

No one employs you for long, because after a while their insurance company tells them not to, but you don't care if you're sacked. You prefer being freelance (masterless knight with a lance for hire), or *ronin* (masterless samurai warrior with a sword for hire) or hired gun, and get to roam the world. The black economy adores you because you always lose the paperwork and you don't give a toss about health-and-safety regulations.

WHEN ARCHERS GO WRONG

You are hopeless at the really serious crime that involves quiet, vicious men in immaculate tailoring, because you are noisy, brash, boast about your exploits, splash your cash about like a sailor and can't keep a secret – even when threatened with a kneecapping. These might do:

Mugger

The simple opportunistic crime you were born for: requires no forward planning or special tools – just daring, physical strength and a quick getaway; yields instant cash for you to lose immediately at the races.

Rustler

Mingle with the herd under cover of the night and cut loose horses, cattle, cars, bikes, anything mobile that you can drive off and sell in the next town's market for cash. No paperwork, instant returns.

CRIMES AND MISDEMEANOURS

How bad could it get?

So what sort of crim would you be, if sociopathy became the new world order? How would you spend your days (or maybe your nights) if you really lived on the Darkside? The thin line between good and bad is the teensiest bit blurry, isn't it, Sagittarius? Especially when you trample all over it with your great hooves. It's the risk, danger and adventure you like, though the loot is always acceptable. You see yourself as a bit of a swashbuckler, so horse thieving, joyriding, ramraiding, gun-running and drug smuggling all appeal, as does a little light arson (though this is usually one of your careless mistakes). You'd really love the camaraderie of an audacious *Ocean's 11*-style heist with a gang of mates, but Scorpio would have to run the caper. And you could be a getaway driver, but last time you drew police attention to yourself (and blew the job) by revving your red Ferrari outside the bank and shouting, 'Whee, can't catch me'.

You usually have no backup plan (or have forgotten it), so are usually caught. In the dock you are restless, impatient, argumentative and a bit sweaty. Your defence relies heavily on rueful grins and shrugged shoulders – you don't mean to be bad, it just comes out that way; and juries (especially if they contain mums with teenage sons) often take pity on you: a mistake, as you will not learn.

When you are banged up, the warders welcome you back, because you are such a card; and you immediately compromise any parole by jumping out of the prison van and being instantly recaptured.

289

AT HOME

château pitstop

If you do have a home, you probably don't remember where it is (although you can always pinpoint which continent, as you're great on the big picture), so home is wherever you throw your hat. You yo-yo between friends, lovers, parents, relatives, student squats, public libraries, park benches, jail (a little light 'drunk and disorderly' will always get you a warm cell for the night), etc., with your empties and your filthy washing, evading anything freedom-sapping, like bills. Luckily you never stay long; sometimes only an unlocked window, an empty fridge and a pile of I.O.U.s show that you have dropped by.

DOMESTIC DISHARMONY

Aries – they burn the place down; so do you, of course, but only by mistake.

Taurus – keep changing the locks, but you always come in through the window anyway.

Gemini – pawn Leo's crowns and tuck the receipts in the hood of your sleeping bag.

Cancer – lock the fridge, so you have to kick it open.

Leo – they throw you out! Just because they own the place.

Virgo – constantly tut-tut under their breath about something they call lack of consideration.

Libra – not speaking to you since the night you mistakenly drank their Eau Sauvage.

Scorpio – glare at you when you pick your nose with their knife; what's that all about?

Sagittarius – is that the one who throws great parties when Virgo's out? Or is that you?

Capricorn – they keep hassling you for your share of the rent (but haven't caught you yet).

Aquarius – they do Jedi mind tricks with your dogs.

Pisces – follow you around tiresomely, picking up the half-empty bottles you throw out

Decor

International Absentee Moderne. While you are galloping about, your partner(s) decorate the home(s) to their taste; after all, you only need a space by the door to stash your backpack and sleeping bag. When finally hobbled, you go for Mongolian Yurt Chic, or the large-dogs-do-furnish-a-room look.

Sharing the Sagittarius stable

Bruising; you love communal living because it means you get to use everybody else's stuff whenever you want – what's the problem? They could use your stuff, if you had any. And you never do any chores; but then don't expect anyone else to, either.

Sagittarius paint chart

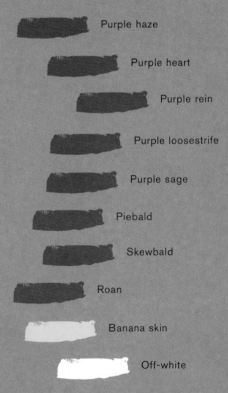

Purple haze

Purple heart

Purple rein

Purple loosestrife

Purple sage

Piebald

Skewbald

Roan

Banana skin

Off-white

PLAYTIME

The darkside of fun

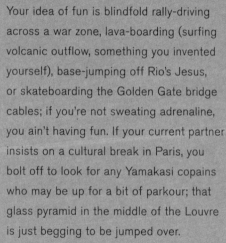

You've never yet booked a return ticket to anywhere because you know you will always come home in an air ambulance, under police escort or in a box. Or, of course, you just won't come back at all.

ZODIAC CULL

Suppose you were marooned on a desert island/up an alp/in a rainforest/at sea with 11 others, each one a different star sign. Who would you eliminate in order to survive? Well, you just love being marooned and wouldn't want to get rid of anybody, but would inadvertently eliminate a few by sheer enthusiasm, and Virgo would explode with frustration. You'd make everyone left hide when you heard the chopper – getting rescued is girlie, and would spoil all the fun you're having.

Your idea of fun is blindfold rally-driving across a war zone, lava-boarding (surfing volcanic outflow, something you invented yourself), base-jumping off Rio's Jesus, or skateboarding the Golden Gate bridge cables; if you're not sweating adrenaline, you ain't having fun. If your current partner insists on a cultural break in Paris, you bolt off to look for any Yamakasi copains who may be up for a bit of parkour; that glass pyramid in the middle of the Louvre is just begging to be jumped over.

If you've drunk the budget, you don't mind at all going hooligan-class, where your loud, drunken, obnoxious behaviour raises no eyebrows – not that you'd care if it did. And if your old mates are still in intensive care from your last jaunt, you go solo and meet a bunch of new ones.

Holidays from hell

★ A five-day coach tour of the tulip fields of the Netherlands; shut in a vehicle with the same 65 people going endlessly across flat lands within the speed limit. You'll empty your hipflask in one.

★ Self-denial and detox at Virgo's favourite spa. You'd do it for half a morning, for the experience, then lead the escape party to the nearest rib shack.

★ Two weeks in challenge-free hyperluxury with Libra and Taurus; after you have swung from every chandelier in the suite, you get frustrated and bored.

Road rage

Mr Toad! That's you riding high on your hog, or in a beat-up, souped-up Boxster, or even on the back of an ex-racehorse,

in fact on anything that moves, fast. You mow down widows and orphans, and blow anything off the road, because you can't see anything but the road. You're always pleased when the cops start after you because you love a race. What map? You navigate by the stars, which is why you don't see the rocket transporter coming the other way.

Gamesmanship

Just because it's a game doesn't mean you don't play to extremes; reckless and hot-headed, you are easily provoked into fouling the opposition, are red-carded within 10 minutes and spend the rest of the game kicking and screaming on the sidelines. You don't take your ball home because you've forgotten you brought it.

BAD COMPANY

Your hall of infamy

You may be feeling a bit emotionally fragile after a session on the Darkside, so to cheer the soul, let's look at a few of the famous, infamous, notorious and just plain bad Sagittarians who might feel the same if they read this book. You will be impressed by the number of rockstars, gunslingers and wild frontier-busters there are; you're in very good bad company. And, despite your formidable (though somehow feckless) Darkside, there are a number of people who appear to want to be you, but who simply don't have the mindless stamina. Think of any impulsive compulsive gamblers who consider Las Vegas too quiet and who have pathologically itchy hooves. All wannabe Sagittarians. If they're not, someone's lying. Look at the panel below if you don't believe me.

WANNABES

Most of us have the odd day when we feel Sagittarian longings, usually at the end of a fruitful evening's bar work; all scallywags, lovable rogues, Australians (at least those working their way around the globe), high-plains drifters, bookies, extreme sportists,

outlaws, freelancers live-fast, die-young, stay-pretty freaks, plus any card sharps who aren't Gemini are all honorary Sagittarians. Quite a few hard-living rockstars (hiya, Keith Richards, Jimi Hendrix) actually are. But consider Jack Kerouac, the badboy beat hero, poet of

the open road and enthusiastic consciousness-alterer? Pisces. And what about Timothy Leary, rogue university prof who dedicated his life to adventures in consciousness and so wished to loose the surly bonds of Earth that he ordered his ashes to be shot into space? Libra.

Billy the Kid *23 November, 1859*

The gunslinging boy wonder (aka William Bonney) was actually born William Henry McCarty Jr. in New York City, but by the time he was 18 he was way out west in Arizona, a-horse thievin', a-cattle rustlin' and a-killin'. He shot and killed at least nine men (legend says 21) and was himself gunned down by Sheriff Pat Garrett in 1881 (although maybe he wasn't, and ran away to Mexico, where he died aged 92).

Ty Cobb *18 December, 1886*

The Georgia Peach (but never peachy off the diamond); the legendary best-ever baseball player and the sport's most detestable human being, according to most aficionados; violent, übercompetitive (he allegedly wore spiked boots) and frequently prosecuted for violent attacks on fans, neighbours and hotel staff.

Lucky Luciano *24 November, 1897*

Sicilian-born celebrity gangster of the 1930s, who came to New York in 1906, got arrested for shoplifting in 1907, went on to run drugs, drink, gambling and prostitution rackets in New York, and founded Murder Inc., the contract-killing arm of the Mafia. He got his nickname from his smart choice of horseflesh.

Jim Morrison *8 December, 1943*

Frontman with legendary Sixties cult-rock psychedelics, The Doors, Morrison (who strutted the stage as the Lizard King) consumed every mind-bending drug known to humanity, cleared the boundaries of reality in a single leap and kicked down the doors of perception. Actually said, "We're more interested in the dark side of life, the evil thing, the night time'. Died poetically in Paris, aged 27.

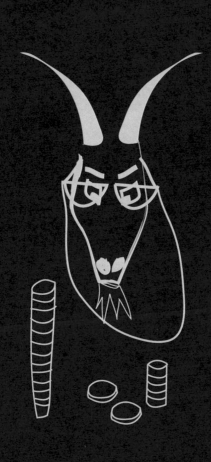

CAPRICORN

22 December ~ 20 January

Capricorn is a feminine, cardinal Earth sign ruled by Saturn. It is the tenth sign on the zodiac wheel, directly opposite Cancer, and is named after the constellation Capricorn (the goat, or as some pedants insist, the sea goat), which bleats and backbites behind the Sun at this time of year.

On the Darkside, this makes you a cold, cruel, petty-minded slave driver with unsuspected yet unquenchable ambition and an addiction to tightfisted penny-pinching.

ANNOYING HABITS

Punctuality

You always arrive 30 minutes early, to impress important people and make underlings feel insecure, unless the inner goat has seized control, when you won't turn up at all because you are busy corrupting innocents.

Toothpaste

It is a truth universally acknowledged that the Capricorn toothpaste tube is always tightly rolled from the bottom up. When it's finished, you unroll it, cut it open and scrape off the last smears.

Temper gauge

0° to boiling point in one second (although you have high Latent Tetchiness levels and are easy to rile). You never forgive a slight and, if shown disrespect, will charge at the offender and headbutt them into a ravine.

PERSONALITY

Petty, parsimonious, pessimistic

Brightsiders have got it in for you, haven't they? You must be familiar with the list (but don't think that's going to stop me rubbing it in): mean, miserly, cruel, cold-hearted, tightfisted, self-opinionated, petty, negative, unforgiving, pessimistic, etc., etc. Scorpio is the only other sign whose Darkside is quite so tediously well documented by the Pollyanna Tendency, but they are sort of redeemed (at least on the Darkside) by their magnetism, erotic overload, etc.; you appear far too respectable to have such a thing as a saving disgrace about you.

Virgo may be the zodiac's perfectionist nitpicker, but you are the one with the stamina and relentless bloody-mindedness to keep wearing away until the world follows The Way of the Goat, because they have lost the will to live. Resistance is exhausted by endless spirit-dulling routine and petty regulations. You very much enjoyed F. Kafka's meticulous accounts of a well-run administrative department and effective judiciary system; if only more people thought that way, your job would be so much easier. A herd of corporate-minded goats can achieve the total desertification of an alpine meadow if they keep nibbling long enough; you can achieve total desertification of the soul using much the same method.

You may bleat that you are insecure inside (so who isn't) but it doesn't help that you come on so ultra-respectable and old-at-heart on the outside. You are a gift to Gemini and Sagittarius since you loathe being teased, embarrassed or made to look undignified. You'd do absolutely anything to preserve your social status (why do you think there are so many blood-soaked net curtains, bizarre gardening accidents and inexplicable and fatal outbreaks of salmonella in respectable leafy suburbs?). You'd also prefer to keep your ruthless, pathological ambition under wraps, in case anyone notices what you are doing and pulls away the ladder.

As for your famous Scrooge gene, that is far too much of a cliché to discuss here. So yes, you are Hon. Sec. of the local branch of the Skinflint Society and author of a monograph on *String Saving for Success*, yadda yadda yadda, but the real reason for all that penny-pinching and wet-blanketing is to conserve your resources and energy for what you actually get up to.

Because the formal, conventional pinstripes and stiff manner are all a front, aren't they? Underneath it all you are a mad square-eyed goat, fourth cousin to the Horned God, the living symbol of mischievous lechery and anarchic goings-on. Nothing can be proved, of course, but the general folk opinion is that you have a timeshare in Pan Demonium, are on cups-of-sugar-borrowing terms with Beelzebub and spend most Sunday nights clustered around a pentangle in the nude. If nothing else, it explains the number of gifted, doomed Capricorn musicians who evidently went down to the crossroads and came to some arrangement with the Prince of Darkness.

Bitch rating

B++. You don't really have the spontaneity to bitch, since it is undignified, but you write excoriating e-mails and sharply worded letters to the more respected newspapers when you feel your status is being impugned. Your inner goat has no such scruples, however, especially after a few cups of black wine.

Collective noun

A procedural tip for non-Capricorns. You may find yourself, for some bizarre zodiacal reason, in a freezing banking hall full of Capricorns. The soft clunk of closing vault doors balances the swish of savings being transferred to higher-yielding accounts. This is an Audit of Capricorns. Bring your own lunch.

FAVE DEADLY SIN

After statistical analyses have been completed, you conclude that the DS that best matches your profile is Avarice, the sophisticated version of Greed. Greed just sounds gross and fat-making, but Avarice is cold accumulation, an insatiable hunger that sucks you dry from the inside, so that you have hollow cheeks and a tiny, tiny heart and squat like a dragon on treasure you can't spend. However, your inner goat makes up for this when let out, going straight for naughty but life-affirming Lust and Gluttony (goats eat anything).

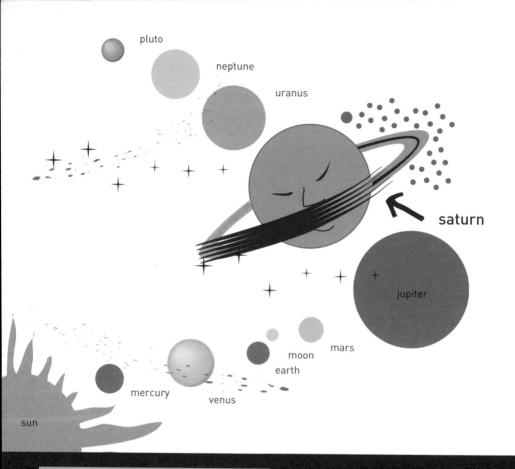

pluto

neptune

uranus

saturn

jupiter

mars

moon

earth

mercury

venus

sun

PLANET PLANET

Every sun sign has a planetary auditor who comes around once a year, crawls all over the books and asks searching questions about petty cash. Before there were telescopes, astrologers could only see five planets in the sky, plus the Moon and Sun, so they counted

these two as planetary rulers. It seemed a good idea at the time. Each planet babysat two zodiac signs – except for the Moon (Cancer's minder) and the Sun (which allows Leo to rule). Your planetary ruler is Saturn, the high-ranking guardian of the solar system's perimeter, until

modern science moved the goal posts and let in any old parvenu planetary riff-raff. You used to have to share it with that weirdo Aquarius until, thankfully, they were snapped up by one of the upstart planets (Uranus). Of course, they left without giving proper notice. No respect.

BLAME YOUR PLANET

Stern, stifling, strong-willed

Twelve of the bank's more desperately feckless customers have just staged a mass suicide in your office because you refused to extend their overdrafts; good riddance – people should learn to live within their means like you do; you have successfully refused entry to another 62 asylum-seeking orphans on an exquisitely obscure technicality you unearthed after 10 hours' hard graft at the paperwork; your petition to ban workplace smiling has attracted another five signatures. It's been a good day. Don't start puffing up with pride, though; you didn't achieve this all by yourself. Thank your planet, Saturn.

Saturn is the sixth rock from the sun, the large (but not as large as Jupiter) dignified one, banded with the rings of office that show just who is second-in-command around here, and accompanied by a grade I personal private secretary (the moon Titan) and 22 administrative assistants (grades 2 and 3). It takes 29½ years to proceed around the sun and return to its original position on our birthchart, so comes back into our lives just when we think we might bust out in a different direction, to point out the restrictive clauses in our contracts.

Saturn is named after a pre-Roman god who taught humanity how to plough and was actually quite fun, with his own raunchy annual festival (Saturnalia) and everything; but he became equated with scary Cronos, son of Uranus and father of the Olympic gods. Cronos castrated his own father to get his hands on power; an example to ambitious sons everywhere.

BAD MOON RISING

The darkside of Capricorn's darkside

It's not all sunshine on the Darkside. You know just how power-crazed and monomaniac your innermost thoughts and secret fantasies are, but where do you think they come from? The Moon, that's where – or whichever area of your birthchart the Moon was moodily plodding when you were born. The Sun is our daytime self; the Moon represents our inner psycho. The nippy little blighter rushes around, plunging in and out of signs every few days, so throughout Capricorn's month in the Sun, the lunar nuisance dodges around like a bent accountant winding up offshore funds, one step ahead of the Inland Revenue. That helps to explain why two Capricorns born only days apart play completely different status symbols, depending on which sign the Moon was bothering at the time.

CATCHING THE MOON

That's all very well, you say, but how do I know where the Moon was when I was born? There are long, complicated (and, frankly, dull) tables called ephemerides that tell you where every planet (and for tedious astrological reasons, the Moon is an honorary planet) stood in the heavens, atmosphere bated, as you made your sorry debut. However, we have provided a Moon itinerary at the back of this book to enable you to get a rough idea. If that sounds like too much hard work, and you have the techno technique, then try visiting the following website: www.alabe.com/freechart. If you know where you were born, and when, they will produce, for *free*, a rough-cut birthchart that will pin your Moon on the zodiac wheel.

Lunatic combinations

Here's what happens to Capricorn when the Moon bustles off to a power lunch.

Moon in Aries – constantly rushing to the end of your rope so fiercely that you have permanent neck burn.

Moon in Taurus – you hate rush; the ladder's not going anywhere, so why not take it one rung at a time?

Moon in Gemini – it's great to look so respectable; it's so much easier to con most of the people most of the time.

Moon in Cancer – you like to point out modestly that it was a goat (Amalthea) that raised baby Zeus (he was ruler of the gods, you know).

Moon in Leo – why can't your revised, hyper-efficient petty cash system be imposed by royal decree?

Moon in Virgo – why is the greasy pole of ambition quite so disgustingly sticky?

Moon in Libra – why tire yourself out scrambling up the unforgiving mountain when you can charm bigger goats into carrying you up?

Moon in Scorpio – Ebenezer Stalin.

Moon in Sagittarius – sometimes you deliberately let your bank account slide into the red just for the sheer hell of it.

Moon in Capricorn – as soon as you get that branch managership, you are going to run a really tight gulag.

Moon in Aquarius – this Earthling body is more efficiently laid out than most, but the thermostat is set a bit low.

Moon in Pisces – the goat most likely to be barbecued over vine leaves on a Greek beach lapped by the wine-dark sea.

BORN UNDER A BAD SIGN

The scum also rises

And another thing. Your sun sign is modified by your rising sign. This is the zodiac sign that was skulking over the horizon at the very minute you were born. If your sun sign is your ego, then your rising sign gives you your public manners (such as they are), your Sunday worst. It's the painted smile behind which the real, disgusting you lurks. Some astrologers maintain that its malign influence affects what you look like. Be afraid.

You consider it in keeping with your position in society that, in the southern hemisphere, for tedious astronomical reasons, there are more people with Capricorn (and Aquarius) rising than any other sign. The zodiac is a wild, unpredictable place and needs as many Capricorns as possible to maintain order, propriety and respectability.

GOING UP

Now pay attention, because the following is quite brain-busting. There are 12 signs of the zodiac, and astrologers like to think of them as occupying a band of sky that spins around the Earth once every 24 hours. (This is a convention; it is not astronomically correct and you will not see the signs if you look up, so don't write in.) So, every two hours or so another sign hauls itself blearily over the eastern horizon. This is going on whatever time of the day or night you were born, and whichever benighted spot on the globe you chose to appear in. These astro-mechanics help to explain why goats born at either end of the same day use different climbing techniques to get up the greasy pole. There are long, nerdy ways to discover your rising sign, but the easiest way is to get hold of a birthchart (see page 304).

Upwardly mobile

If your rising sign is Capricorn, your public persona is a dull sourpuss trudging along just slightly behind the times. This is to distract the rest of us from your plans to force the world to balance its books. Here's what happens when other zodiacal upstarts rise above their station.

Aries rising

Regimental goat.

Taurus rising

You patronize multistar restaurants, but take home everybody's leftovers in a doggy bag so that you don't have to buy groceries for the rest of the month.

Gemini rising

You twinkle nimbly to the top of K2, where you are the first to open a lucrative oxygen-mask and hot-soup concession.

Cancer rising

Your rope isn't tethered to anything; you stay in the meadow because it's home and you fear adventure.

Leo rising

Goat royale. Dazzle herdmates with your gorgeous gilded horns so that they fund your every excess without a bleat.

Virgo rising

Your little hooves are raw from the constant laundering of money.

Libra rising

Fluffy little angora goat, with your slotty little eye on the main chance.

Scorpio rising

You appear darkly, hypnotically sadistic; actually you're just boringly sadistic.

Sagittarius rising

Leap fearlessly from crag to crag, safely covered by a rock-solid insurance policy.

Aquarius rising

You avoid the herd and always climb solo.

Pisces rising

Silly billy; always forgetting to bring your cash, so others have to buy your drinks.

DON'T YOU LOVE ME, BABY?

Venus and Capricorn

Just how much of a high-maintenance tease or bunny-boiler you are may depend on where the solar system's heartless tart (Venus) was blushingly dropping her handkerchief when you were born (*see below*). Oh, and Venus also has a say in how harmoniously you blend in with the world, but what do words like harmony have to do with the Darkside? Now, for astrological reasons that will fry your brain if I explain them here (basically, Venus is far too luxury-loving to move too far away from the Sun, and her orbital rate is in bed with Earth's), Venus only ever appears in your sun sign, or two signs on either side of it. In your case, goats, that means Venus will be in Capricorn, Scorpio, Sagittarius, Aquarius or Pisces. And this is what it does to your love and lust life.

MAKE LOVE AND WAR

Venus is the girlie planet of lurve, right? And Mars is planet lad, the warlord. You may also have a sneaking feeling that men are from Mars and women are from Venus. Don't be upset if I tell you this is not true. All of us, of all genders, have a stake in both planets. Where they are in your birthchart has what I shall call consequences. You may think your sun sign makes you a born babe-magnet, but Venus in a chilly sign will cut you off at the knees; you may think that your sun sign means you are the twin soul of the dove of peace, but you may go red-eyed with bloodlust when beaten to a parking space. Mars will be somewhere irascible. You'll need a birthchart (*see page 304*) to find out what Venus and Mars were getting up to when you were born. It is far too complicated – and, frankly, dull – to work out here.

Venus in Capricorn

Love objects are unsuspicious when you invite them out, since they expect nothing more than a stupefying evening comparing the performance of mutual offshore funds with long-term unit trusts. Are they in for a big surprise!

Venus in Scorpio

As founder and president of your local Satanic Society, you get first choice of all the virgins willingly offering themselves up in sacrifice to the Horned One.

Venus in Sagittarius

Between conferences at the Shanghai Bank, you pull the love object into the glass-walled lift, press the up button and feel the Earth move away.

Venus in Aquarius

Get your people to call the beloved's people, to find a time slot that fits your separate agendas. Schedule a two-minute lust window. Fulfill obligations while streaming the FTSE averages via your hands-free headset.

Venus in Pisces

You play hard to get, dodging elusively behind the more accessible rocks, then let yourself be caught and tied, bleating prettily until a substantial pre-nup is agreed (because you have been so hurt before). You behave so badly with their best friends that they are forced to leave you; then you sue for breach of contract.

ARE YOU LOOKING AT ME?

Mars and Capricorn

Capricorns avoid direct physical violence, preferring purges and show trials instead. But just how confrontational, threatening, paranoid and gagging for a fight you are depends on which area of your birthchart the bruiser planet Mars is being held back in by his mates (leave it, Mars, he's not worth it). Mars is the next planet out from Earth, but paces its orbit rather more slowly (presumably to get some effective eyeballing in). It takes 2½ years for Mars to get around, and on the way it spends about two months of quality menacing time in each sign. As a Capricorn, you crack down hard on Deviant Thought, and action taken in defence of the status quo is always justified. If you find yourself fighting just for fun, or new ideas, check out Mars' alibi at the time of your birth.

Mars in Aries

A ferocious head-butting psycho, best kept on a short rope, unless needed for

Mars in Gemini

You love leading the Crown prosecution at show trials; there's no defence, the

Mars in Leo

War is good; it's nature's way of thinning down the field and getting rid of broken reeds so that efficient, organized rulers like yourself can take command.

Mars in Virgo

You have always thought a purge the most efficient way to rid the body politic of enemies and parasites, and are only too happy to administer one personally.

Mars in Libra

You've drawn up two equally efficient war plans, Code Red and Code Blue, and now you can't make up your mind which one goes best with your jackboots.

Mars in Scorpio

Plan and execute an exemplary campaign (well within the defence budget), show no mercy and take no prisoners (except a few to use as examples); a career tyrant.

Mars in Sagittarius

It's traditional for the Resistance or the Maquis to hide out in the hills to plot revenge and daring, unexpected sabotage raids; and you are very traditional.

Mars in Capricorn

In the right hands, bureaucracy can be as effective as a neutron bomb (kills people, leaves property intact); so your weapon of choice is Smart Paperwork.

Mars in Aquarius

You avoid actual fighting, but plot the key battles using your collection of vintage lead soldiers; when the war is over, you'll be able to sell them for a fortune.

Mars in Pisces

You stride into the fray looking fierce and organized; you mislay your detailed orders, cop some friendly fire because you are lost, or shoot yourself in the foot.

Capricorn

Cancer

POLAR BEARS

Your polar sign sits on the opposite side of the zodiac wheel, six signs away, giving you knowing looks. You have a dark umbilical link with it. If Darkside you is your evil twin, then your polar sign is your evil twin's evil twin. It's got your number – but then you've got

its, so that's alright, isn't it? Brightside astrologers maintain that there is a strong complementary relationship between you and your polar sign, and that this relationship is positive and fruitful, especially at work, because you share the same energy quality (cardinal)

Well, excuse me; on the Darkside it's more like the tension felt in the world's money pits just before the trading bells ring. Lean, lone and hungry, red-eyed traders stand like jackals downwind from carrion, each ready to eat the other; all want the same thing: more.

WHO'S GOT YOUR NUMBER?

check out the Opposition

Your polar opposite sign is Cancer: the snappy, soft-bellied, success-phobic sentimentalist. (For more about your darkly fascinating opposite number, *see pages 104–135.*) What would an upwardly mobile, tough-minded, tunnel-visioned, pragmatist like you want with an unreliable mood-driven despair-junkie like your average Cancer? How do you have this – shall we say – understanding? Well, like good cop and bad cop, or arch villain and superhero, you need each other to make the Darkside work for you. It's all about elements (undesirable ones, of course). You are Earth; Cancer is Water. That makes mud – Cancer likes to wallow in it; you get to work drying it out, employing illegal immigrant labour and cornering the market in cheap pottery piggy banks.

As you sit at midnight in your icy offices (it may be 20° below, but no way are you switching on the heating before January), preparing the next batch of P45s for the old retainers you promised your dad you'd keep on (as if!), or composing terse e-mails threatening to withdraw canteen privileges from the entire workforce until whoever took a biscuit from the executive biscuit tin returns it, can't you sense within yourself the reproachful gaze of two beady little eyes?

Respect your inner Cancerian – it rounds off your jagged bits and prompts you to behave at least in public as if you give a toss for other people's needs and feelings, so you are less likely to be shot by a crazed underling. Careful, though: get too soft and you'll end up as scapegoat.

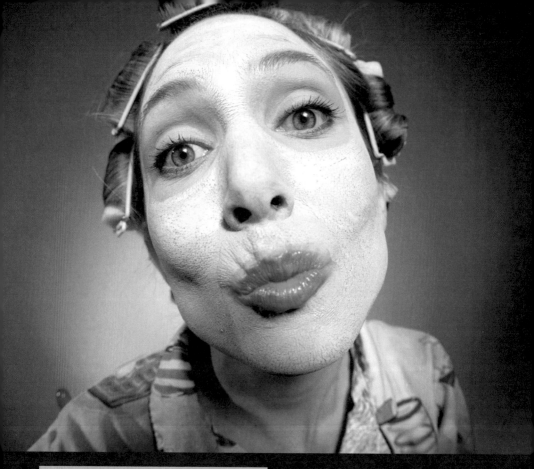

DARKSIDE DATE

Naturally you will get an assignation with a young person because you are a respected member of society, with whom it is an honour and a privilege to go out. You make the arrangements through the proper channels, via a reputable agency or trusted family members. More adventurous Capricorns might try speed dating, which eliminates the waffle and waste you cannot abide, or even mail order. You take them to lunch where you always have lunch and order what you always order (Dutch treat). You quiz them about their academic qualifications, fiscal status, current employment, prospects and long-term plans, then whisk them off to the free exhibition (*A Hundred Years of the Spokeshave*) at the local museum. As dusk falls, you shake hands and hurry home to check their family tree.

SEX

You can't judge a book ...

It's Saturday night, time for your weekly bout of connubial unpleasantness, so it's on with the buttoned-up-to-the-neck pyjamas and off with the light as you buckle down to your contractual obligations. You do this without fail every week, regardless of whether a partner is present; it's all over very quickly (you know exactly what is going to happen and when), so you can soon get back to your petit point. Indeed, some of you have developed a technique that allows you to continue with the less taxing stitches throughout the entire two minutes.

What a nice respectable cover story; but some of us have not forgotten that you are, underneath all those layers of bedtime flannel, a goat – a randy lascivious long-eyed lecher. Twitch aside the polyester sheets fast enough, and we catch a fleeting glimpse of your inner satyr, part man, part horse but mostly goat (horns, you see, and cloven hooves), notorious for its unquenchable lust and the enormity of its schlong. So don't come the repressed libidophobe with me.

What kind of love rat are you?

You don't dump (you have a binding agreement) unless betrayed, when your revenge is terrible and reaches down the generations. However, few people ever even know that they are the object of your affection (and therefore prospective dumpees), for you despise flirting and never utter the L-word again after you have fulfilled statutory demands by saying it once, usually out of anyone's hearing.

INCOMPATIBILITY RATING

Aries – you know what they say about separating the sheep from the goats? Well, it's true.

Taurus – they do it their way; you do it your way.

Gemini – tease you mercilessly in front of the neighbours.

Cancer – they take pity on lame ducks; you shoot them.

Leo – you grovel ingratiatingly to royalty; they walk all over you.

Virgo – nothing either one of you does is ever good enough for the other one.

Libra – they are your trophy partner; you are their meal ticket.

Scorpio – despise you because your ambition is so obvious.

Sagittarius – saw through the rungs of your career ladder.

Capricorn – who is this rude, self-opinionated curmudgeon?

Aquarius – they're on Mt Chalk; you're on Mt Cheese.

Pisces –always slide off the hook just when you think you've got their life organized for them.

RELATIONSHIPS

Friends in high places

You are unlikely to be at a party (unless your inner goat has chewed through its rope) because you despise wasting your valuable time and resources on fun and levity that yield no tangible returns. Frankly, you'd rather be at home gloating over your assets. You've given up on friends because they do not appreciate your help, even though they need it since your methods are so much more efficient than theirs; remember that time when you kindly used your power and influence at the bank to cancel all Libra's credit cards because you knew they had exceeded their limit and were incurring punitive interest charges? And they called you an interfering m**********r? Well, really.

But you are obsessed with status and respectability, and you realize that, however velcro-clad your little goat hooves are, you need help negotiating some of the trickier traverses of the social mountain; so you cultivate useful acquaintances on strategic ledges. Brightsiders say you are a terrible judge of character; you say why waste time on character when only social standing counts? What's wrong with obscene grovelling to appalling people who are higher up than you and might throw down a rope? You'd have invited Augusto Pinochet and Pol Pot around for Sunday brunch if you'd thought it would make you look good at the golf club.

You approve of marriage (you approve of any institution): it's a very sensible way to tie up money and property to your advantage. What's love got to do with it?

You don't have time to waste on idle dreams as Mr Terwilliger has asked you to present your report ('Micromanaging the Catering Interface') to the board, and it does not do to set a bad example to the workforce, but when you get a minute between meetings, consider:

Loss adjuster

Sneering at people who fitted substandard burglar alarms or forgot to lock the bathroom window, and writing damning reports, so insurance companies can pay out on the Scrooge scale and as late as possible.

Politician

A natural for a self-important, self-opinionated status junkie with the stamina to do the spadework on substeering committees until called to office; then you can draft laws to make us all do things your way.

WORK

Respect my authority!

You make a point of getting into the office just that strategic half hour before everyone else, and are always seen to be the last to leave. The boss appears impressed, and the rest of the workforce starts the day feeling surly and inadequate, which is just how you like it, for it makes you look better – although they get their own back by bribing Gemini to tease you, as they know it will provoke a flurry of pompous e-mails that can be quoted in the pub after work.

It doesn't really matter what the work is, as long as it revolves round a greasy pole you can climb up, because although you show the world the dull, neat exterior of a harmless office drudge, inside you seethe with the kind of high-voltage ambition the Macbeths could only dream

of. On the way up you brown-nose the boss class while trampling on the heads of those poor saps who gave you a leg up in the early days, or whose good ideas you have passed off as your own. When hoisted to middle management level, you issue Mao-style directives insisting on respect for your authority and devise a Five Year Plan only you can administer.

Your aim is power, not glory; you don't want to be the front person (Leo can do that); as number two, you get to make all the real decisions, and this gives you a chance to make life hell for all those smartarses who laughed at you in the first paragraph. Plus, if you are number two in a dubious organization and the law catches up with you, you can simply tell them you were just following orders.

WHEN GOATS GO WRONG

Successful top-of-the-range career crime demands a tough mind, rigorous attention to planning and detail, and a high degree of organization. It offers a chance for anyone to work their way up from nothing, and punishes slackers and incompetents. Very you.

Insider trader

How can this be against the law? You are simply taking advantage of unpublished information you happen to have come across to buy and sell shares and get ahead of the game. Isn't that just sensible?

Pimp/madam

Your inner goat knows all about lust and lechery, and how it can part temporarily blinded fools from their money; your outer goat understands how to harness and organize this Dionysiac power to make it pay.

CRIMES AND MISDEMEANOURS

How bad could it get?

So what sort of crim would you be, if sociopathy became the new world order? How would you spend your days (or maybe your nights) if you really lived on the Darkside? You would only consider white-collar crime, and then only with a properly run syndicate that offered ample opportunity for preferment. You'd do well at corporate crime, the kind that depends on the co-ordinated collusion of every key executive in the company and involves so much money and top-level corruption that governments can't afford to recognize it as crime, and everyone gets away with it: rigging LIBOR rates for example; mis-selling of more or less anything by the entire banking system; pension fund rip-offery; global oil conglomerate market fixing. The world, currently, is your pearl-stuffed oyster.

You respect law and order, because people are feckless and disorganized and need to be told, and it's true that the state system keeps inefficient amateur criminals off the streets and out of your hair. However, sometimes it deviates from your personal code, so naturally you are obliged to follow your own, superior way. You explain all this in court, where you conduct your own defence at great length, with flipcharts and spreadsheets, correcting the judge on minor points of procedure. When you are sent down, you find you have a lot in common with the guards and that working the hierarchy to your advantage couldn't be simpler. And assiduous networking with strategic co-inmates guarantees employment after you get early release for good behaviour.

AT HOME

Bleak house

Although you have made it clear that your residences are open to business contacts only, acquaintances who have found out where you live sometimes make the mistake of dropping in. After you have checked via the one-way spyhole that they are dressed respectably enough to impress the neighbours, you unlock the doors, letting out a welcoming blast of cold air. Your guests blunder about at first, because of the low wattage of the few light bulbs you allow, but eventually find upright wooden chairs to sit on (upholstery and soft furnishings weaken the character). They leave soon afterwards.

DOMESTIC DISHARMONY

Aries – use your cash-stuffed mattresses for trampolines.

Taurus – they insist on using the oven to bake cakes to their own recipes, rather than yours.

Gemini – live rent-free because they know about the pentangle and the black altar in the cellar.

Cancer – always feeding your breakfast stale crusts and bacon rinds to the birdies.

Leo – run up enormous fuel bills and ignore all the gilt-edged invoices you deliver by hand.

Virgo – constantly tut-tut under their breath about something they call a hot water supply.

Libra – couriers clutter the front path with silk cushions and fur rugs sent by their sugar daddies.

Scorpio – they despise you for wallowing in luxury.

Sagittarius – use the back of the chores rota to calculate the odds on you throwing them out.

Capricorn – the coroner will record the first known deaths by spontaneous hypothermia.

Aquarius – absentmindedly crack the combination to your vaults via their Playstation 4.

Pisces – stay warm by drinking your secret stash of single malt.

Decor

Because you own a lot of residences (tax losses, foreclosures, investments), you buy a job lot of unlabelled paint at a fire sale and decorate them all at once. Your main residence is home to your prized collection of Early Counting House Gothic escritoires, arranged in rows; modern flatpacks just don't provide enough secret drawers for hiding money in.

Sharing the Capricorn establishment

It will probably help to have spent time in German youth hostels, reform school or boot camp: the routine, the rosters, the inspection parade won't come as such a shock, and they'll know enough to keep quiet and avoid double latrine duty.

Capricorn paint chart

Payne's grey

Pinstripe

Grey eminence

Field grey

Grey matter

Pale black

Light black

Dark white

Greenback

Bluenose

PLAYTIME

The darkside of fun

It is one of your many rules that holidays should be planned ruthlessly to prevent dangerous outbreaks of fun, spontaneity or a budget overrun of more than 0.02 per cent (you're not a complete killjoy).

ZODIAC CULL

Suppose you were marooned on a desert island/up an alp/in a rainforest/at sea with 11 others, each one a different star sign. Who would you eliminate in order to survive? Bind and gag Sagittarius and Gemini, for they're not taking this seriously; shoot Pisces for their own good. Then set up an escape committee, requisition resources, draw up duty rosters and draft a stiffly worded letter suing the holiday company for criminal neglect. You'd be quite sorry when rescue came, but first up the ladder.

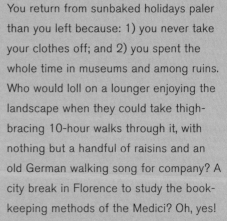

You return from sunbaked holidays paler than you left because: 1) you never take your clothes off; and 2) you spent the whole time in museums and among ruins. Who would loll on a lounger enjoying the landscape when they could take thigh-bracing 10-hour walks through it, with nothing but a handful of raisins and an old German walking song for company? A city break in Florence to study the book-keeping methods of the Medici? Oh, yes!

You hyperprogramme your leisure time with improving activities, because you're afraid that if you relax for one second, the pagan goat locked in the cellar of your soul will bust out and force you to drink the bar dry, dance on the tables and act lewd; you also know that Gemini will take photographs and blackmail you.

Holidays from hell

★ A week in Vegas with Sagittarius and Gemini; the sight of all that money being thrown away for fun would scar you for life.

★ A month in unknown territory with Pisces, who is lost, and Aries; this cuts out a lot of options, because you have a very narrow definition of 'known'.

★ Two weeks in a Danish nudist camp with health-obsessed Virgo; they would have to drug you and cut you out of your clothes with a laser gun.

Road rage

Your drive a car just slightly larger than you need and with more hidden extras than your neighbour's. You never break down or run out of petrol, and like to sweep past feckless grasshoppers who do, covering them in dust. Everybody else's failure to follow lane discipline has you reaching for your shotgun, but as you tell the judge, that is not road rage – just good citizenship. You have a road atlas, three maps of different scales, two satnavs and a GPS watch, so there's no chance of wandering off the straight and narrow.

Gamesmanship

You don't like team games, as people will not play them to your rules, however often you call time out and patiently re-explain the Offside Amendment (b) (1985). Annoyingly, games are often relocated at very short notice, but you never get the message. You don't take your ball home, for that would be childish and undignified. You invoice for it later.

BAD COMPANY

Your hall of infamy

You may be feeling a bit emotionally fragile after a session on the Darkside, so to cheer the soul, let's look at a few of the famous, infamous, notorious and just plain bad Capricorns who might feel the same if they read this book. You will be seriously impressed by the number of power-crazed tyrants and cruel-minded perverts who share your office; you're in very good bad company. And, despite your formidable (though tiny-hearted) Darkside, there are a number of people who appear to want to be you, but who have failed to follow the correct registration procedure. Think of any rigid-minded tightwads, with an exaggerated respect for hierarchy and a pathological inability to relax. All wannabe Capricorns. If they're not, someone's lying. Look at the panel below if you don't believe me.

WANNABES

The interesting thing about Capricorn is that quite a few people you think ought to be actually are. Right-wing politicians? I give you Tricky Dicky Nixon and Fulgencio Batista of Cuba. Sherlock 'you know my methods, Watson' Holmes? Holmesian fanatics have fixed his birthday as 6 January, 1854. Ebenezer Scrooge? Oh, please. Devious bankers who aren't Taurus, devious accountants who aren't Virgo, goatherds, people who re-use teabags more than twice and recycle birthday cards and prison-camp kommandants are all honorary Capricorns. And although I can find no reliable d.o.b. for Alexei Stakhanov, the Russian miner who in 1935 allegedly cut 14 times more coal in one shift than anyone else, and so set Stalin's industrial treadmill in motion, he was certainly a goat in spirit.

Edgar Allan Poe *19 January, 1809*

American Gothic writer and Darkside aficionado, addicted to the thrill of pain, torture, decadence, sickness, premature burial and ravens. Also invented the detective story.

Hermann Göring
12 January, 1893

Nazi. As early as 1933 he had invented the Gestapo and set up concentration camps to contain those people who did not live up to the Nazi ideal (i.e. almost everybody). He glittered less fiercely when the Luftwaffe – German airforce – (of whom he was in charge) failed to deliver during World War II.

Mao Zedong *26 December, 1893*

Ruthless, blunt-speaking peasant who fought his way up the bamboo pole to rule the People's Republic of Communist China in 1949, throwing friends, allies, wives and children to the wolves, and punishing everyone who deviated to the left or right of his path.

J. Edgar Hoover *1 January x, 1895*

Director of the FBI, father of the G-Men and relentless witch-hunter of pinkos, deviants and civil rights activists. Allegedly a closet transvestite and homosexual all along.

Charles Addams
7 January, 1912

Known as 'Chill' to his friends, Addams grew up on Elm Street (in Westfield, New Jersey) and as a boy liked visiting graveyards. Best known for his cartoon take on domestic life with the gothically undead Addams Family. He collected medieval crossbows.

AQUARIUS

21 January ~ 19 February

Aquarius is a masculine, fixed
Air sign ruled by Uranus. It is the
eleventh sign on the zodiac wheel,
directly opposite Leo, and is named
after the constellation Aquarius (the
water carrier), which looks down its
nose and takes notes behind the
Sun at this time of year.

On the Darkside, this makes you
a chilly, detached, eccentric loner,
with perverse voyeuristic habits
and a shard of ice in your heart.

Punctuality

You refuse to follow anyone else's agenda, so never turn up on time or even on day. People blame it on your legendary but suspect absentmindedness, but you know it's your way of controlling the situation.

Toothpaste

You don't use toothpaste, mostly because you've usually lost the tube (last seen as a bookmark), but clean your teeth at the lab with the handheld sonar gun. They glow a bit in the dark, but it's a good look.

Temper gauge

0° to boiling point in .0001 sec. since you do not suffer fools gladly, but like to give people a chance to defend themselves. No red-faced shouting (not logical), just cool insults and deletion of offender from your database.

PERSONALITY

Aloof, arrogant, alien

Well, waterboys, you have set things up well on the Brightside, making sure everyone knows you are a cool, detached, distant, offbeat, freedom-loving loner because, after your extensive study of human nature, you know that nothing is more irresistible to us grubby, hot, sweaty little Earthlings than a cool, detached, etc. loner, drifting in and out of our dull little lives. It's a great bit of symbiosis: we all think that maybe we will be the one who will bring you down to Earth, and you just love being worshipped from afar.

But it's not a Brightside pose, is it? You don't care that your Darkside is on display because, insulated in your space suit, you don't feel the consequences of your words or actions. You really are a chilly-hearted, disengaged observer of the human condition, who has never knowingly reacted spontaneously to any experience. Whatever you're doing, the inner you is busy making observations and taking notes. You even do it when you are on your own; in fact, you find yourself and your reactions to stimuli endlessly fascinating. Your diaries are written to give you something sensational to read on the return trip to Betelgeuse.

Not that you think what other people do is dull; *au contraire*, you're the one outside the neighbour's house with the night-vision binos and the infrared camera; you say legitimate research, the judge says voyeur. Perverse is how you like it; you don't do routine or reliable, and although you want everybody else to show how much they need you, you'd

rather drink rocket coolant than let them know you needed them. You are cranky and surly when it would actually be much more productive to be charming and cooperative (your annual work review, for example); cold and standoffish to your own family, and kind and forgiving to your drinking mates down on Skid Row (they make you feel so deliciously superior). You like to signal your contrariness by dressing in eccentric garments to ensure that we all recognize your fascinating otherness.

As for the absentmindedness – the I-am-far-too-intellectual-and-otherworldly-to-remember-what-day-it-is-or-to-wipe-my-own-bum-or-do-the-supermarket-run routine? It's just a very good act. You get out of all the dull stuff, like social engagements or work; you don't have to keep telling tedious people like your spouse what you are up to; and some gullible sap (there's always one) will cook your meals and wash your socks – all you have to do is come up with a work of unsurpassably staggering genius every now and again. And that's insultingly easy: you just log on and steal one; dull-brained people say plagiarize, you say homage. If you can't be bothered to do that, and people find you out as the parasitical drone you are, then you just shrug and point to the logo on your T-shirt (Take Me or Leave Me).

And it's no good telling us that you are an offworlder, ignorant of Earthling ways. You have been here quite long enough now.

Bitch rating

A--. Theoretically a high-ranker, but you don't bother much because, for a smart one-liner king like you, it's just shooting fish in a very small barrel; but if you find a worthy foe, and there is an appreciative audience on hand, you come on like Cyrano de Bergerac and pulp their ego to mush with vicious sarcasm.

Collective noun

A technical tip for non-Aquarians. You may find yourself, for some bizarre zodiacal reason, on the frosty observation deck of a space station full of Aquarians, each sealed in their own individual space pod. Logic gates can be heard closing in the distance. This is a Spock of Aquarians. Wear thermal underwear.

FAVE DEADLY SIN

It's fascinating what humans devise to beat themselves up with – must be some sort of ritual psychodrama. All the sins are a bit crude and obvious, and require an engagement of the flesh that you don't really do, but finding out which ones fit you looks like fun – a bit like knowing your Sun sign – and you love a good mind game. So perhaps the one called Sloth, because you can be a tad languid, and maybe Pride, but that's rather academic, for you obviously *are* superior to everyone else, not just swanning around thinking you are.

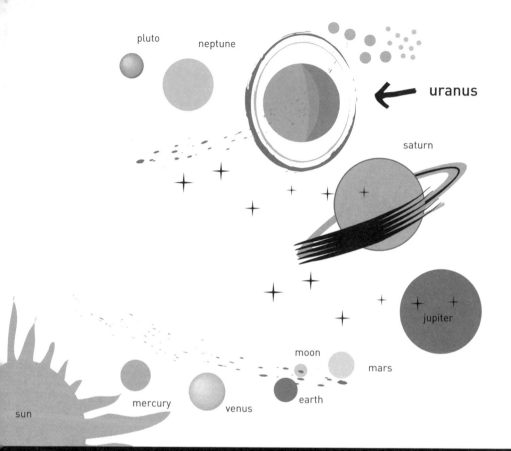

pluto

neptune

uranus

saturn

jupiter

moon

mars

earth

venus

mercury

sun

PLANET PLANET

Every sun sign has a backroom planet, a theoretician floating in a think tank whose job it is to work out how things ought to be, but not necessarily to make them so. Before there were telescopes, astrologers could only see five planets in the sky, plus the Moon and Sun, so they

counted these two as planetary rulers. It seemed a good idea at the time. Each planet babysat two zodiac signs – except for the Moon (Cancer's minder) and the Sun (which allows Leo to rule). Yours is Uranus. You used to share Saturn with that gloomy creep Capricorn until

1781, when William Herschel peered through his telescope and saw Uranus (can we get all the puerile jokes over with now, please? Thank you). It's the first modern planet, discovered by science, brain and hard sums – not just by staring at the night sky in a drippy, romantic manner

BLAME YOUR PLANET

Space oddity

Aquarius and Saturn was never a good look (although it does compute with the opinionated grumpiness, surliness and stuff); Uranus is so much more on your wavelength: the cosmic generator of crankiness, wilful eccentricity and very odd changes in direction. So even though you don't give a toss about what others think of your behaviour, you now have a get-out: whenever you are tediously going up the down escalator to show just how zany you are, blinding mice in the name of research or blanking your mates because you are playing *Assassin's Creed Syndicate* in a parallel universe, you can put the blame firmly on Uranus.

This planetary oddball is the seventh rock from the sun and four times bigger than Earth; it takes 84 years to loop the void, spending seven years (see – a weird, mystic number already) in each sign, slightly longer than is bearable. What is really bonkers about it is that it tilts 98° – just call me Planet Sideways – so that its poles take it in turns to face the sun; hypothetically, you sunbathe at the north or south pole and build igloos on the equator. It's smothered in icy clouds of gas, and has no significant internal heat source, just like you don't. It's got 15 mates, or moons, and a set of rings like Saturn, only they are the dark mysterious kind that don't show up on film.

It's named after the Greek god Oeranos (sky), partner of Gaia (Earth) and father of the Titans. The Greeks ignored him – he didn't get a single temple, which suits you, as you don't do deference.

BAD MOON RISING

The darkside of Aquarius's darkside

It's not all sunshine on the Darkside. You know just how power-crazed and monomaniac your innermost thoughts and secret fantasies are, but where do you think they come from? The Moon, that's where – or whichever area of your birthchart the Moon was moodily plodding when you were born. The Sun is our daytime self; the Moon represents our inner psycho. The nippy little blighter rushes around, plunging in and out of signs every few days, so throughout Aquarius's month in the Sun, the lunar nuisance dodges around like a free electron in a particle accelerator. That helps to explain why two Aquarians born only days apart set up experiments using completely different apparatus, depending on which sign the Moon was bothering at the time.

CATCHING THE MOON

That's all very well, you say, but how do I know where the Moon was when I was born? There are long, complicated (and, frankly, dull) tables called ephemerides that tell you where every planet (and for tedious astrological reasons, the Moon is an honorary planet) stood in the heavens, atmosphere bated, as you made your sorry debut. However, we have provided a Moon itinerary at the back of this book to enable you to get a rough idea. If that sounds like too much hard work, and you have the techno technique, then try visiting the following website: www.alabe.com/freechart. If you know where you were born, and when, they will produce, for *free*, a rough-cut birthchart that will pin your Moon on the zodiac wheel.

Lunatic combinations

Here's what happens to Aquarius when the Moon goes absent without leave.

Moon in Aries – Starship trooper; exterminate first, ask questions later, but don't listen to the answers.

Moon in Taurus – you like to express your eccentricity in unusual food combos: sardines in a *latte* anyone?

Moon in Gemini – you encourage the idea that you are absent-minded and unworldly, then clean up at the card table.

Moon in Cancer – you creep into the lab at night to give the rats extra food; they all die of fatty degeneration and your research funding is cut off.

Moon in Leo – you pose just upstage of the bright lights, because you know you cast a more imposing shadow that way.

Moon in Virgo – always relieved to get back to the ship's decontamination unit.

Moon in Libra – playing it cool gives you time to calculate which sap is more likely to fund your urgent shoe research.

Moon in Scorpio – Dr Strangelove.

Moon in Sagittarius – boring safety routines are for wimps; let's just attach this wire to that terminal and that wire to this terminal and …

Moon in Capricorn – deep inside, a part of you wishes you could for once wear an unremarkable suit and discreet tie.

Moon in Aquarius – so unbearably cool you slash your wrists on the cutting edge; it's a good job you don't bleed.

Moon in Pisces – the zodiac's ice-cream bar: hard and icy on the outside, wet and gooey on the inside.

BORN UNDER A BAD SIGN

The scum also rises

And another thing. Your sun sign is modified by your rising sign. This is the zodiac sign that was skulking over the horizon at the very minute you were born. If your sun sign is your ego, then your rising sign gives you your public manners (such as they are), your Sunday worst. It's the painted smile behind which the real, disgusting you lurks. Some astrologers maintain that its malign influence affects what you look like. Be afraid.

You of course already know from your research that in the southern hemisphere, for tedious astronomical reasons, there are more people with Aquarius (and Capricorn) rising than any other sign. This is statistically fascinating and indicates that colony ships from the Orion sector made first landfall on Australia's Nullarbor Plain, as suspected.

GOING UP

Now pay attention, because the following is quite brain-busting. There are 12 signs of the zodiac, and astrologers like to think of them as occupying a band of sky that spins around the Earth once every 24 hours. (This is a convention; it is not astronomically correct and you will not see the signs if you look up, so don't write in.) So, every two hours or so another sign hauls itself blearily over the eastern horizon. This is going on whatever time of the day or night you were born, and whichever benighted spot on the globe you chose to appear in. These astro-mechanics help to explain why water-carriers born at either end of the same day use entirely different systems of logic. There are long, nerdy ways to discover your rising sign, but the easiest way is to get hold of a birthchart (see page 336).

Upwardly mobile

If your rising sign is Aquarius, your public persona is an off-beam loner, with odd socks and a lobster on a lead. This is to distract the rest of us from your plans to stop the world so that you can get off. Here's what happens when other zodiacal upstarts rise above their station.

Aries rising
Rambo.

Taurus rising
You like to look dull and respectable, because it means no one follows you home and discovers the landing site.

Gemini rising
With all your local knowledge and street talk, you could almost pass for an Earthling, but you're just a tad too clever.

Cancer rising
When you watch crabs dancing sideways on the beach at night, it reminds you of the great parties you hated going to, back in the days of the pan-galactic alliance.

Leo rising
You wear gold lamé and go everywhere with a brace of ruby-collared leopards; no one will notice your extra head.

Virgo rising
A person could eat their dinner off your laboratory floor; in fact, you insist.

Libra rising
You are the pioneer of geek chic; desperate fashionistas doorstep you for next season's daring new look.

Scorpio rising
You appear darkly, hypnotically perverse; actually, you're just perverse.

Sagittarius rising
Everyone knows you're from Sirius; so?

Capricorn rising
So repressed and conventional that we all know you must have another, secret life.

Pisces rising
Cold fish.

DON'T YOU LOVE ME, BABY?

Venus and Aquarius

Just how much of a high-maintenance tease or bunny-boiler you are may depend on where the solar system's heartless tart (Venus) was blushingly dropping her handkerchief when you were born (*see below*). Oh, and Venus also has a say in how harmoniously you blend in with the rest of the world, but what do words like harmony have to do with the Darkside? Now, for astrological reasons that will fry your brain if I explain them here (basically, Venus is far too luxury-loving to move too far away from the Sun, and her orbital rate is in bed with Earth's), Venus only ever appears in your sun sign, or two signs on either side of it. In your case, waterboys, that means Venus will be in Aquarius, Sagittarius, Capricorn, Pisces or Aries. And this is what it does to your love and lust life.

MAKE LOVE AND WAR

Venus is the girlie planet of lurve, right? And Mars is planet lad, the warlord. You may also have a sneaking feeling that men are from Mars and women are from Venus. Don't be upset if I tell you this is not true. All of us, of all genders, have a stake in both planets. Where they are in your birthchart has what I shall call consequences. You may think your sun sign makes you a born babe-magnet, but Venus in a chilly sign will cut you off at the knees; you may think that your sun sign means you are the twin soul of the dove of peace, but you may go red-eyed with bloodlust when beaten to a parking space. Mars will be somewhere irascible. You'll need a birthchart (*see page 336*) to find out what Venus and Mars were getting up to when you were born. It is far too complicated – and, frankly, dull – to work out here.

Venus in Aquarius

You can't be doing with all this physical neediness; you like a partner who is online, in tight underwear and on the other side of the world. You always use your mouse, as it's good to have a free hand. What's gender got to do with it?

Venus in Sagittarius

Love, oh careless love. Strap yourself to the love object and take them free falling; you do the calcs for a safe landing on the way down, on the back of your P45, which blows away in the slipstream. So what? You've never missed the ground yet.

Venus in Capricorn

You only consider scientific geniuses, rock stars and conceptual artists as lovers; you gain a layer of celeb gloss, and when they're rich, famous and dead, you take over the estate as well as the royalties.

Venus in Pisces

Weak, clingy, slippery, cold, calculating little libido; overconfident lovers think you are a crushable pushover until you go kissing and tweeting on Gawker.

Venus in Aries

You've got this great new micro-calculator to notch up the conquests; it doubles as a camera, so you can e-mail hotshots to the beloved, who will be dumped by the time they pick them up. You must move on, but it will give them something to remember you by – as will the rash.

ARE YOU LOOKING AT ME?

Mars and Aquarius

Aquarians do not do violence or physical contact, preferring to set phasers on stun from an accurately computed distance. But just how confrontational, threatening, paranoid and gagging for a fight you are depends on which area of your birthchart the bruiser planet Mars is being held back in by his mates (leave it, Mars, he's not worth it). Mars is the next planet out from Earth, but paces its orbit rather more slowly (presumably to get some effective eyeballing in). It takes 2½ years for Mars to get around, and on the way it spends about two months of quality menacing time in each sign. As an Aquarian, you always go for mindgames over wargames, so if you find yourself feeling hot-eyed and murderous, or even feeling anything at all, check out Mars' alibi at the time of your birth.

Mars in Aries

Fierce, impetuous and aggressive, but in your own eccentric way; you will only fight using authentic Civil War weapons.

Mars in Taurus

Death Star. It takes you a long time to reach warp speed, but when you do, you hunt down your enemies relentlessly and vaporize them, very slowly.

Mars in Gemini

Out in the field, nipping from war zone to war zone and posing sad teddy bears in the ruins before you do your piece to camera, to add pathos and make trouble.

Mars in Cancer

You cruise with defensive shields up at all times; so if you do meet an enemy, you have nothing left in the locker.

Mars in Leo

You pilot the gold-hulled flagship space cruiser, and draw up the battle plans, but don't fight yourself, because that would be illogical – you are in charge.

Mars in Virgo

You approve of battles in deep space because there is a vacuum out there, and everything is sterile. People have no idea how difficult it is to get bloodstains off co-polymer-based body armour.

Mars in Libra

You sign non-violence pacts with the Klingons and the Geckoids; watch them eat each other; then betray the winner.

Mars in Scorpio

There is nothing and nobody you will not sacrifice to gain complete control of the universe. Goodbye, mother, spouse and children. It's nothing personal.

Mars in Sagittarius

You love a good slapfest, but can't be doing with all that reality stuff; prefer to challenge enemies to marathon sessions on your Playstation beat-em-ups.

Mars in Capricorn

In space no one can hear you scream, which is how you like it, as the other prisoners get antsy if they hear what you are doing to traitors and rebels.

Mars in Aquarius

You don't care for all that engagement-in-battle mess, so blast everything with your Annihilation Ray, then go and rebuild the universe in another part of your head.

Mars in Pisces

You sit in the Space Ranger Lounge, cursing your broken leg and malfunctioning hyperdrive until it's all over. Smash open a celebratory bottle with your crutch.

Aquarius

Leo

POLAR BEARS

Your polar sign sits on the opposite side of the zodiac wheel, six signs away, giving you knowing looks. You have a dark umbilical link with it. If Darkside you is your evil twin, then your polar sign is your evil twin's evil twin. It's got your number – but then you've got

its, so that's alright, isn't it? Brightside astrologers maintain that there is a strong complementary relationship between you and your polar sign, and that this relationship is positive and fruitful, especially at work, because you share the same energy quality

(fixed). Well, excuse me; on the Darkside it's more like the tension generated during a classic Vader/Skywalker encounter, when two sides of the force clash (OK, OK, they're both dark forces here – are you a Virgo or something?). First to drop their light saber is a wuss

WHO'S GOT YOUR NUMBER?

check out the opposition

Your polar opposite sign is Leo: self-centred, self-satisfied and self-indulgent. (For more about your darkly fascinating opposite number, *see pages 136–167*.) What would a dispassionate, disdainful remote-controller like you want with such a posturing limelight-hogger like your average Leo? How is it that you have this – er, what shall we call it – understanding? Well, like good cop and bad cop, or arch villain and superhero, you need each other to make the Dark side work for you. It's all about elements (undesirable ones, of course). You are Air; Leo is Fire. Leo thinks this means more torchlight for their parade; you know that if bush fires rage fiercely enough, the mother ship will be able to see your signal from deep space.

You come on as an icon of cool, too glamorously ironic to be contaminated by the despicable neediness of the rest of the zodiac. Every time you get near a spontaneous outburst, your Inner Editor activates the defensive shields, so that you can look on untouched while others tear themselves apart. It's logical, but isn't it a bit, well, sterile? Don't you sometimes just want to get down and dirty?

Respect your inner Leo; it provides that orange glow deep inside, the tiny flame that hungers for fame, celebrity and adoration, and melts the ice-shard in your heart just enough to make you care about another individual, and want them to love you and not see you as a displaced Vulcan. Don't get too loved up in there, though, or the hyperdrive will go into meltdown.

DARKSIDE DATE

You always get a date, or at least a close encounter of some kind, because there is always somebody somewhere who goes for the oddball. You just need to use the scientific approach to maximize your hit-rate. Hang around at LoTR conventions, Trekkie fests, cult recruitment drives, crop circle workshops, re-enactment society meetings, downtown Roswell, or any university physics block, and you are bound to meet the kind of people who will give you the time of day (even if it is in Venusian). Or just stalk the chatrooms. Your ideal date is with a group of young, impressionable cross-dressing ufologists whom you take to your favourite fetish club, where you end the night tucking £10 notes between the bum cheeks of nude chess grandmasters as they make provocative opening gambits.

SEX

cool and kinky

You're not used to Earthling bodies and have never learned how to activate the direct feed that links sensation to brain. There is always time to evaluate and edit sense data as they come in, so you never have emotionally unprotected sex or have been swept away by lust. This means you are always in control, which is good, but it also means you get a teensy bit bored and fidgety waiting for your partner to come down off the ceiling or wake up.

Pass the time drilling a hole through to next door's bedroom, to see how they do it; if they are any good, you can record it with your spy-grade miniature digital camera and download it directly onto your local cable porn channel. Or invite a few friends around to try a few themes and variations. Even better, dress up in each other's underwear and play Invasion of the Body Snatchers. Warning: don't get caught taking notes on the job; no one wants to know they are raw material for a doctoral thesis or an airport bonkbuster.

What kind of love rat are you?

You are unlikely to have a long-term partner to dump, because you despise clingy dependants just as much as you loathe jealous control freaks (you do all the controlling around here), and there's not much in between. You'd rather not dump, as it invalidates the experiment, but if you have to, you mindgame lovers into behaving badly so that you can sack them without guilt. You wipe your data banks, and blank exes whenever you see them again, especially if they are in tears.

Aries – they think you're playing hard-to-get, so won't go away.

Taurus – they want to possess your soul; have you got one?

Gemini – is it you they love, or your enviable penumbra of cool? Like you care.

Cancer – suspect your absent-mindedness may be a front.

Leo – textbook delusions of grandeur: fascinating.

Virgo – dull case of obsessive-compulsive disorder centred on matching up your socks.

Libra – seduce all your friends and colleagues; you take notes.

Scorpio – textbook delusions of power: you're writing a paper.

Sagittarius – one sniff of commitment and they're off; you've already left.

Capricorn – they want you to get a proper respectable job.

Aquarius – balanced equation: you don't care; they don't care.

Pisces – wet and clingy and have to be frozen off, like warts.

RELATIONSHIPS

Group therapy

It's a neighbourhood barbecue, guests flutter around the flames in fluorescent Hawaiian shirts, sarongs and shades; but who is that enigmatic lone wolf wearing an ex-Russian army greatcoat that last saw duty in Stalingrad, kung-fu slippers and a spotty bandanna? That's you, that is, looking glamorously, eccentrically different, and making damned sure all the straights can see you looking glamorously, eccentrically different. (You work on the Heisenberg Principle: the observer affects the experimental process.) If you are the lone outsider you'd like us to think you are, how come you are always at the centre of the circle (alright, slightly to one side, and maybe it's an ellipse), talking too loudly about cool stuff you'd like us to think you know all about?

People think you are friendly because you hang around with so many groups, but that is because you need a large enough statistical sample to make the data you are collecting viable. It's no strain to interact with groups, but you are bored by any individual's feelings (except your own, which you find fascinating). Sometimes you just duck out (maybe for years). Brightsiders say this is because you like your privacy; actually you are back at base, writing up your field notes. Plus Earthlings are essentially weak, and weak people drain your energy cells, so you need to get away to recharge.

You may get married, so that you can experience at first hand a primitive cultural ritual, but you know you'd never get it quite right, and it wouldn't mean anything.

DREAM JOBS

As far as you're concerned, work is the stuff physicists measure in joules; what you're doing is just drudgery; but don't sit there maliciously reprograming the MD's organizer, downloading porn and randomly changing passwords and access codes; consider these options instead:

Mad scientist

Someone gives you funding to order up lots of shiny apparatus, play around with ideas all day long and grow a beard; and all they want in return is a smallish, itsy-bitsy, little doomsday weapon; sounds good to you

Croupier

They may look like toys, but the roulette wheel, the dice and the pack of cards are all portals to a secret cosmos of probability, numbers, systems and chance; and only you have the keys! For this, even you will wear a tux

WORK

You cannot be serious

You'd rather spend your time on your pioneering research/Time Machine/That Difficult Second Novel, but a waterboy's gotta drink, and if you don't have state funding or private patronage, any old McJob will have to do. Best-case scenario would be as a techie, because only other techies know what you are talking about, and the boss can't tell whether you are working or not, and daren't ask.

Infuriatingly, you can work out the OS of any job in about 10 seconds (it didn't take you that long to realize that every admin job, however uptitled, is an aspect of filing); but you're a sarcastically bolshy routine-phobe who spits on the corporate ethic. You're never on time, customize your uniform, loathe being overseen and get sneery and surly filling in those self-assessment forms (121b: how do you rate your ability to fill in assessment forms?). Bosses hate you because they suspect, rightly, you could do their job in your sleep if you felt like it, and they lie awake at night wondering why you don't feel like it. So you are regularly sacked, usually in your absence because you forgot your shift dates, but you don't care.

Colleagues are awed by your insolent, independent swagger, but go off you when they come across the notebook containing the outline of a searing indictment of petty-minded office life (obviously a storyboard for a reality TV show) listing all their quirks, idiosyncrasies and catchphrases, and all the grubby water-cooler secrets they told you in confidence because you seemed so nice and friendly.

WHEN WATERBOYS GO WRONG

In the Organization they call you
Brains, and Mr Big's orders are
that you are not to be messed
with, even though you're weedy,
geeky, arrogant, annoying, off-
the-wall and a physical wreck;
this is because you are a genius
at the 21st-century techie crime
successful Mr Bigs now commit

Computer hacker

Cybercrime is money from home
for you. Not that you do it for the
money; you just like knocking
through firewalls, cracking
codes and bluffing your way
into impenetrable systems. It's a
Swiss bank system; so what?

Stalker

Restraining orders mean
nothing to you; as long as
you've got a satellite link, bugs
and access to a computer
network, you can make life hell
for anyone: every breath they
take, you'll be watching them

CRIMES AND MISDEMEANOURS

How bad could it get?

So what sort of crim would you be, if sociopathy became the new world order? How would you spend your days (or maybe nights) if you really lived on the Darkside? Well, as an impartial observer, you find the whole crime scene fascinating, a dark mirror to the Brightside social structure, with rules, organizations, etiquette, hierarchical structure and so on. Moral codes are all relative, so of course you plunge in and give it a try, for research purposes; there's not much you won't do, except violence and returning library books too late, and you reckon a quick biog and a couple of authentic thrillers dashed off after the event will pay any legal bills.

Problem is that you are, as always, too clever by half. Your schemes are so convoluted and littered with unnecessary dead ends, red herrings and false scents that the Brightsiders employ serious Harvard-brained coppers (Aquarius or Scorpio), who enjoy this kind of game as much as you do. When caught by a bright-eyed waterboy, you tend to shake hands and say, 'Well played, sir'.

So you get your day in court, even though you are above the crude local legal system and would certainly have diplomatic immunity, if only Earth had ratified the treaty with your home planet. You smile a lot, take notes assiduously at the trial and unnerve the judge. When you go to prison (or a secure psychiatric unit, if the judge felt really unnerved), you spend time observing the system, then organize a rooftop protest to improve inmates' rights. When you get bored, you beam up.

AT HOME

Domestic science

You may well have a normal house, but who's to know, as you've been in the shed since 1984, perfecting cold fusion in a bucket. If you live alone, as so many of you do, you use the kitchen for brewing rocket fuel and the bathroom for your gamma-wave detection array; the bedroom houses your mainframe and you sleep with the dog. Artistic Aquarians cannot access the muse unless they live in a freezing boho garret with just a desk, a pencil and mice to train if things get slack. Many young waterboys live happily in the tiny area just behind a keyboard. You are always pleased to see visitors, but few show up.

DOMESTIC DISHARMONY

Aries – they've used up all your nitroglycerine on some hare-brained project of their own.

Taurus – keep trying to store gardening tools in the shed.

Gemini – pirate all your software and sell it to schoolkids; give your name when arrested.

Cancer – they iron the bohemian creases out of your labcoats.

Leo – tear down the posters of Che and Mao, not realizing they are what keep the walls up.

Virgo – constantly tut-tut under their breath about something they call domestic routine.

Libra – hide their Agent Provocateur catalogue from you.

Scorpio – they've got the only sterile room, but won't let you use it for your anthrax cultures.

Sagittarius – you're working on ways to harness their energy to run the refrigeration plant.

Capricorn – too impressed by your PhDs to throw you out.

Aquarius – you've never met them, as their shed is in the front garden and yours is in back.

Pisces – drank a whole batch of your experimental homebrew and are now hermaphrodite.

Decor

Where there aren't books, papers, revolutionary posters and cannibalized computer peripherals, there are solar-powered fridges (in the developmental phase), stuff in petri dishes, paperclips linked together to demonstrate the superstring theory and a cat (cats love you); plus blackboard paint on the walls and plenty of chalk.

Sharing the Aquarian research facility

Don't tell new roommates what happened to the old roommates before they move in; you could mention that the house may blow up (or take off) at any moment, but point out that at least that means they won't have to do any more dull chores.

Aquarius paint chart

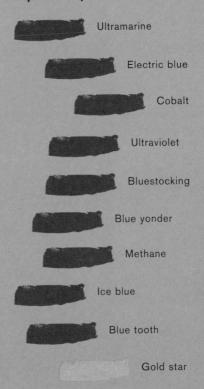

Ultramarine

Electric blue

Cobalt

Ultraviolet

Bluestocking

Blue yonder

Methane

Ice blue

Blue tooth

Gold star

PLAYTIME

The darkside of fun

Everywhere you go, you always take your perverse urge to be off-centre with you. A bucket-and-spade holiday? You take an old Buzz Aldrin replica space helmet and a deflagrating spoon. Activity holidays?

ZODIAC CULL

Suppose you were marooned on a desert island/up an alp/in a rainforest/ at sea with 11 others, each one a different star sign. Who would you eliminate in order to survive? A very interesting experiment; it would be bad methodology to terminate any subject in such a small statistical sample, but you can make useful observations about the percentage that self-destruct and those who try to kill you. And radio signals will be stronger out here in the wilderness, so you can mayday the mother ship.

Painting in Provence? Too ordinary; you go for website designing in Kabul, or amoeba rehab in Arkansas. You are saving up for one of those zero-gravity jaunts they do in Siberia.

You set off by unlicensed cargo ship, crop-duster or camel to remote edges of the world, but only if you are seen doing it, or the experiment is invalidated. You dress in a smart three-piece suit with polished shoes to look different when you get there, but bring back ethnic garments with unpronouncable names to wear at board meetings to look different when you get back. On holiday your inner Leo comes out to sunbathe, and you yearn to be worshipped by the locals, just like the deluded Aztecs worshipped Cortés as their Lost White God, Quetzalcoatl.

Holidays from hell

★ Honeymoon; trapped in an alien cultural construct with someone who evidently expects you to express feelings, and listen to them talk about theirs.

★ A remote retreat where you see no one; how can you be withdrawn, weird and wacko if there are no conventional straights to compare and contrast with?

★ A Science Fiction Convention, thronged by thousands who really shouldn't wear tight lycra; the rest of the zodiac think this is just up your street, so of course you keep away.

Road rage

You'll drive anything, but prefer a perverse ride: deconsecrated hot-dog van, lime-green hearse, cult cult-bike, a mule down the King's Road. You don't do road rage (you don't notice anyone else on the road) but you're always speeding (because you're so used to warping into hyperdrive). When the cops pull you over, you make it worse for yourself by being snotty, superior and evasive (of course you've got a licence, you're cleared to pilot intergalactic space freighters) and get thrown in jail. You only carry a star map and the latest EEG of your alpha waves; hey, the world is round – how can you get lost?

Gamesmanship

You only play games you have made up yourself, with very complex rules others couldn't possibly understand. If people don't want to play, you don't care. They can keep the spheroid; you can't use it.

BAD COMPANY
Your hall of infamy

Even you may be feeling a bit emotionally fragile after a session on the Darkside, so to cheer the soul, let's look at a few of the famous, infamous, notorious and just plain bad Aquarians who might feel the same if they read this book. You will be impressed by the number of resolute outsiders and chilled-out weirdos there are; you're in very good bad company. And, despite your formidable (though somehow disengaged) Darkside, there are a number of people who appear to want to be you, but who have downloaded the wrong software. Think of anyone too cool and disdainful to mingle with the mob, who is allergic to sensible routine and who sees the rest of humanity as their private lab rats. All wannabe Aquarians. If they're not, someone's lying. Look at the panel below if you don't believe me.

WANNABES

Albert Einstein, humanity's very own absent-minded professor, absent-mindedly pointing out how atomic power works? A hardwired Aquarian, surely? Negative, Captain: Pisces. Well, what about Marcel Duchamp, anti-artist and iconoclast (you know, moustache and rudery on the *Mona Lisa*) and all-round bourgeoisie basher? Leo (but then that's Aquarius's opposite sign, so you can see how it happened). Salvador Dali, painter, surrealist and eccentric dresser? Safe waterboy, wouldn't you say? Taurus. (Yes, who'd have thought it – but he was Spanish, so maybe it's a bull thing). All astronauts are honorary Aquarians, and Buzz Aldrin really is one; and the number of writers (detached observers of the human condition) who ought to be Aquarius, and are Aquarius, is scary. Especially Virginia Woolf.

Tom Paine *29 January, 1737*

Career revolutionary born in Norfolk, England; thrown out of every European country for publishing his eccentric ideas and theories (abolition of monarchy and slavery, sexual equality, public education, the poor to get regular food, that sort of thing). Very popular in the US, where his pamphlet, *Common Sense*, inspired the Declaration of Independence (1776); a must-have at every A-list revolution, freedom fight and popular insurrection.

Lord George Byron
22 January, 1788

Eccentric British poet; he invented the cool, floppy-shirted, floppy-haired, bad, mad, etc. hero; besieged by women, in spite (or because) of being a short bastard with a club foot. Died fighting in the Greek War of Independence.

Eva Braun *6 February, 1912*

Hitler's mistress, although you'd never have known; the duo rarely displayed intimacy and she chose to spend most of her time alone in his isolated alpine retreat, Berchtesgaden; yet she poisoned herself to die with him. Strange.

James Dean *8 February, 1931*

Achingly cool (even after all these years) moody screen supericon, who said little, died young, and stayed pretty; a template for doomed youth since his death aged 24.

David Lynch *20 January, 1946*

Mysterious, eccentric independent filmmaker and artist, auteur of TV's most bizarre soap, *Twin Peaks*, and cult movies *Eraserhead*, *Blue Velvet* and *Wild at Heart*; he knows what he means, but he isn't going to tell us.

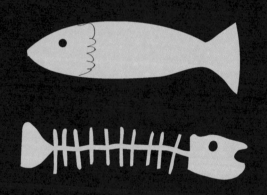

PISCES

20 February ~ 20 March

Pisces is a feminine, mutable Water sign ruled by Neptune. It is the twelfth sign on the zodiac wheel, directly opposite Virgo, and is named after the constellation Pisces (the fish), which drifts and fantasizes behind the Sun at this time of year.

On the Darkside, this makes you a slippery, manipulative, unreliable reality-dodger with delusions of adequacy and an addiction to sentimentality and self-destruction.

Punctuality

You're not late as such, but you get lost, can't remember where you're going, or what day it is. It's whoever you're meeting's fault for putting you under so much pressure; stop off at a pub for a consoling drink or several.

Toothpaste

You squeeze from the middle and leave the cap off, but are usually using a can of shaving gel or haemorrhoid cream because you don't do small print; blame the bathroom's owner when you throw up.

Temper gauge

0° to boiling point in a minute or two, building up a good head of steam to drive the whinge engine, which can go for weeks at a time but not in any logical direction; often runs off the rails or over innocent bystanders.

PERSONALITY

confused, chaotic, contradictory

Brightsiders describe you as two fish tied together and swimming in opposite directions. Not really a good start, is it? They say this conflicting image represents your reach-for-the-stars-side and your degradation-junkie Darkside, pulling each other every which way (they don't mention that the rope that ties you together is what usually garrottes other zodiac signs who get involved with you). This kind of implies that your Darkside is separate from your Brightside, which suits you because it means you can deny its existence and, at the same time, blame it every time you mess up. (Yes, I know that is confused and contradictory, but confused and contradictory is what you are.) But it's not true, is it? Both your fish have dark underbellies.

You have candy-coloured dreams in which you are the handsome hero on a white horse who rides in and saves everybody, asking nothing but everlasting gratitude and unconditional love in return; this explains your Brightside rep for clustering around sickbeds, retraining as an alternative therapist or marriage counsellor so that you can make it all better for the sad and inadequate. Let's pause and savour that magnificent irony for a moment before wondering what you are really up to. Emotional tourism and vicarious wallowing spring to mind, mainly because if by chance you do manage to get anyone back on their feet and they start succeeding at life, you get insanely jealous and start pricking their brave new little balloon of self-esteem.

Your natural habitat is murky emotional depths, where you drift about vaguely, moaning about the intolerable pressure the world puts you under (possibly someone has asked you the time). And because you have the willpower of a marshmallow, whenever you feel cosmically hard done by, which is most of the time – you didn't ask to be born, you whinge adolescently – you climb into a bottle or book a holiday in the Altered States of Fantasia. Staring at life through a glass darkly (or just through a glass), you appear helpless and put upon, but you're not: you know the manipulative value of martyrdom and suicide threats. If rumbled, you come over all Virgo, and escape into hypochondria or start sweating obsessively about the small stuff.

Anyone who has to deal with you should always carry a tape recorder, for anything mutually agreed two minutes ago you will deny utterly two minutes later (although you will then deny that it's your voice on the tape). Your instantaneous mood changes make Cancer look like an emotional Mt Rushmore. You set out on a sentence (e.g. pass the salt, please) full of optimism and jollity; by the time you get to the end, you are one with Eeyore and everybody else has lost the will to live. What you want now is never what you will want in one minute, or what you did want three minutes ago. Persistence of vision is nature's way of letting us see the world as a constant picture rather than a flicker of separate images; you don't have it.

Bitch rating

A-. Stealth-class submarine bitchery; you're so wishy-washy topside, people underestimate the powerful Emotional Location System that allows you to hook directly into others' weakest points and go in with a spiteful trident. You always hit below the waterline, and leave a slow corrosive poison in the victim's system.

Collective noun

An angling tip for non-Pisceans. You may find yourself, for some bizarre zodiacal reason, in a damp, windowless drinking club full of Pisceans. Mournful eyes stare at you accusingly as tears splash steadily into beer. You are dissolving in a Whinge of Pisceans. Don't smack them with a wet fish – that's just what they want.

FAVE DEADLY SIN

As you are a weak-willed sensationalist, you have regularly been led astray by all seven DSs, often all at the same time (which may explain some of your mood changes, but is still no excuse). Anger and Lust seem uncomfortably proactive and positive for you, and Greed is a bit too much like hard work, so Envy, Sloth and Gluttony are your solid drinking crew – especially Envy, since you could have been a contender if only your cruel parents hadn't held you back, and everybody else in the world hadn't made your life an absolute misery.

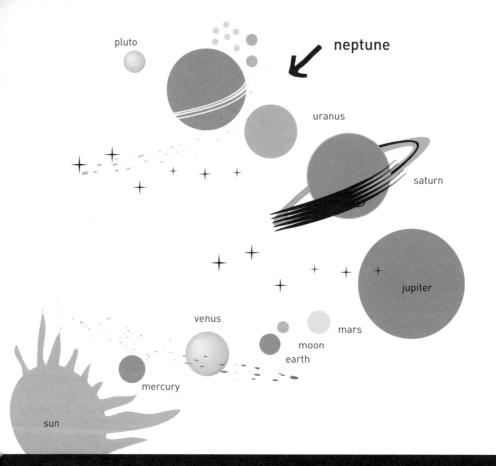

pluto

neptune

uranus

saturn

jupiter

venus

mars

moon

earth

mercury

sun

PLANET PLANET

Every sun sign has a planetary waster, whose function it is to irritate everybody, blag tenners, make drunken promises and fall asleep at the wheel. Before there were telescopes, astrologers could only see five planets in the sky, plus the Moon and Sun, so they counted

these two as planetary rulers. It seemed a good idea at the time. Each planet babysat two zodiac signs – except for the Moon (Cancer's minder) and the Sun (which allows Leo to rule). Your ruler is Neptune. You used to share Jupiter with that loony, hyperactive, riskophiliac

Sagittarius (though it was great having someone so easy to blame for everything). Then in 1846 the astronomical arm of Interpol, led by J. G. Galle, finally apprehended Neptune – first seen by Galileo in 1613, but not recognized for the cosmic nuisance it actually was.

BLAME YOUR PLANET

Ball of confusion

Pisces and Jupiter were never going to make it through the night; the Jolly Gas Giant is far too positive, although it does explain the occasional red flash of ambition glimpsed as you turn with the tide. Neptune's much more your sort of thing: unfocused, nebulous and wet. Since you're a Black Belt blameshifter, you don't need me to tell you what to do when you've behaved really badly, again.

Neptune, the eighth rock from the sun, is huge, yet somehow insubstantial, a whirling ball of cold wetness (molten rock, water, fluid gases), and the windiest planet in the solar system. It took three people (an Englishman, a Frenchman and a German) to find it and persuade it to come home. They worked out where it must be because the erratic behaviour of its orbit-buddy, Uranus, meant that something, somewhere was leading it astray: guess who? Neptune's famous for its intermittent and unpredictable hazes, an unreliable number of moons and a faint, half-hearted ring system, parts of which have drifted off. It leans sideways and takes about 165 years to lurch around the Sun, sponging off each sign in turn for about 13 years – although it feels like longer.

It's named after Neptune, the Roman version of the Greek Poseidon, god of the sea, wine and horses, the permanently foul-tempered, grumpy and hungover brother of Zeus. You can often see him painted on the insides of ancient Greek wine bowls, sloshing steadily through a sea of wine – your kind of god.

BAD MOON RISING

The darkside of Pisces's darkside

It's not all sunshine on the Darkside. You know just how power-crazed and monomaniac your innermost thoughts and secret fantasies are, but where do you think they come from? The Moon, that's where – or whichever area of your birthchart the Moon was moodily plodding when you were born. The Sun is our daytime self; the Moon represents our inner psycho. The nippy little blighter rushes around, plunging in and out of signs every few days, so throughout Pisces's month in the Sun, the lunar nuisance dodges around like a junkie whose main man has gone AWOL. That helps to explain why two Pisceans born only days apart fail to make any kind of decision about completely different urgent matters, depending on which sign the Moon was bothering at the time.

CATCHING THE MOON

That's all very well, you say, but how do I know where the Moon was when I was born? There are long, complicated (and, frankly, dull) tables called ephemerides that tell you where every planet (and for tedious astrological reasons, the Moon is an honorary planet) stood in the heavens, atmosphere bated, as you made your sorry debut. However, we have provided a Moon itinerary at the back of this book to enable you to get a rough idea. If that sounds like too much hard work, and you have the techno technique, then try visiting the following website: www.alabe.com/freechart. If you know where you were born, and when, they will produce, for *free*, a rough-cut birthchart that will pin your Moon on the zodiac wheel.

Lunatic combinations

Here's what happens to Pisces when the Moon lurches off on a lost weekend.

Moon in Aries – never let the fact that you don't know what you are doing prevent you from doing it ASAP.

Moon in Taurus – it looks like you're drifting aimlessly, but you're invisibly chained to a huge block of chocolate that anchors you to the seabed.

Moon in Gemini – so lovably unworldly and confused, you're always walking off with other people's wallets/car keys.

Moon in Cancer – no one dares speak to you, because they never know which mood-swing system is in operation.

Moon in Leo – ragingly jealous of the emperor's new clothes, which should belong to you, as ruler of Neverland.

Moon in Virgo – every Friday night, you stand up in a dismal back room and announce to everybody that you are a lifelong abuser of Herbal Tisanes.

Moon in Libra – what's so great about being away with the fairies is that someone else will always do the dull and dirty stuff before you come back.

Moon in Scorpio – hidden depths suck in those who surf your obvious shallows.

Moon in Sagittarius – you go with the flow most likely to take you over the rapids.

Moon in Capricorn – when you swim at a certain angle, the observant can spot a flash of steely resolve under your scales.

Moon in Aquarius – you appreciate the zen of swimming around an empty fish bowl.

Moon in Pisces – so wet your friends have to carry you around in a bucket.

BORN UNDER A BAD SIGN

The scum also rises

And another thing. Your sun sign is modified by your rising sign. This is the zodiac sign that was skulking over the horizon at the very minute you were born. If your sun sign is your ego, then your rising sign gives you your public manners (such as they are), your Sunday worst. It's the painted smile behind which the real, disgusting you lurks. Some astrologers maintain that its malign influence affects what you look like. Be afraid.

You'll have another reason to feel sorry for yourself when I tell you that, in the northern hemisphere, for tedious astronomical reasons, there are fewer people with Pisces (and Aries) rising, or ascending, than any other sign; it's just as well, because Fantasy Island, where you spend most of your time, is already crammed to the gills.

GOING UP

Now pay attention, because the following is quite brain-busting. There are 12 signs of the zodiac, and astrologers like to think of them as occupying a band of sky that spins around the Earth once every 24 hours. (This is a convention; it is not astronomically correct and you

will not see the signs if you look up, so don't write in.) So, every two hours or so another sign hauls itself blearily over the eastern horizon. This is going on whatever time of the day or night you were born, and whichever benighted spot on the globe you chose to appear

in. These astro-mechanics help to explain why fish born at either end of the same day swim aimlessly around completely different pagodas. There are long, nerdy ways to discover your rising sign, but the easiest way is to get hold of a birthchart (see page 368).

Upwardly mobile

If your rising sign is Pisces, your public persona is a sentimental, clingy, dependent victim with no visible grip on reality. This is to distract the rest of us from your plans to make us so sorry for you that we give you the world on a plate and let you play forever. Here's what happens when other zodiacal upstarts rise above their station.

Aries rising

You thrash around tetchily in your tank, creating huge waves and loads of backwash, but never actually do anything.

Taurus rising

Stuffed fish; preferably with almonds, black olives and serrano ham.

Gemini rising

Angler fish; you get the goods, and the Usual Suspects get the blame.

Cancer rising

Always worrying, quite rightly, about how easy you are to fillet.

Leo rising

The Chinese worship golden carp, you know; more of this kind of attitude.

Virgo rising

The light bouncing off your gleaming, polished fish bowl lures many ships onto the rocks when the moon is dark.

Libra rising

Sharkskin slingbacks and handbag.

Scorpio rising

You appear darkly, hypnotically emotional; actually, you're just *bouillabaisse*.

Sagittarius rising

Like the noble salmon, you leap obstacles and fight against the current to reach your goal, but can't remember why.

Capricorn rising

You lurk at the bottom of wishing wells to catch the pennies of the gullible.

Aquarius rising

Brain sturgeon.

DON'T YOU LOVE ME, BABY?

Venus and Pisces

Just how much of a high-maintenance tease or bunny-boiler you are may depend on where the solar system's heartless tart (Venus) was dropping her handkerchief when you were born (*see below*). Oh, and Venus also has a say in how harmoniously you blend in with the rest of the world, but what do words like harmony have to do with the Darkside? Now, for astrological reasons that will fry your brain if I explain them here (basically, Venus is far too luxury-loving to move too far away from the Sun, and her orbital rate is in bed with Earth's), Venus only ever appears in your sun sign, or two signs on either side of it. In your case, fish, that means Venus will be in Pisces, Capricorn, Aquarius, Aries or Taurus. And this is what it does to your love and lust life.

MAKE LOVE AND WAR

Venus is the girlie planet of lurve, right? And Mars is planet lad, the warlord. You may also have a sneaking feeling that men are from Mars and women are from Venus. Don't be upset if I tell you this is not true. All of us, of all genders, have a stake in the love. When the

are in your birthchart has what I shall call consequences. You may think your sun sign makes you a born babe-magnet, but Venus in a chilly sign will cut you off at the knees; you may think that your sun sign means you are the twin soul of the

red-eyed with bloodlust when beaten to a parking space. Mars will be somewhere irascible. You'll need a birthchart (*see page 368*) to find out what Venus and Mars were getting up to when you were born. It is far too complicated – and,

Venus in Pisces

Adrift on a sea of schmaltz, you cling to your lover like a limpet with dependency issues, and overload the fragile love boat with a cargo of foul cuddly toys and little heart-shaped cushions with cutesy pet names stitched on them. When a luxury liner passes in the night, you jump ship.

Venus in Capricorn

You woo your lover with rosy-tinted couplets, but make sure you keep copies (and the copyright) so you can clean up in the lucrative T-shirt/mug/calendar/ Valentine card/fridge-magnet market.

Venus in Aquarius

You take all your lovers swimming with the dolphins in the moonlight; they think it is poetically romantic; you are pleased to find a way to build up a statistically viable sample for your research paper on 'The Effect of Light Levels on Non-Verbal Intermammalian Communication'.

Venus in Aries

You suck in your swim bladder, stiffen your dorsal fin, and predate on all the pretty young fish in the Atlantic; when you've got them hooked, you do a runner to your feeding grounds in the Pacific.

Venus in Taurus

You grapple your lover to your bosom with high-tensile fishing line, but provide hand-woven keepnets so they have somewhere to relax in while you are away diving for sunken treasure.

ARE YOU LOOKING AT ME?

Mars and Pisces

Pisces have no armour and can't risk a straightforward fight, so rely on manipulation and the tyranny of the weak instead. But just how confrontational, threatening, paranoid and gagging for a fight you are depends on which area of your birthchart the bruiser planet Mars is being held back in by his mates (leave it, Mars, he's not worth it). Mars is the next planet out from Earth, but paces its orbit rather more slowly (presumably to get some effective eyeballing in). It takes 2½ years for Mars to get around, and on the way it spends about two months of quality menacing time in each sign. As a Pisces, you are so intensely annoying that few can resist the urge to give you a good slap, but if you find yourself getting your retaliation in first, check out Mars' alibi at the time of your birth.

Mars in Aries
You know those Siamese fighting fish, so out of touch with reality that they attack their own image in a mirror? Familiar?

Mars in Taurus
You hang silently like a pike among the murky reeds at the bottom of a stagnant pond until someone stirs up the mud; then show them your Jaws impression.

Mars in Gemini
You fight in fits and starts, like those puffer fish who blow themselves up to twice their normal size to look fierce, but can't be bothered to keep it up.

Mars in Cancer
Either the Walrus or the Carpenter; tears of pity stream down your shell, yet you carry on massacring the oysters.

Mars in Leo

If you feel people are not appreciating you, you send a gunboat to show that you are the Big Fish in this particular pond.

Mars in Virgo

You devise an intricate fishing quota system that no one but you understands; then fight to the death when it is ignored.

Mars in Libra

Always triggering diplomatic incidents as, during any hostile situation, no one pays enough attention to you; you are forced to reveal A's secret plans to B (and vice versa); when it hits the fan, blame C.

Mars in Scorpio

You are the *agent provocateur* sent in to spread alarm and despondency, as you home in on everyone's shameful secret weaknesses and use them to drain people's will to live, let alone fight.

Mars in Sagittarius

You swarm around in the rigging with a knife between your teeth scanning the horizon for a shipload of cut-throat desperadoes who will heave to and just make your day.

Mars in Capricorn

You blockade enemy ports and cut the oxygen lines of divers sent to sabotage your fleet: simple, ruthless, cost-effective.

Mars in Aquarius

Far below the fussing and fighting, insulated in your submarine, you look through the periscope window and target enemies several oceans away.

Mars in Pisces

You follow whoever shouts loudest or offers most rum, get confused, harpoon several of your shipmates by mistake, then claim that bigger pirates made you do it.

Pisces

Virgo

POLAR BEARS

Your polar sign sits on the opposite side of the zodiac wheel, six signs away, giving you knowing looks. You have a dark umbilical link with it. If Darkside you is your evil twin, then your polar sign is your evil twin's evil twin. It's got your number – but then

you've got its, so that's alright, isn't it? Brightside astrologers maintain that there is a strong complementary relationship between you and your polar sign, and that this relationship is positive and fruitful, especially at work, because you share the same energy quality,

(mutable). Well, excuse me; on the Darkside it's more like the tension between Captain Ahab and Moby-Dick (yes, I *know* Moby's not a fish), chasing each other around the watery globe, forever blaming each other for the pattern of their lives. It can only end in tears

WHO'S GOT YOUR NUMBER?

check out the opposition

Your polar opposite sign is Virgo: the naggy, hyperorganized, detail-obsessed bleachaholic. (For more about your darkly fascinating opposite number, *see pages 168–199*.) What would a self-deluded, dysfunctional escapist like you want with an anal-retentive despiser-of-the-weak like your average Virgo? How do you have this – shall we say – understanding? Well, like good cop and bad cop, or arch villain and superhero, you need each other to make the Darkside work for you. It's all about elements (undesirable ones, of course). You are Water; Virgo is Earth. Put them together and you get mud; it always makes you pine for the gutter, where you have spent so much quality time; but Virgo uses it to cure all those nasty psychosomatic rashes.

Don't you wonder, as you drift about the world in a haze of aimless confusion, why someone as unable to run their own life as you are has not simply dissolved in their own juices? (Probably not; you've only got a short little attention span.) Or what the mysterious force is that helps you occasionally get things done (and no one, least of all you, knows how)?

Respect your inner Virgo; it cleans a little patch in your fish bowl so that at least one beam of real light penetrates the murk every now and then, and nags you into remembering that fish do have a backbone, even if it's bendy and made of cartilage. Don't get too organized in there; if you start making lists of all the terrible things you've done, you'll have to shoot yourself, or have another drink.

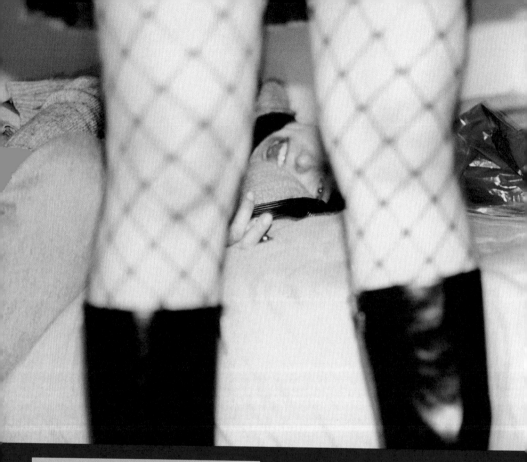

DARKSIDE DATE

You always get a date because you are totally indiscriminate; anything with a pulse will get your juices flowing, and you sometimes think that maybe you're being a teensy bit too picky and dead-ist. Your signature seduction technique is emotional blackmail ('I've only got six months to live' is always a winner). Your ideal date is with your partner's best friend, whom you take to a murky wine bar, where you don't let them get a drink in edgeways as you tell them how misunderstood you are, stare into their eyes and sob that they have always been the one. Once you have scored, you deny it all – even when the photographs are produced – then blame your partner for being so horrible that you had to find comfort elsewhere. If you don't have a partner to deceive, your ideal date is anyone who'll buy you a drink.

SEX

Let's pretend

You love someone to take charge, lash you to the bedpost with your own fishnet stockings and give you a sound spanking because you have been very naughty; or dress you up as a great big baby and force a Chardonnay-dipped dummy into your mouth; or make you shuffle around on hands and knees playing doggies, fetching your leash between your teeth and doing what Master says. If that's all a bit expensive, you can always just stay at home and dress up as doctors and nurses, or prisoners and warders. It's not for the sex (although you quite like sex, and 90 seconds is plenty long enough for your attention span). You do it: a) to stop being yourself, and dissolve into someone else; and b) to abase yourself and make someone else responsible for you.

You are tooth-achingly sentimental; lovers shrink before the accusing, beady-eyed stare of the 2,000 cuddly toys that cram your boudoir, and go red in the dark at the thought of the pet names (Bunny Blubbikins) you give them. And you always confuse sex (OK) with love and affection (yes! yes! yes!), which is why Scorpio always fools you.

What kind of love rat are you?

Supreme – you are one with the rat-force. If things are the least bit difficult, you feel under pressure (your partner asks you what you want for dinner), or if a better offer swims by, you simply drift off, leaving partners, children, debtors, etc. to tread water. You never feel guilty because it's always everyone else's fault.

INCOMPATIBILITY RATING

Aries – they take it out on you when the world confuses them.

Taurus – you despise people who have no control around addictive substances (cake).

Gemini – they cheat on you with your best friend, then disappear.

Cancer – it's just all mood swings and self-pity with them.

Leo – they demand unconditional attention; so unreasonable.

Virgo – try to organize your life, so you are forced to run away with their best friend.

Libra – just so unreliable.

Scorpio – they make spiteful remarks and try to control you by manipulating your emotions.

Sagittarius – spend most of their life hanging around in bars.

Capricorn – won't pay off your credit card bill, so you are forced to turn to a life of crime.

Aquarius – sneer when you say the stars are God's daisy chain.

Pisces – blame you for every little thing that goes wrong.

RELATIONSHIPS

The kindness of strangers

Quantity is the only thing that will absorb all the neediness you pump out, and that will generate enough energy to replace all that you absorb, so you swim around with a huge school of acquaintances. Because you have a nano-attention span, and can't be bothered to do any work on existing relationships, you are always looking for a New Best Friend. Your New Best Friend can do no wrong: he (or she) really understands the supersensitive inner you; is never harsh or critical of your lost weekends and your inability to hold down a job, like all your Old Best Friends were; you know he is a perfect, superhuman being who walks on water. When the water inevitably reaches his knees, you launch a few spite-laden torpedoes at his weak points, then drift off to look for a new New Best Friend. You target the sick, ugly, outcast or psychologically damaged, because you think they will be grateful and fulfill some of your many needs: constant unconditional affection, someone else's emotional depths to splash around in, and a chance to be co-dependent – your lifestyle of choice.

At the same time (nobody said this was easy) you need a hero to feed off (like the cleaner fish that floss food from sharks' teeth), who will let you be a doormat so that you can get yourself off the boring hook of personal responsibility.

Brightsiders claim you're a romantic, but you're just a sentimental drifter. You float in and out of relationships and marriages without a second thought, pulled by the strongest current.

DREAM JOBS

Where's the fun in dreaming about a job, here in dreary old reality? You are a pro, you need a dream job in Fantasy World; so I consulted the J. Walter Mitty Corporation, Fantasy World's leading headhunting agency, and they suggested that you might like to be considered for:

World dictator

When you are world dictator, you can make every one of your fantasies a reality and then, because you won't want them any longer, you can command all your subjects to think up some lovely new ones.

World's greatest lover

It's not what you think: it's you floating in a bath of champagne while beautiful people of all sexes sob and weep in sheer adoration of your sensitive self, pushing *tsunamis* of affection at you, however badly you behave.

WORK

The curse of the drinking classes

No one understands. You are an artiste. It may say 'clerk' in your job description, but you are in fact a misunderstood genius. Brightsiders say you are creative (salon talk for unemployable), so you think this gives you licence to stare blankly at the wall for hours at a time, or even close your eyes to await the muse. The snoring is always a giveaway, and the slumping slack-jawed and drooling on your desk. And I wouldn't trust you in the caring professions (another dumb Brightside suggestion) since it is obviously just a ruse to get near the pharmaceuticals.

So is there anything you can do? Well, not a lot. You should never work with heavy machinery – you'll forget about it, and drift off to the water cooler for some juicy gossip (you are the master grinder at the rumour mill); or in anything that really matters, such as neurosurgery or air-traffic control, where concentration and steady hands are needed. Your lack of energy and co-ordination, and a pig-headed adolescent determination to buck the system, man, don't help. When you are not praised extravagantly for the work you imagine you have done, you feel hard done by, sulk, bitch and go to the pub for the rest of the day or week.

Yet you are ambitious and want to get on, as long as it does not involve doing anything; no one in their right mind would make you an executive, unless they wanted to run down the company for tax reasons, but you'd be an excellent slavish sycophantic number two to a dictatorial boss, so you can do tyranny by proxy.

WHEN FISH GO WRONG

You're too incompetent to work on your own, so ingratiate yourself into a gang, where you start at the bottom as the expendable gofer. If you survive, Mr Big may eventually let you light his cigar, or use you as a bootscraper. You may even make it to one of these:

Drug baron

You know the market and just how much money can be wrung from the streets, and Mr Big bankrolls you; all goes well until you transgress the Unwritten Law and start sampling you own merchandise again. Dumbo!

Pirate

Strictly the old-fashioned kind; this one has it all: romance, rum, dressing up, a fast ship for dramatic escapes, more rum, affection – everybody loves a pirate, as long as they don't actually meet one – and rum.

CRIMES AND MISDEMEANOURS

How bad could it get?

So what sort of crim would you be, if sociopathy became the new world order? How would you spend your days (or maybe your nights) if you really lived on the Darkside? You are a pushover for the romance of crime, the fantasies of wealth and power that fog the brains of most doomed petty criminals, the adolescent buzz of getting one over on the suits; you see yourself as a dashing Robin Hood sort of person (except that, after you have stolen from the rich, the poor would have to whistle for it). You are magnetically drawn to degradation and the lower depths, and would do anything to join a street gang, but your crimes would be small-time (robbery to fund one of your addictions, unconvincing bogus charity scams) or inadvertent (skipping bail, spilling snakebite venom on your electronic tag and deactivating it). When caught (inevitably) you squeal immediately and give up all the gang's secrets.

You weren't paying attention when they explained about the law, but just as you resent the laws of physics applying to you, so you resent any man-made justice applying to you. When you go to court you sob, lie and bluster, and push the emotional manipulation buttons (your poor white-haired old granny, brave legless little Timmy who depends on you, etc.) and swear on your baby's eyes that you were out of town and didn't do it. The judge nominates you for an Oscar.

Jail suits you just fine: no decisions, no responsibilities and big-time villains to get in with. Steel bars don't mean a thing to an escapist of your calibre.

AT HOME

Underwater grotty

Guests who can get the door open (it's blocked by a sea of brown envelopes and final demands) should bring a scuba kit and a torch; watery light filters through grimy light-bulbs and the odd patch of cleaned window pane that you use to look out for bailiffs. There is squelching underfoot. Since you have kept everything you've ever acquired, and gone out of your way to take in other people's junk, closet doors and drawers bulge with the strain, and in the darker corners random heaps of un-nameable stuff spontaneously generate, flourish and collapse, like ancient civilizations. Life on Earth probably started like this.

DOMESTIC DISHARMONY

Aries – you just lose the house keys; they throw them away.

Taurus – well, they shouldn't leave their caviar in the fridge when you're hungry.

Gemini – you suspect there's more than one person in their room, but it's too dark to see.

Cancer – dump your collection of string-that-might-come-in-handy, and bring in their own

Leo – make you buy new light-bulbs just so they can see themselves in the mirror.

Virgo – constantly tut-tut under their breath about something they call unspeakable chaos.

Libra – have an ongoing affair with the pest control squad.

Scorpio – never in, but lots of strange people come around after dark and leave packages

Sagittarius – pour all your tropical fish into the bath because they say they don't like to see animals confined.

Capricorn – won't pay their utility bill until they see a utility.

Aquarius – making a fortune out of that anti-retrovirus culture they found under the bath mat.

Pisces – you've never seen them, they're always in rehab

Decor

You and your partner decide to paint the bathroom pink. They paint the bathroom pink. You explode irritably and say you meant pea green. They paint it pea green. You explode irritably and cry, 'Who chose that foul colour?' As they didn't tape the conversation, they can't prove that you did, and you deny it. They paint the whole house beige, and leave. You love beige, the colour of indecision.

Sharing the Pisces fish bowl

Not recommended; lightning mood swings make you impossible to live with unless of course you find another fish and synchronize your whinging. Desperate house mates should bring their own rose-tinted virtual-reality helmet.

Pisces paint chart

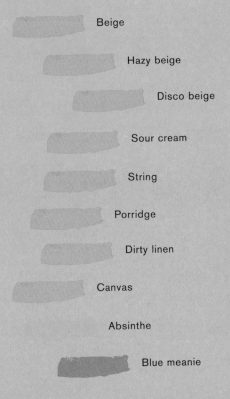

Beige

Hazy beige

Disco beige

Sour cream

String

Porridge

Dirty linen

Canvas

Absinthe

Blue meanie

PLAYTIME

The darkside of fun

When you go on holiday, the rest of us hold our collective breath waiting for reports of accidental killings, international incidents caused by misunderstandings and confusion, unprecedented citywide traffic jams and unexpected drug busts; fortunately for us, you rarely go, because all that planning, booking tickets, getting a passport stuff is so boring. No one takes you on holiday more than once, for you are a self-indulgent, nervous breakdown-inducing liability. On a guided tour, you wander off up a sleazy alley, fall in with thieves and the whole group has to spend three days getting your bail. You never read dull signs like 'Quicksand' or 'No Swimming Here', and after the fourth incident, the emergency services tar and feather you. (You blame everyone else for not reading the signs to you.) And you are always the one who holds up the plane for two hours because you don't listen to public announcements and you are too busy gargling in Duty Free.

ZODIAC CULL

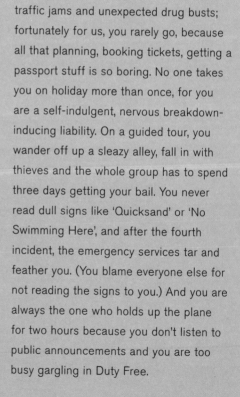

Suppose you were marooned on a desert island/up an alp/in a rainforest/ at sea with 11 others, each one a different star sign. Who would you eliminate in order to survive? Of course, it was you who got them all into this fine mess to start with, but that doesn't stop you blaming everyone else for making you do it. You keep out of Aries's way, but suck up to Cancer and Leo, playing weak and dependent so that they have to look after you until rescue comes, when you say it was all their fault.

Holidays from hell

★ Anywhere that you have to come back from by the same route you went (or anywhere you have to come back from at all) – interferes with drifting.

★ Anywhere that does not have an alcohol or controlled substance *du pays*.

★ Anywhere with your family; they make constant demands on your time, and for some reason everyone gets mad when you leave the kids on the bus…

Road rage

You no longer have a driving licence because either you lost it down the back seat of your previous car, or they took it away from you, just because you were drunk/stoned/doing 110 in a 30 m.p.h zone while going the wrong way up a

one-way street (what signs?); but hey, that doesn't mean you don't drive. Of course you do road rage – everyone else except you drives so badly, and don't they know that the Highway Code does not apply to you? You have loads of maps (including a 1976 street guide to Medicine Hat, and a hand-drawn chart of the sea roads of Southampton), but you always get lost (often on the tricky trip between home and garage); still, you can blame the maps.

Gamesmanship

Since you don't do rules, you cheat and foul your way through the game, successfully shifting any blame onto your team's best player, who gets sent off. What? You always take home your ball, and anybody else's that you can get away with.

BAD COMPANY

Your hall of infamy

You may be feeling a bit emotionally fragile after a session on the Darkside, so to cheer the soul, let's look at a few of the famous, infamous, notorious and just plain bad Pisceans who might feel the same if they read this book. You will be impressed by the number of fantasists, cultmongers and lost souls there are; you're in good bad company. And, despite your formidable (though somehow nebulous) Darkside, there are a number of people who appear to want to be you, but who got waylaid and cast adrift. Think of any self-indulgent emotional sponges, permanently switched to self-destruct mode, who can't get to the end of a sentence without running into a mood swing. All wannabe Pisceans. If they're not, someone's lying. Look at the panel below if you don't believe me.

WANNABES

Honorary status of course to junkies of all kinds, groupies, gullible cult members, actors, wimps and weeds, but what about Baron Hieronymus von Münchhausen, real-life Prussian army officer and fantasist's fantasist? Even has a syndrome named after him — the one

where you make yourself ill to get attention. Fish to the gills, wouldn't you say? Taurus. Alright, then consider J. M. Barrie, inventor of *Peter Pan* (the boy who wouldn't grow up) and promulgator of the belief that a fairy is born every time a baby laughs for the first

time? Yuck, but no fish: Taurus again. Then surely Blanche Dubois, Tennessee Williams's fictional faded southern belle, a reality-dodger who relies on the kindness of strangers and slugs of Jack to get by? No: Gemini (according to the script – but of course she did lie about her age)

Buffalo Bill *26 February, 1846*
Although he was a real Iowa-born frontiersman
and worked as a trail scout, Pony Express
rider, buffalo hunter, hotelier (!) and railroad
owner, Bill (William Frederick Cody) is best
remembered for his Wild West Circus, which
brought the fantasy of the wide open spaces
to city folk, including Queen Victoria.

Adolf Eichmann *19 March, 1906*
Hitler worshipper and architect of the Final
Solution, the Nazi plan to exterminate all
Jewish people in Europe. Abandoned family
and escaped to Argentina at the end of World
War II, but was caught, tried and executed in
1962; claimed he was 'only following orders'
(a textbook Pisces manoeuvre). He wasn't
alone: other high-ranking Nazi fish include
Joseph Mengele and Albert Speer.

L. Ron Hubbard *13 March, 1911*
Successful pulp SF writer, Lafayette (for
that is his name) went on to found a fiercely
evangelical self-help cult – scientology – which
has no basis in known fact, science, myth or
religion. Did he believe it? Was it all a cynical
money mill? Whatever – he hooked all those
self-indulgent Hollywood types, didn't he?

Lou Reed *2 March, 1942*
Survivor and musician from the Warhol Factory,
whose oeuvre drew heavily on his adventures
on the wild side of altered states; obsessed with
dead, professional Goth, Edgar Allan Poe.

Kurt Cobain *20 February, 1967*
Hypersensitive Nirvana frontman who lost
himself in gloom, grunge and sickness,
despite being the object of adoration.

CATCHING THE MOON

If you can't wait to get a birthchart, here is a rough way to find out where the Moon was lurking when you were born. All you need is your date of birth – see overleaf for instructions.

				JAN	FEB	MAR	APR	MAY
1941	1960	1979	1998	aqu	**ari**	ari	**gem**	can
1942	1961	1980	1999	gem	**leo**	leo	**lib**	sco
1943	1962	1981	2000	sco	**sag**	cap	**aqu**	ari
1944	1963	1982	2001	pis	**tau**	tau	**can**	leo
1945	1964	1983	2002	leo	**vir**	lib	**sco**	sag
1946	1965	1984	2003	sag	**cap**	aqu	**pis**	tau
1947	1966	1985	2004	ari	**gem**	gem	**leo**	vir
1948	1967	1986	2005	vir	**sco**	sco	**cap**	aqu
1949	1968	1987	2006	cap	**pis**	pis	**tau**	gem
1950	1969	1988	2007	tau	**can**	can	**vir**	lib
1951	1970	1989	2008	lib	**sag**	sag	**aqu**	pis
1952	1971	1990	2009	pis	**ari**	tau	**gem**	can
1953	1972	1991	2010	can	**vir**	vir	**lib**	sag
1954	1973	1992	2011	sco	**cap**	cap	**pis**	ari
1955	1974	1993	2012	ari	**tau**	gem	**leo**	vir
1956	1975	1994	2013	leo	**lib**	lib	**sag**	cap
1957	1976	1995	2014	cap	**aqu**	pis	**ari**	tau
1958	1977	1996	2015	tau	**can**	can	**vir**	lib
1959	1978	1997	2016	lib	**sco**	sag	**cap**	aqu

TABLE 1 YEAR AND MONTH OF BIRTH

JUNE	JULY	AUG	SEPT	OCT	NOV	DEC
leo	**vir**	sco	**cap**	aqu	**ari**	tau
cap	**aqu**	ari	**cap**	tau	**gem**	leo
tau	**gem**	leo	**lib**	sco	**sag**	cap
lib	**sco**	sag	**aqu**	pis	**tau**	gem
aqu	**pis**	tau	**can**	leo	**vir**	lib
gem	**leo**	vir	**sco**	sag	**aqu**	pis
sco	**sag**	aqu	**pis**	ari	**gem**	can
pis	**tau**	gem	**leo**	vir	**lib**	sag
leo	**vir**	sco	**sag**	cap	**pis**	ari
sag	**cap**	pis	**ari**	gem	**can**	leo
tau	**gem**	can	**vir**	lib	**sag**	cap
vir	**lib**	sag	**cap**	aqu	**ari**	tau
cap	**pis**	ari	**gem**	can	**vir**	lib
gem	**can**	vir	**sco**	sag	**cap**	aqu
lib	**sco**	cap	**pis**	ari	**tau**	can
pis	**ari**	tau	**can**	leo	**lib**	sco
can	**leo**	lib	**sco**	cap	**aqu**	ari
sag	**cap**	aqu	**ari**	tau	**can**	leo
ari	**tau**	can	**leo**	tau	**can**	leo

THIS IS WHAT YOU DO

★ Look up the year and month of your birth in table 1. Note which sign is indicated – this is not your sun sign, so don't get antsy.

★ Now look at table 2 to check the date on which you fell to Earth. There is a number opposite it – remember it.

★ Look at table 3, the zodiac wheel, and find the sign that was indicated in table 1.

★ Count anticlockwise from this sign, following the number indicated in table 2 (including the start sign). This is your moon sign.

TABLE 2 DATE OF BIRTH

DATE	NO.	DATE	NO.	DATE	NO.	DATE	NO.	DATE	NO.
1	0	7	3	13	5	19	8	25	11
2	1	8	3	14	6	20	9	26	11
3	1	9	4	15	6	21	9	27	12
4	1	10	4	16	7	22	10	28	12
5	2	11	5	17	7	23	10	29	1
6	2	12	5	18	8	24	10	30	1
								31	2

TABLE 3

ZODIAC WHEEL

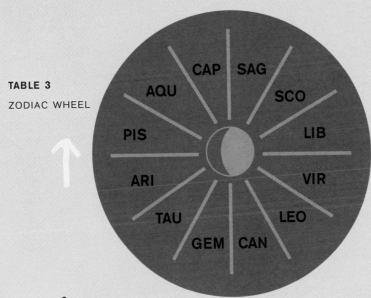

AN EXAMPLE TO US ALL

You were born in March 1972, so your star sign (in table 1) is VIRGO.

You were born on the 17th day of March, so (according to table 2) you have to count 7.

Counting anticlockwise for seven signs (in table 3) from (and including) VIRGO delivers you to ... PISCES.

You are therefore a Moon-in-Pisces Pisces. Bad luck!

RESOURCES

Books

These books were selected because they are informative, entertaining and great for readers starting out on the astro trail.

Arroyo, Stephen, *Chart Interpretation Handbook: Guidelines for Understanding the Essential of the Birth Chart*, CRCS Publications, 1990
★ Serious stuff, but quite penetrable.

Burk, Kevin, *Astrology: Understanding the Birth Chart*, Llewellyn Publications, 2001
★ All the essentials, but requires a bit of previous reading, and you have to know more than just your birthday.

Farebrother, Sue Merlyn, *Astrology Decoded*, Rider, 2013
★ Basics, history, context and a thorough step-by-step teaching workout.

Fenton Sasha, *Sasha Fenton's Planets in Astrology*, Zambezi Publishing 2014
★ Excellent guide to how the planets behave and what you can blame them for.

Fenton, Sasha, *Sasha Fenton's Rising Signs*, Zambezi Publishing 2nd revised edition 2009
★ Still going and still spot on; a marvellous intro to rising signs. Very clear and jargon free.

Gerwick-Brodeur, Madeleine, and Lenard, Lisa, *The Complete Idiot's Guide to Astrology*, Alpha Books, 4th Edition 2007
★ All the basics, entertainingly covered, in CIG style.

Goodman, Linda, *Linda Goodman's Sun Signs*, Taplinger Publishing Company, 1968
★ Vintage and venerable and still right on the money.

Orion, Rae, *Astrology for Dummies*, John Wiley, 2nd ed, 2007
★ Stalwart stuff from Orion and the Dummies team.

Rogers-Gallagher, Kim, *Astrology for the Light Side of the Brain*, ACS Publications July 2013
★ A fun and informative walk on the Brightside.

Sakoian, Frances and Acker, Louis S, *The Astrologer's Handbook*, Quill reprint 2001
★ Long in the astro tooth, but much loved and respected, and essential for newbies who want to build their own astroverse.

Starsky, Stella, and Cox, Quinn *Sextrology: The Astrology of Sex and the Sexes*, William Morrow, 2004
★ Sizzling, seductive and sophisticated; not your usual astro tome…

Tompkins, Sue, *The Contemporary Astrologer's Handbook: An In-Depth Guide to Interpreting your Horoscope*, LSA/Flare 2010 (Kindle edition)
★ Solid stuff from the co-founder of the London School of Astrology; an excellent primer for first timers.

Woolfolk, Joanna Martine, *The Only Astrology Book You'll Ever Need*, Taylor Trade Publishing, 21st Edition, 2012
★ What it says on the jacket; except for this book of course…

Other books by Stella Hyde

Darkside Zodiac in Love, Red Wheel/Weiser, 2007
★ Like this book, only focusing on the battlefield of love and relationships.

Darkside Zodiac at Work, Red Wheel/Weiser, 2007
★ Like this book, only focusing on the warzone that is work.

Websites

Always Astrology
http://www.alwaysastrology.com
Elegant site covering most options; free birthchart, in depth coverage planets in the signs and a Learn Astrology section.

Astrodienst
http://www.astro.com
A well-organized, user-friendly site set up by Swiss Alois Treindl; a bit optimistic for us Darksiders but extremely useful.

Astrolabe
http://www.alabe.com/freechart
Free computer-generated birthcharts – good for finding the positions of the planets on your natal chart; they offer a standardized interpretation and should be used as starter guides.

Astrology.com
http://www.astrology.com
Probably the biggest site in the world; slick and commercial and with an increasing taller pay wall, but still a useful entry for the wary.

Astrolutely
http://www.astrolutely.com
Clear, comprehensive site. Free week, month and year reports (short but sweet) and more if you pay; pleasingly devoid of jargon and woo-woo.

Cafe Astrology
http://www.cafeastrology.com
Lovely stylish site run by Annie Heese and Adam Banks; covers everything you may want to ask, and has a great uncluttered design and is easy to navigate. Lots of free stuff.

Blogs

All the main astrologers have their own blogs and are easy to find, but these are fun:

http://darkstarastrology.com/

http://sasstrology.com

http://www.elsaelsa.com

http://rubyslipper.ca

http://astrologyguru.tumblr.com

Apps
Big sites such as astrology.com offer apps, and there are lots of 'predictive' fun apps out there that don't offer much insight, but you will be safe with these two.

★ *TimePassages*
AstroGraph Software

★ *Daily Horoscope*
Horoscope by Comitic

Fellow Darksiders

Finally, let's hear it for our Brothers and Sisters in Darkness. Here are a couple of sites with a pleasingly gloomy approach:

http://www.astrotheme.com/files/black-zodiac.php

https://zodiacrealm7.wordpress.com/category/the-dark-side-of-the-zodiac

INDEX

ACKNOWLEDGEMENTS

The author and publishers would like to thank the following for permission to reproduce photographs:
Corbis: © Bettmann page 103, © Hulton-Deutsch Collection page 263, © Memory Shop page 295, © S.I.N.
page 391; Patrik Giardino page 10, Immo Klink page 378, Thom Lang page 74, LWA-Dann Tardif page 26
Getty Images: Herman Agopian page 106, Karen Beard page 298, Van Cohen page 250, Tobi Corney page 330,
Robert Daly page 362, Andrew K. Davey page 282, Terry Doyle page 346, Britt Erlanson page 266, Tim Flach
page 58, Karan Kapoor page 90, James McEntee page 218, Jim Naughten page 186, Carl Posey page 122,
Duane Rieder page 154, Chip Simons page 314, Ann Summa page 138,
Kellie Walsh page 234, Tonwen Jones: pages 42, 170, 202.